The International Organizations
and World Order Dictionary

THE INTERNATIONAL ORGANIZATIONS AND WORLD ORDER DICTIONARY

Sheikh R. Ali
North Carolina Central University

Santa Barbara, California
Oxford, England

4

Library of Congress Cataloging-in-Publication Data
Ali, Sheikh Rustum.
   The international organizations and world order dictionary /
Sheikh R. Ali.
     p. cm—(Clio dictionaries in political science)
   Includes bibliographical references and index.
   1. International agencies—Dictionaries. 2. International
relations—Dictionaries. I. Title. II. Series.
   JX1995.A4595 1992   341.2′03—dc20   91-38953

ISBN 0-87436-572-4 (alk. paper)

99 98 97 96 95 94 93 92   10 9 8 7 6 5 4 3 2 1 (cloth)

ABC-CLIO, Inc.
130 Cremona Drive, P.O. Box 1911
Santa Barbara, California 93116-1911

This book is printed on acid-free paper ∞ .
Manufactured in the United States of America

06/15/92

To Louis Ed. and Betty Hodges
with affection and admiration
and the hope that our friendship
will continue to blossom
and bear more fruit.

Clio Dictionaries in Political Science

The International Law Dictionary
Robert L. Bledsoe and Boleslaw A. Boczek

The International Organizations and World Order Dictionary
Sheikh R. Ali

The International Relations Dictionary, Fourth Edition
Jack C. Plano and Roy Olton

The Latin American Political Dictionary
Ernest E. Rossi and Jack C. Plano

The Middle East Political Dictionary
Lawrence Ziring

The Peace and Nuclear War Dictionary
Sheikh R. Ali

The Presidential-Congressional Political Dictionary
Jeffrey M. Elliot and Sheikh R. Ali

The Public Administration Dictionary, Second Edition
Ralph C. Chandler and Jack C. Plano

The Public Policy Dictionary
Earl R. Kruschke and Byron M. Jackson

The Soviet and East European Political Dictionary
Barbara P. McCrea, Jack C. Plano, and George Klein

The State and Local Government Political Dictionary
Jeffrey M. Elliot and Sheikh R. Ali

The Urban Politics Dictionary
John W. Smith and John S. Klemanski

SERIES STATEMENT

Language precision is the primary tool of every scientific discipline. That aphorism serves as the guideline for this series of political dictionaries. Although each book in the series relates to a specific topical or regional area in the discipline of political science, entries in the dictionaries also emphasize history, geography, economics, sociology, philosophy, and religion.

This dictionary series incorporates special features designed to help the reader overcome any language barriers that may impede a full understanding of the subject matter. For example, the concepts included in each volume were selected to complement the subject matter found in existing texts and other books.

Entries in all volumes include an up-to-date definition plus a paragraph of *Significance* in which the authors discuss and analyze the term's historical and current relevance. Most entries are also cross-referenced providing the reader an opportunity to seek additional information related to the subject of inquiry. A comprehensive index, found in both hardcover and paperback editions, allows the reader to locate major entries and other concepts, events, and institutions discussed within these entries.

The political and social sciences suffer more than most disciplines from semantic confusion. This is attributable, *inter alia,* to the popularization of the language, and to the focus on many diverse foreign political and social systems. This dictionary series is dedicated to overcoming some of this confusion through careful writing of thorough, accurate definitions for the central concepts, institutions, and events that comprise the basic knowledge of each of the subject fields. New titles in the series will be issued periodically, including some in related social science disciplines.

—Jack C. Plano
Series Editor

CONTENTS

A NOTE ON HOW TO USE THIS BOOK

The International Organizations and World Order Dictionary is organized so that entries and supplementary data can be located easily and quickly. Items are arranged alphabetically throughout, rather than grouped into chapters. When doubtful about how to locate an entry, consult the general index. For study purposes, numerous entries have also been subsumed under major topical headings in the index, affording the reader access to broad classes of related information.

The reader can also fully explore a topic by employing the extensive cross-references included in all entries. Many entries can be found as subsidiary terms, but in each case the concept is related to the main entry.

The author has adopted the format of this book to provide the reader a variety of useful applications. These include its use as (1) a *dictionary* and ready *reference guide* to the universal language of International Organizations; (2) a *study guide* for introductory courses in International Institutions, the United Nations, International Relations, International Law, Peace Studies, Policy Sciences, or for any specialized course in these areas; (3) a *supplement to a textbook* or a group of paperback monographs adopted for use in these courses; (4) a *source of review material* for political science, international relations, and history majors enrolled in advanced courses; and (5) a *social science aid* for use in economics, education, government, policy sciences, and journalism.

PREFACE

In a world of nation-states, and in a global organization like the United Nations with a membership of sovereign entities, the missions of international organizations are numerous and overlapping. As a result one can see the arena of the community of nations only in part, not as a whole. Further, international bodies have been so encumbered by power politics, so buffeted by the winds of nationalism, and so beset by financial crises that it has become almost impossible to gain a clear picture of their operations.

The United Nations provides the world with a primary instrument for the conduct of complicated multinational negotiations on issues that involve the interests of many parties. Effective multilateral diplomacy within the UN framework, however, requires a realistic look at the organization's capabilities and limitations. Troublesome questions persist about its ability to live up to its founding principles, values, and ideals. The problems of double standards, politicization, national egos, and bloc voting continue to haunt the United Nations and compromise its capacity to act.

The capacity of international organizations to attain their ultimate goals of peacekeeping and peace building can, therefore, be evaluated effectively only if one observes their responses to evolutionary change in the behavior of national and international systems.

Since international organizations are still in a developing stage, any transformation of peace from formal goal to peace as an operational program depends on the degree of institutional evolution. The process of evolutionary change is constantly hampered by existing international and national systems. Present international phenomena are not conducive to the drastic changes in international organizations that would be required to initiate an operational peace program. At the national level, resistance to changes that involve a transfer of a country's authority to the international arena is most intense. That is why within international organizations themselves the difficulties in securing change are multiplied.

International organizations have become institutions which, although remaining the creatures of their members (nation-states), also have lives of their own. For example, they give visible and continuing expression to certain canons of behavior that members have agreed to observe. International organizations also provide a setting in which states may confer and debate and through which, in consequence, something approaching a "world public opinion" can be formulated. In itself noncoercive, this consensus may nonetheless exercise a moral pressure that states cannot easily ignore.

International organizations are not an end in themselves. Rather they are a means chosen by governments for achieving common ends. Consequently these questions must always be asked with respect to the method itself: How effective is it in achieving its purpose? What are the conditions of its success? What impact does it have upon the world community, or more particularly, on the attitudes of its members?

Since the establishment of the United Nations in 1945, international organizations have witnessed a vast increase in both the membership and the concerns of the peoples of the world. International organizations have registered a solid list of accomplishments. Peace-keeping forces sent into the field have contained hostilities. Peoples formerly under colonial rule have attained independence and full sovereignty. Refugees have been provided shelter and relief. Many legal instruments have been adopted to promote respect for human rights. International law has been expanded and codified. Many diseases have been wiped from the face of the earth. International organizations have been active in eradicating poverty and hunger from the world. They have been busy in reviewing major problems and policy issues affecting the world food situation and recommending remedial action. The international financial institutions and organizations have helped raise standards of living in developing countries by channeling financial resources to those countries from developed nations.

The new climate of international cooperation between the United States and the Soviet Union, which set the stage for the extraordinary response in 1990–1991 of the UN Security Council to the Persian Gulf crisis, demonstrated the need and potentialities of collective action more than ever before. The fundamental principles which have been espoused by the United Nations for almost five decades are taking root in places as diverse as Eastern Europe, Southern Africa, and Central America. The United Nations, no longer relegated to the sidelines, has become a central catalyst for peaceful change and respect for the values of democracy, human rights, and self-determination worldwide.

The International Organizations and World Order Dictionary is predicated on the belief that survival in today's world is a race between awareness and catastrophe, between anarchy and collectivity. With this objective in mind, the author has systematically selected and organized nearly 300 entries to complement and occasionally supplement most standard works on the subject of international organizations. Thus the instructor and the student can employ this dictionary as a teaching/learning tool for unifying courses developed around individual readings. In selecting terms for inclusion, the author has been discriminating rather than exhaustive; only those terms that are considered to be most pertinent to an understanding of the field of international organizations, both public and private, were selected. While we have tried to incorporate accurately all relevant and up-to-date data on subject matter, it should be remembered that changes affecting international organizations occur almost every day. We would, therefore, appreciate readers calling any sins of omission or commission to our attention. The author is indebted to many fine scholars, writers, and informed persons whose works he has consulted in preparing this book. He is also grateful to his students, who have often challenged him to be concise and precise, to identify actors and institutions, and to analyze the significance of current international events.

Finally, the author wishes to express his deepest appreciation to the series editor, Jack C. Plano, a noted lexicographer, who first developed the unique two-paragraph format for political dictionaries 30 years ago and who has authored, coauthored, and edited more than 40 books. His careful editing has saved the author from stylistic errors and verbosity. The author especially thanks his friend and colleague Marion C. Salinger, who reviewed and critiqued the original manuscript. Further, it is a better book because of the efforts of Heather Cameron, Vice President, ABC-CLIO, who inspired the project. Last but hardly least, this volume is for the author's wife, Rina, who showed once again unusual patience and tolerance during the completion of the undertaking.

Sheikh R. Ali
North Carolina Central University

The International Organizations and World Order Dictionary

A

Achaean League   A confederation of cities and towns of Achaea
and other places in the Peloponnesus, in ancient southern Greece.
The Achaean League, composed of 12 cities, flourished in Achaea
during the time of Herodotus (fifth century B.C.) and survived
through the fourth century B.C. The 12 cities formed a religious
confederacy, meeting in Poseidon's sanctuary at Helice. Following the
war between Rome and the Achaeans in 146 B.C., Achaea was administered by Rome as part of the Macedonian province; the League was
disbanded during the period of Macedonian domination. In 280 B.C.,
while Macedonia was torn by internal struggles, the ten surviving cities
of Achaea once again renewed their federation. This second league
was a federal union of independent states, each having equal power in
the council of government. The league was totally defeated by the
Romans at Corinth in 146 B.C. and was dissolved that same year. *See
also* CONCERT OF EUROPE.

Significance   The Achaean League attempted to develop a system
that would encourage cooperation among members and discourage
conflict and discord. This early league introduced more than a century of efficient government into south-central Greece. Another notable achievement of the league was an initiative to combine city
autonomy with an organized central administration, and it made dis-
cernible progress in the institution of representative government. The
league prescribed uniform standards and coinage, commissioned
federal courts and invoked confederal authority, and also levied taxes
and fined tax evaders. Under the league, each city maintained strict
autonomy. Issues relating to foreign policy, federal taxes, and offense
against the league were referred to a council. The league's attempts
at "early and rudimentary peace efforts"[1] have continued, in varying degrees, up to the present day. It may be said to have been an

3

endeavor far ahead of its time, in an era when international cooperation was not the order of the day. The ideas found in the Achaean
League are being applied today in the United Nations and the European Community, and have been suggested by observers as a compromise system for the Union of Soviet Socialist Republics (USSR).

Administrative Tribunal   A UN court of justice created to hear
and pass judgment on complaints alleging nonobservance of contracts
of employment or terms of appointment brought by staff members
of international organizations. Established in 1946 by the General
Assembly, the Administrative Tribunal is open to all UN personnel
and employees of selected specialized agencies. The tribunal normally
reviews cases only after they have been heard by the Joint Appeals
Board. It was established by the General Assembly of the United
Nations in 1949 and is composed of seven members, no two of whom
may be nationals of the same state. The number of appointees to the
tribunal varies; three members constitute the tribunal for the consideration of a particular case. The jurisdiction of the tribunal is largely
confined to disputes between officials of the organizations themselves.
See also UNITED NATIONS INTERNATIONAL COURT OF JUSTICE (ICJ).

Significance   The Administrative Tribunal hears cases after other
internal recourse procedures have been exhausted. For example, disputes are first heard by the Appeals Board, an advisory body on which
staff and administration are represented. The International Court of
Justice (ICJ) functions as a court of appeal for decisions issued by the
Administrative Tribunal. Thus a recourse is provided for international civil servants as employees of international organizations, because they are not protected by national laws of their own countries.
The tribunal provides a mechanism for staff members of the United
Nations, the International Civil Aviation Organization (ICAO), and
the International Maritime Organization (IMO) to seek redress. The
Administrative Tribunal was used first in 1952, when the UN secretary-
general dismissed or suspended a number of secretariat employees
who were citizens of the United States. The grounds for dismissal
were the refusal of the staff members to testify before a U.S. federal
grand jury or before congressional committees on questions of sub-
version. Twenty-one of these former employees appealed their cases
to the Administrative Tribunal. The tribunal awarded compensation to 11 of those dismissed. Disputes in other organizations,
such as the International Labor Organization (ILO), the Food and
Agricultural Organization (FAO), the United Nations Educational,
Scientific and Cultural Organization (UNESCO), the World Health

Organization (WHO), the International Telecommunication Union (ITU), the World Meteorological Organization (WMO), the International Atomic Energy Agency (IAEA), the Universal Postal Union (UPU), and the World Intellectual Property Organization (WIPO), fall under the jurisdiction of the Administrative Tribunal of ILO. The United Nations has been discussing the feasibility of merging its own and ILO's tribunal into one.

Afghan Civil War   A protracted insurgency by Afghan guerrillas against the Soviet-backed regime of Afghanistan. The Afghan Civil War was instigated by the Soviet invasion of Afghanistan on December 27, 1979. Thereupon the Afghan guerrillas, known as *mujahiddin* (holy warriors), attacked Soviet emplacements and convoys in small engagements. Meanwhile the Afghan army, supported by Soviet troops, met with stiff resistance from the insurgents and from the underground opposition, both partly financed and, via Pakistan, armed by the U.S. Central Intelligence Agency (CIA). Resistance to the Soviet military presence and the marxist Afghan government spread to the major cities, including the capital, Kabul. The insurgents and other rightists organized joint protest strikes in the country; they assassinated many family members of government officials. In return the young militia of the ruling Khalq-Parcham coalition arrested and executed insurgents in the cities. The purge and counterpurge continued until the Afghan guerrilla war ended on February 15, 1989, when the Soviet troops withdrew from Afghanistan, as provided in the 1988 Geneva Accord. (The Afghan Civil War still continues to some extent.) The United Nations established three Good Offices Missions for Afghanistan and Pakistan (UNGOMAP) bases on the Afghan-Pakistan border, at Torkham, Chaman, and Parachinar, to facilitate monitoring of cross-border activity. *See also* PEACEKEEPING FORCES: UNITED NATIONS GOOD OFFICES MISSION IN AFGHANISTAN AND PAKISTAN (UNGOMAP); VIETNAM WAR.

Significance   The decade-long Afghan Civil War between the local insurgents and more than 100,000 Soviet troops and the Soviet-supported Afghan army proved a major trauma for the people of Afghanistan. In the Soviet Union the effects of escalating military costs and over 13,000 young military casualties were felt at every level of the society. The 1989 Soviet withdrawal from Afghanistan was one of the most dramatic developments since the end of World War II. Unable to overcome fierce mujahiddin resistance, the Soviet leadership under President Mikhail Gorbachev opted to cut Moscow's military losses with the assistance of UN diplomacy. The ultimate impact of the Soviet withdrawal on regional states, such as Pakistan and Iran, and the cessation of hostilities in Afghanistan remains uncertain because many Afghan refugees who fled to those countries are afraid to go back home so long as the pro-Soviet Najibullah regime remains in power. Another unsolved problem facing the consultative council of the seven Pakistan-based parties who are opposed to the Najibullah regime is its inability to force him to abdicate. Until that happens and the resistance alliance is able to move inside Afghanistan and form a government acceptable to the people of Afghanistan, there will be no solution to the vexing Afghan situation. The factional division and conflict among the resistance forces and the fact that the Najibullah regime has significant support in the country may also prolong the limited civil war in Afghanistan.

African Development Bank (ADB)   A multilateral and regional financial institution set up in 1964 to promote economic development in Africa. The African Development Bank has its headquarters in Abidjan, Ivory Coast; all African countries except South Africa are members. Its initial capital was $250 million. Under the aegis of the Economic Commission for Africa (ECA), an agreement was drawn up by a committee of experts from nine African countries. Unlike other regional development organizations, membership in the bank was originally limited to African countries, but a decision was taken in 1979 to admit nonregional members while still emphasizing its avowed set of principles aimed at preserving the African character of the institution. The primary functions of the ADB are: to provide loans (directly or indirectly) for financing national and multinational projects; to encourage public and private investment; to assist member countries in improving the utilization of their resources; to enhance the economic systems and to promote the balanced growth of foreign trade; to extend technical assistance; and to cooperate with those economic institutions in Africa and outside that support African economic development. *See also* ASIAN DEVELOPMENT BANK (ADB); INTERNATIONAL BANK FOR RECONSTRUCTION AND DEVELOPMENT (IBRD).

Significance   The African Development Bank was formed to promote regional interests through loans in support of specific projects. Initially the relatively small capital formation was due to the restraint of an all-African membership, which was at one and the same time (as Riggs and Plano maintain) "contributors to and beneficiaries of the bank's resources."[2] However, this situation has improved since 1979 when membership in the bank was extended to non-African countries.

Since then, over two dozen nonregional, mostly industrial nations have joined the organization as nonborrowing members. This has meant that despite the best intentions on the part of African members, the non-African influence over policy decisions has become dominant. The ADB has also developed close links with several regional and extraregional political, financial, and technical institutions: the Food and Agricultural Organization (FAO), the International Bank for Reconstruction and Development (IBRD), the International Labor Organization (ILO), the Organization of African Unity (OAU), the United Nations Educational, Scientific and Cultural Organization (UNESCO), and the World Health Organization (WHO), among others. Although the magnitude of developmental problems facing its members still daunts the ADB, it has managed to play an important role in African economic development through a supporting unit called the African Development Fund, which secures capital for the bank.[3]

African-Caribbean-Pacific Community (ACP)   An organization of African, Caribbean, and Pacific nations formed in 1975 to promote the economic development of its members. The African-Caribbean-Pacific Community is loosely associated with the European Economic Community (EEC). Forty-four of the 66 ACP members are from Africa and the rest are from the Caribbean and the Pacific regions. Algeria, Egypt, Libya, Morocco, Tunisia, Angola, and South Africa are not members. The relationship between the ACP and the EEC was established by two treaties signed in Lomé, Togo, in 1975 and 1979; their basic objective was to establish favorable trade relations with EEC countries. Other aims are to promote and strengthen the existing solidarity of the ACP group; to contribute to the development of greater and closer trade, economic, and cultural relations among the member states and among Third World nations in general; and to develop collective self-reliance. *See also* AFRICAN DEVELOPMENT BANK (ADB); EUROPEAN ECONOMIC COMMUNITY (EEC).

Significance   The African-Caribbean-Pacific Community agreement, which replaced the Yaoundi and Arusha conventions, offered privileged access to the European market, economic development aid, a price stabilization fund for commodities, and a new basis for industrial cooperation. The ACP is dominated by the African states, and it brought Francophone and Anglophone states together. The ACP proved to be most beneficial to African members, since over 50 percent of their exports go to Europe—most of which is duty-free. The organization came into being with euphoric hopes that it marked the beginning of the New International Economic Order (NIEO), which would ensure greater benefits to poor countries. This has not yet been achieved, but over the years the ACP and the EEC have taken definite steps toward improving trade arrangements.

Afro-Asian People's Solidarity Conference   A historic meeting of African and Asian representatives held at Bandung, Indonesia, in 1955. The Afro-Asian People's Solidarity Conference, often called the Bandung Conference after its location, was organized at the initiative of Indonesia and was supported by Burma, India, Pakistan, and Sri Lanka. It was an ad hoc meeting for the discussion of common problems and, in its final communiqué, put forward resolutions on matters such as economic needs, cultural cooperation, human rights, the search for self-determination by dependent peoples, and world peace. The conference also adopted the Indian *Panchsheel* or five principles of coexistence, which were (1) mutual respect for territorial integrity and sovereignty, (2) nonaggression, (3) noninterference in the internal affairs of others, (4) equality and mutual support, and (5) peaceful coexistence. In 1958 the second Afro-Asian Solidarity Conference was held in Cairo, Egypt, setting up a permanent council to meet annually and to be composed of one representative from each national committee. It also established a permanent secretariat. *See also* ASSOCIATION OF SOUTHEAST ASIAN NATIONS (ASEAN); SOUTH ASIAN ASSOCIATION FOR REGIONAL COOPERATION (SAARC).

Significance   The Afro-Asian People's Solidarity Conference was the first major gathering of Third World states. Since this meeting other conferences of Third World nations have been held, notably the series of nonaligned conferences. The nonaligned movement (a large group of nations that actively refuses to be politically or militarily associated with either the West or the Soviet bloc), which thereafter became a third force in world politics, has its origin in Bandung at the Afro-Asian People's Solidarity Conference. Most of the representatives at the Bandung Conference had the West in mind when the meeting resolved that "Colonialism in all its manifestations is an evil which should speedily be brought to an end." Although the conference was financed by participating governments, "peoples" rather than states were represented at the 1958 Cairo conference with 400 participants from 46 different peoples of Africa and Asia. During the following decade, as decolonization progressed and friction among the members increased, the concept of Afro-Asian solidarity became less meaningful. In 1965 another solidarity conference was scheduled to be held in Algiers, Algeria, but it was postponed indefinitely.

Since then the original dream of Afro-Asian people's solidarity has remained dormant.

Aggression   An attack or intervention by one country against another. Aggression may be the first act of hostility leading to a confrontation or war. In a political sense, aggression refers to any manifestation of an expansive policy; in a military sense, it is the initial use of armed forces of one nation against the territorial integrity and sovereignty of another nation; and from a legal point of view, aggression is the use of military force by one or more governments in violation of obligations under the UN Charter or other international agreements. The term *aggression* has appeared in many treaties and declarations, including the League of Nations Covenant (Article 10) and the UN Charter (Article 39). The League of Nations found Japan to be an aggressor in Manchuria in 1933, and the United Nations found North Korea and the People's Republic of China to be aggressors in South Korea in 1950 and 1951. *See also* LEAGUE OF NATIONS; UNITED NATIONS (UN).

Significance   *Aggression,* like any other term in the social sciences, is most difficult to define. Although the Charter of the United Nations does not specifically define aggression, the UN General Assembly came up with a compromise formula, adopted on December 14, 1974, and reflecting a fair degree of international consensus. General Assembly Resolution 3314 (XXIX) adopted, without voting, a definition of aggression that contained a number of ambiguities, such as "the use of armed force by a State against the sovereignty, territorial integrity or political independence of another State, or in any other manner inconsistent with the Charter of the United Nations."[4] The reason the General Assembly made the description so open was that there was no universally acceptable definition of aggression, and, as the preamble states, "the question whether an act of aggression has been committed must be considered in the light of all the circumstances of each particular case." Such efforts by scholars and international organizations will continue as long as there is no universally acceptable definition of aggression. There is also "unprovoked" aggression—a phraseology found in many treaties. Whether provoked or not, aggressors frequently cite provocation as justification.

Alliance   An agreement between two or more states for close coordination of efforts in order to reach security goals, or to advance mutual interests. An alliance between two or more states develops whenever a basis exists for cooperative participation of the partners against another country or group of countries. Alliances may be bilateral or multilateral, military or economic, political or cultural, and secret or open. All alliances have one common goal—to augment the collective resolve against nonallied nations. Alliances have long been a part of the European state system. For instance, Britain allied herself with different countries in the nineteenth century in an effort to maintain the balance of power in Europe. The two major alliances of the early twentieth century were the Triple Alliance of Germany, Austria-Hungary, and Italy and the Triple Entente of Britain, France, and Russia. Some contemporary multilateral alliances are the North Atlantic Treaty Organization, the Warsaw Treaty Organization, the Organization of American States, the Organization of African Unity, and the League of Arab States. *See also* NORTH ATLANTIC TREATY ORGANIZATION (NATO); WARSAW TREATY ORGANIZATION (WTO).

Significance   Although alliances have existed throughout history, recent alliances have been marked by substantial longevity. Alliances serve to coordinate the individual member's plans and actions with those of its partners. In the years following World War II the United States formed extensive networks of alliances. These were the Rio Pact in Latin America, the Central Treaty Organization (CENTO) in the Middle East, the Southeast Asia Treaty Organization (SEATO) in Asia, the Australia, New Zealand, and United States Pact (ANZUS) in the Pacific, as well as the North Atlantic Treaty Organization (NATO) in Western Europe. The alliance rivalry between NATO and the Warsaw Treaty Organization (WTO) produced a major arms race. Major questions facing the state system in the 1990s include the following: What is the role of alliances in this new world? Do alliances help the peace or are they likely to increase the danger of war? Now that the WTO has been dissolved (first the military structure, followed by the economic side, and finally the political aspect were all disbanded one after another in 1991), what is the future role of NATO?

Amazon Pact   A treaty to coordinate the development of the Amazon River basin and to protect the region's environment through rational utilization of resources. The Amazon Pact (or Amazon Cooperation Treaty) aims at fostering cooperation in the Amazon basin with a view to accelerating the harmonious socioeconomic development of the members' Amazon territories and to stimulate the relevant initiatives and projects included in national economic plans. Eight nations are parties to the 1978 treaty: Bolivia, Brazil, Colombia, Ecuador, Guyana, Peru, Suriname, and Venezuela. The treaty provisions include (1) free navigation of all rivers in the Amazon region, (2) the rational use of the region's water resources, (3) the right of each nation to develop its Amazon territory so long as it does not cause any harmful impact on the territories of other members, (4) the development of cooperative research on the river basin, (5) the improvement of health and the building of a transportation and communication infrastructure, and (6) the promotion of tourism. The principal vehicle created by this treaty is a high-level meeting of the region's foreign ministers, under the auspices of an Amazon Cooperation Council. *See also* RHINE RIVER COMMISSION.

Significance The Amazon Pact has contributed markedly to the ecological protection and rational utilization of the resources of the region. It has set an example of how nations, despite their political differences, can unite to cope with common ecological and economic problems. Although the Amazon Pact is not an example of a strongly integrated movement, it does focus on encouraging some measure of regional cooperation and has reduced the possibility of political and military hostilities in the region. To a limited extent it has also succeeded in raising the standard of living for people of the region, in protecting the varieties of animal and vegetable life, and in developing renewable conventional and nonconventional energy sources.

Ambassador The highest-ranking permanent diplomatic representative of one country to another. An ambassador is usually called a "permanent representative" when assigned to an international organization such as the United Nations. At the Congress of Vienna in 1815, three types of diplomats were recognized and a fourth was added by the Congress of Aix-la-Chapelle in 1818. These were (1) ambassadors, including papal legates and nuncios, who represent the person and dignity of the sovereign and are entitled to personal access to the sovereign to whom they are accredited; (2) ministers plenipotentiary and envoys extraordinary, including papal internuncios, who are accredited to foreign heads of state but do not represent the person and dignity of the head of their own states; (3) ministers resident, who are accredited to the head of the state but rank below the previous class; and (4) chargés d'affaires, who are accredited to the foreign minister of their host country. Today, however, these distinctions no longer exist. They are all called "diplomats" and follow a rule of precedence according to the seniority of their posts. The senior ambassador is the dean of the diplomatic corps and sees that diplomatic privileges and immunities are observed. *See also* CONGRESS OF VIENNA.

Significance   The term *ambassador* originally was associated with the monarchy, and treaties could be negotiated by the ambassadors. Medieval ambassadors were sent abroad for limited periods to accomplish a specific purpose. In the past, an ambassador often exercised considerable discretionary authority, although in principle he was bound by instructions from his government. With modern communication, however, an ambassador can receive frequent instructions, and his chief functions now are to represent his country, report about the nation to which he is accredited, and conduct negotiations. Beyond carrying out these functions, ambassadors are expected to cultivate ties with a wide variety of contacts and to keep themselves well versed about their host country. Previously, ambassadors were almost always aristocratic or wealthy male favorites of the rulers. Their ranks have been broadened increasingly over time to include professionally trained diplomats, including women and representatives of minority communities.

Amnesty International   An organization that seeks to mobilize international public opinion to apply pressure on governments to alter their nation's inhumane policies. Amnesty International is an international nongovernmental organization (INGO). Founded in London in 1961, with statutes amended in 1981, Amnesty International conducts research and organizes worldwide action by local members on behalf of prisoners held in countries other than their own. Local groups appeal for release of prisoners of conscience, join campaigns highlighting political imprisonment and detention without trial, and participate in urgent action networks to bring about immediate pressure in cases where torture, disappearance, or execution is feared. Sometimes observers are sent to monitor trials and missions, visit designated countries to interview prisoners, or hold talks with government officials. Amnesty International has over 200,000 individual members from 95 countries, many of whom participate in one of the 2,671 local groups.[5] Through local publicity, it has been successful in getting 50 percent of designated "prisoners of conscience" released within a short time.[6] *See also* INTERNATIONAL NONGOVERNMENTAL ORGANIZATIONS (INGOS).

Significance   Amnesty International has worked painstakingly for 30 years to gather and verify information on individuals who have been imprisoned for political reasons. It is often able to send its representatives to observe trials and interview individuals whom Amnesty International considers "prisoners of conscience." It also has had some successes in gaining release of internationally celebrated political prisoners and has gained credibility for its efforts to eradicate torture. The organization is well respected in the world not only as a source of information but also for its role in encouraging governmental action to vindicate basic human rights. Among many other accomplishments, Amnesty International held a major conference for the abolition of the death penalty in 1977, making revelations regarding the practices of some governments in imprisoning political enemies and helping to create worldwide sympathy for Soviet Jews, who in past years were prevented by their government from emigrating. For its contribution to "secure the journal for freedom, for justice, and thereby also for peace in the world," Amnesty International received the Nobel Peace Prize in 1977. On the occasion of the thirtieth anniversary of the Universal Declaration of Human Rights in 1978, the organization was awarded the United Nations Human Rights Prize for "outstanding achievement in the field of human rights."

Andean Common Market   An economic group within the legal framework of the Latin American Free Trade Association (LAFTA). The Andean Common Market aims at strengthening the smaller economies of the Andean subregion through trade liberalization, industrial specialization agreements, common policies for regulating foreign investment, a common external tariff, and special measures to favor the least-developed members. Parties to the Andean Common Market include Bolivia, Chile, Colombia, Ecuador, Peru, and Venezuela (Venezuela did not join the group until 1973). In response to LAFTA's failure to develop a common market on the European model, the signatories to the Andean Common Market met in Bogotá, Colombia, in 1966 and declared their intention to expedite Andean economic integration within the larger structure of LAFTA. Although actually signed in Bogotá, the pact establishing the common market is officially known as the Cartagena Agreement in honor of the city where the conclusive negotiations took place. Chile was an original member but withdrew in 1976 after a dispute over the common rules governing foreign investment. *See also* LATIN AMERICAN FREE TRADE ASSOCIATION (LAFTA).

Significance   The Andean Common Market promotes balanced and harmonious development of member countries and seeks to accelerate their growth through economic and social integration in such a way as to reduce existing differences. To achieve these objectives, the common market has adopted harmonization of economic and social policies, intensification of subregional industrialization through sectoral programming, acceleration of trade liberalization, use of a common external tariff, development of agriculture and agro-industries, channeling of capital resources from within and outside the subregion toward investment financing, and granting of preferential treatment to Bolivia and Ecuador. The Andean group has succeeded in eliminating almost all internal tariffs, and a common external tariff has been established. The Andean Common Market rejects the free trade, laissez-faire, competitive model of economic integration and instead supports the idea of regional cooperation and central planning as the best approach to modernization and economic development for its members.

Antarctic Treaty   An international agreement to demilitarize the continent of Antarctica. The Antarctic Treaty bans all weapons and military activities and prevents deployment of any nuclear weapons in Antarctica. Signed in 1959, this treaty became effective in 1961, following ratification by the member nations—Argentina, Australia, Belgium, Britain, Chile, France, Japan, New Zealand, Norway, South Africa, the Soviet Union, and the United States. Since the treaty came into force, Brazil, China, India, Uruguay, Poland, and West Germany have become full members. The major provisions of the treaty are (1) the prohibition of all military activity on the Antarctic continent; (2) the prohibition of nuclear explosions or dumping of radioactive wastes on the continent; (3) the right to inspect each other's installations to safeguard against violations; (4) the nonrecognition of existing territorial claims, and agreement that new claims may be made; and (5) the responsibility to settle disputes peacefully and to cooperate in scientific investigations on the continent. Unresolved disputes under the treaty will be "referred to the International Court of Justice for settlement."[7] *See also* ARMS CONTROL AND DISARMAMENT.

Significance   The Antarctic Treaty was the first major arms control agreement to demilitarize and internationalize the Antarctic continent and was the first disarmament accord concluded by the superpowers following World War II, serving as a model for later agreement. Antarctica is the only remaining unexploited continent and one whose resources are largely unknown. The Soviet Union operates the majority of research stations in Antarctica and, with new processes of mineral extraction, promises to make the continent an area of competitive exploitation. A number of inspections have been conducted by national observers, but no violations of the treaty provisions have been reported. The Antarctic Treaty provides that upon the request of any of the consultative parties a review conference will be held 30 years after the inception of the treaty. As of late 1991, the treaty is being reviewed for possible revision.

Arab Bank for Economic Development in Africa (BADEA)   An international financial institution formed by the League of Arab States in 1973 to contribute to economic development in Africa. BADEA finances infrastructural, industrial, and agricultural projects and provides technical assistance to aid African countries faced with the results of devastatingly high oil prices. The decision to establish the bank was made in Algiers, Algeria, at the sixth summit meeting of the Arab states in 1973, and the founding agreement was signed in Cairo, Egypt, in 1974. The basic purpose of BADEA is to provide loans to national and regional institutions for financing national and international projects, provide technical cooperation, supply expertise, and coordinate financial assistance. Some funds have been channeled into the African Development Bank (ADB) and to the southern African liberation movements. The structure of BADEA is similar to that of other international financial organizations; the bank is headquartered in Khartoum, the Sudan. Eighteen Arab states have subscribed $1.5 billion—over half coming from Saudi Arabia, Libya, Kuwait, Iraq, and the United Arab Emirates (UAE). *See also* LEAGUE OF ARAB STATES; ORGANIZATION OF AFRICAN UNITY (OAU).

Significance   The Arab Bank for Economic Development in Africa has been playing an active role in promoting Arab investment in Africa and in coordinating Arab assistance for economic development. The recipient Africans have been critical as to the fairness of BADEA in channeling investment funds and economic assistance to participating nations. The Arab states prefer to channel aid through national institutions and to selected African Muslim countries, rather than through BADEA. Racial and religious bias is evident in Arab assistance to Africa because of the Arab philosophy of aiding predominantly Muslim nations first. The Arab donors prefer to prioritize their charitable contributions to their co-religionists and then to dispense remaining funds to others. Many African leaders have stated that the Arab states ought to channel their aid through the African Development Bank (ADB), which, unlike BADEA, has black Africans on the board of directors.

Arab Monetary Fund   A financial organization to assist all Arab countries in coping with balance of payments and other financial difficulties. The Arab Monetary Fund is intended to develop an overall policy of monetary/economic integration and thereby promote economic development among the Arab countries. Its main objectives are (1) to correct disequilibria in the balance of payments of member states; (2) to assist in the elimination of restrictions on current payments between member states; (3) to establish such policies and modes of Arab monetary cooperation as may achieve Arab economic integration as early as possible; (4) to promote the development of Arab financial markets; (5) to study ways to initiate the use of the Arab dinar as a unit of account, thus paving the way for the creation of a unified Arab currency; (6) to coordinate the position of member states in dealing with international monetary and economic problems; and (7) to settle current payments between member states in order to promote trade among them. *See also* INTERNATIONAL MONETARY FUND (IMF).

Significance   The Arab Monetary Fund operates both as a bank and as a loan fund similar to the International Monetary Fund (IMF). Its operations are carried out through its capital resources. The establishment of a general reserve fund and, if necessary, of special reserve funds, is envisaged by the agreement. The Arab Monetary Fund uses its own unit of account, the Arab Accounting dinar (AAD), which is expressed in relationship to the special drawing rights (SDRs) created by the IMF. The fund maintains close working relations with other economic and financial organizations and agencies of Arab countries. But it is still far from achieving its major political objectives, the promotion of Arab economic integration and the introduction of a unified Arab international currency.

Arab-Israeli Wars   A series of four military conflicts between the Arab nations and Israel. The Arab-Israeli wars occurred in 1948, 1956, 1967, and 1973. Following the creation of the state of Israel by the United Nations in 1948, a war broke out between Israel and Egypt, Jordan, Syria, Iraq, and Lebanon. The Arab armies, despite their numerical superiority, could not match the strength of the opposing forces; the Israelis succeeded in beating back the Arab advance or in holding firm. When Britain and France attacked Egypt in 1956 to seize the Suez Canal, which Egyptian President Gamal Abdul Nasser had nationalized, Israel used that opportunity to strike at Egypt and the fedayeen bases in the Gaza Strip and Sinai peninsula, thus causing the second round of Arab-Israeli war. Israel swept through the Sinai to the Suez Canal, destroying the fedayeen bases in the process. The Arab-Israeli war of 1967 was precipitated by Egypt and lasted only six days; Israel captured territory three times its own size, swelling its narrow defense perimeter to include the Sinai peninsula and Gaza, the Golan Heights, and the West Bank of the Jordan River. The fourth round of the Arab-Israeli war is sometimes referred to as the Ramadan War or the Yom Kippur War, because it began during a period of both Muslim and Jewish holidays of fasting. After initial

successes, the Arab armies of Egypt and Syria were beaten back by
Israel in 1973. *See also* PEACEKEEPING FORCES: UNITED NATIONS EMER-
GENCY FORCE I (UNEF I); PEACEKEEPING FORCES: UNITED NATIONS
EMERGENCY FORCE II (UNEF II).

Significance   In sum, the four Arab-Israeli wars have had important consequences: (1) they demonstrated the Israeli resolve to survive
at any cost; (2) they revealed the weakness and poor training of the
Arab armies; (3) despite public pronouncements to maintain unity,
the Arabs were often divided on how to resolve the Arab-Palestinian-
Israeli conflicts; (4) Israel has occupied and absorbed all of Palestine
although the United Nations allocated only about one-third to the new
Jewish nation; (5) Israel has earned its right to exist and the Palestine
Liberation Organization recognizes this fact; (6) Israel and Egypt
signed a peace treaty at Camp David and established diplomatic relations. With the signing of the Camp David Accords in 1979, Israel's
strategic and diplomatic position improved enormously. Without
Egypt as its leader, an Arab coalition is unlikely to seriously threaten
the dominance of Israel and its occupation of Palestine. Yet, the other
Arab states in the vicinity remain technically at war with Israel, although a UN-imposed truce is in effect.

Arbitration   A process for settling legal disputes between states by
a judicial procedure based on respect for law, using arbitrators or
judges acceptable to the parties and on terms chosen by the parties in
conflict. Arbitration is to be contrasted with conciliation or mediation,
in which the role of the third party is to persuade the parties to the
conflict to accept a settlement, rather than, as in arbitration or adjudication, to impose a binding decision upon them. As defined in The
Hague Convention of 1907, international arbitration has for its ob-
jects the settlement of disputes between states by judges of their own
choice. Article 2 (3) and Chapter VI of the UN Charter stress that
states have an unfettered freedom to choose any peaceful means to
settle their disputes. Many bilateral treaties between states contain
obligations to settle disputes by peaceful means. International arbitration usually looks to the settlement of existing disputes; states have
rarely entered into agreements to settle all their future disputes by
arbitration, although many treaties include provisions requiring arbitration of issues arising out of treaty implementation. *See also* HAGUE
PEACE CONFERENCES.

Significance   Arbitration provides a valuable, though infrequently
used, process for the resolution of disputes. It is but one of a number

of peaceful settlement procedures available for settling conflicts, and it has a special role to play where disputes involve technical legal issues. Arbitration is clearly not a process that can be thrust upon parties in conflict; its effectiveness rests on the political will of states to refer the conflict to arbitration and to honor the arbitral decision. If a state agrees to settle a dispute by arbitration, it will then likely accept the arbitrator's decision even though negative to its interests. The extension of the arbitral process to the settlement of disputes between states is in part a problem in reconciling conflicting values of sovereign and independent nations, and in part a problem arising from the growth of the body of international law. If the dispute is of a legal nature, it is susceptible to decision by international law. If, however, it is of a political character, good offices, mediation, and conciliation will likely be used as more appropriate tools in seeking a settlement.

Arms Control and Disarmament   Agreements involving measures to reduce or eliminate specific classes of weapons, general armaments, or armed forces. Arms control characterizes all measures relating to stabilizing the quantity and quality of certain aspects of weapons, while disarmament seeks to eradicate arms. Although these terms are sometimes used interchangeably, arms control differs from disarmament in that its main objective is to stabilize rather than to limit or eliminate arms. According to Thomas Schelling and Morton Halperin, the objectives of arms control are (1) to reduce the risk of war, (2) to reduce destructiveness when war occurs, and (3) to reduce the cost of providing an adequate military defense.[8] Disarmament negotiations, on the other hand, have been used to seek destruction or reduction of specific types of armaments or the universal limitation of armaments. *See also* UNITED NATIONS: DISARMAMENT.

Significance   Arms control and disarmament sound similar, but a vast difference exists in their applications. Both measures seek to reduce tension and the likelihood of war. Arms control and disarmament "may even appear the same phenomenon. Indeed, the definitions of [these] terms overlap each other to some extent and are controversial."[9] Any arms control agreements short of disarmament will permit the continuation of certain military activities while eliminating or reducing others. Full and complete disarmament would, on the other hand, completely eliminate all armed forces and armaments under international control. In view of the reduction of East-West tensions in recent years, an end to the worldwide confrontation between the superpowers and other major powers for supremacy can now be visualized. Consequently, disarmament proposals among nations may move in positive directions. Whether this "peaceful" situation will last long or is only temporary will depend upon the success of many current arms control discussions and disarmament negotiations. While full and complete disarmament is unlikely in an imperfect world, substantial reductions in war-making potential will increase security and greatly reduce the likelihood of war.

Asian Development Bank (ADB)   A financial institution to foster economic growth and cooperation in the Asian and Pacific region. The Asian Development Bank aims to contribute to the progress of developing countries by lending funds, promoting investments, and providing technical assistance. It was established in 1966 under the auspices of the United Nations Economic Commission for Asia and the Far East (ECAFE), currently the UN Economic and Social Commission for Asia and the Pacific (ESCAP). The bank, with headquarters in Manila, Philippines, had an initial capital of $1.1 billion. In addition to 32 member countries within the ESCAP region, all developing nations of the area, plus Australia, New Zealand, and Japan and 15 other developed countries outside the region—including Canada, France, Italy, Germany, the United Kingdom, and the United States—are participants in the activities of the bank. There are also several socialist members of the bank, including Vietnam, Laos, Kampuchea, and China. Taiwan is also a member with a new name, Taipei-China. *See also* AFRICAN DEVELOPMENT BANK (ADB).

Significance   The Asian Development Bank promotes investment of public and private capital in the Asian and Pacific region for development purposes and cooperates with the United Nations, its organizational arms, and its subsidiaries. It also cooperates with public and private international organizations and other international institutions, as well as any national entities concerned with investment and development funds in the region. The bank's operations provide financing of specific projects in agriculture, agro-industry, energy, industrial and nonfuel minerals, development banks, transport and communications, water supply and sanitation, urban development, education, health, and population control. It has offered loans and other inducements to member countries to help them accelerate industrialization and restructure their economies. However, the ADB needs a substantial increase in its capital resources. New initiatives are required because of cuts being made by several aid donors, especially the United States.

Association of Southeast Asian Nations (ASEAN)   A regional organization to accelerate economic growth, social progress, and cultural development in Southeast Asia. The Association of Southeast Asian Nations was established in 1967 in Bangkok, Thailand, at a meeting of the foreign ministers of the five founding members— Indonesia, Malaysia, the Philippines, Singapore, and Thailand. Brunei joined in 1984, and Papua New Guinea is an observer. The aims of ASEAN are (1) economic growth and social and cultural development through joint efforts undertaken in the spirit of equality and partnership; (2) provision of mutual assistance in training and research facilities in the educational, professional, technical, and administrative fields; and (3) promotion of political stability in the region and the development of close links with other international and regional organizations with similar objectives. *See also* REGIONAL COOPERATION FOR DEVELOPMENT (RCD).

Significance   The Association of Southeast Asian Nations coordinates the positions of its members and takes common stands in international affairs whenever possible. But the functions and powers of the association, in conformity with its basic features, are rather limited in scope and subject to consensus with regard to decision making. Many crises in the region have placed severe strains on the cohesion of ASEAN and upon its credibility. It is an organization whose powers relate chiefly to the promotion of voluntary efforts at coordination. ASEAN has failed to create a zone of peace and neutrality in the region, although it called for the conclusion of a treaty establishing a nuclear-free zone. However, the association has quite successfully developed relations with other international economic organizations. Walter Jones maintains that "the global economic impact of ASEAN has been so great that the United States has had to respond with its own Pacific Basin initiative."[10]

Atlantic Charter   A program of post–World War II reconstruction announced by President Franklin Roosevelt and Prime Minister Winston Churchill after their meeting on the British battleship *Prince of Wales* in the Atlantic Ocean in August 1941. The Atlantic Charter proclaimed the principles that were to guide the two countries in their search for a just peace and stable world order after the defeat of Germany. The principles of the charter were freedom from fear and want, and freedom of speech and religion; the application of the principle of self-determination in all territorial changes; the right of all peoples to choose the form of government under which they live; equal access to trade and the raw materials essential to prosperity;

peace and security for all states; freedom of the seas; renunciation of the use of force; establishment of a permanent system of general security; and disarmament of all aggressor nations that threaten the peace. Other major nations—China, France, and the Soviet Union—also embattled in World War II subscribed to a common program of purposes and principles embodied in the Atlantic Charter and agreed to pursue the war policy, each employing its full military and economic power against the common enemy. Although the United States would not be at war against the Axis Powers for four months, the Atlantic Charter demonstrated an increasingly active role as the nation turned from neutrality to involvement. *See also* CHARTER OF THE UNITED NATIONS.

Significance   The relatively novel dimensions of international organization were expressed in the Atlantic Charter while World War II was still raging. In January 1942, representatives of 26 nations approved the plan, although they did not formally ratify the Atlantic Charter. Then followed the Moscow Declaration of October 1943, which recognized the necessity of establishing, at the earliest practicable date, a general international organization based on the principle of sovereign equality of all peace-loving states. The United Nations system, it was understood, would implement the ideas and ideals of the Atlantic Charter. Then followed a series of conferences in various places in the United States, including Hot Springs, Atlantic City, Bretton Woods, Dumbarton Oaks, and San Francisco, to work out the details of postwar reconstruction and establishment of peace and stability in the world. The system of general security as proclaimed by the Atlantic Charter took shape in the establishment of the United Nations, and worldwide political and economic collaboration has been fostered on an unprecedented scale thereafter. The Atlantic Charter served as a forerunner of the Charter of the United Nations. In 1991, President George Bush restated the principles and ideals of the Atlantic Charter in calling for common action against Iraq and the establishment of a postwar (Gulf War) new world order.

Australia, New Zealand, and United States Pact (ANZUS)   A security treaty to coordinate the defense of the contracting parties in order to preserve peace in the Pacific region. The ANZUS pact, between Australia, New Zealand, and the United States, was signed in San Francisco in 1951. The treaty, which was supposed to remain in force indefinitely, was suspended in 1986 because of the United States' objection to the New Zealand government's decision not to allow port calls by nuclear-armed ships. However, commitments between the

United States and Australia were mutually reaffirmed, and ANZUS continues to govern security relations between Australia and the United States. Prior to the breakup of the treaty, the contracting parties had affirmed their desire to live in peace with all peoples and all governments. The aims of the signers of the pact were to declare publicly their sense of unity against any potential aggressor, to further their efforts for collective defense, and to coordinate their policies. The agreement further provided for exchange of strategic intelligence, scientific and technical assistance in defense matters, supply of defense equipment, combined ground, air, and naval exercises, and visits by military aircraft and naval vessels. *See also* SOUTHEAST ASIA TREATY ORGANIZATION (SEATO).

Significance   The Australia, New Zealand, and United States pact was intended to be a first step toward the development of a comprehensive system of regional security in the Pacific. In case of aggression, each party was bound to act according to its constitutional processes, because an attack against any party constituted a danger to the safety of the others. This defense was further developed by the creation of the Southeast Asia Treaty Organization (SEATO) in 1954. Although SEATO was dissolved in 1977, ANZUS remained in force until 1986. ANZUS was supplemented by numerous bilateral pacts between the United States, Japan, the Philippines, Taiwan, and South Korea. The United States, in the years following World War II, formed a more extensive global set of defense alliances than any other country; ANZUS was one such pact intended to implement the American policy of containment. The U.S. policy toward the Soviet Union during that period was predicated on the doctrine of containment of Soviet power within its existing bounds. Such a policy also meant that the United States assumed the previous role of the United Kingdom by undertaking to protect two Commonwealth nations—Australia and New Zealand.

B

Bank for International Settlements (BIS)   A financial institution to promote cooperation between central banks, to provide facilities for international financial operations, and to act as an agent in international financial settlements. The Bank for International Settlements was established in 1930 at the initiative of those governments participating at The Hague Conference. The conference was attended by Germany and the Creditors' Powers, and discussions focused on reparations and other problems arising out of World War I. Under an intergovernmental convention, the Swiss government undertook to establish the Bank in Basel, Switzerland. The BIS buys and sells gold on its own account and accepts custody of gold for the accounts of central banks. It also receives short-term deposits and utilizes these for lending purposes. The members of the bank are the central banks of 25 countries: Albania, Austria, Belgium, Bulgaria, Czechoslovakia, Denmark, Finland, France, Germany, Greece, Hungary, Iceland, the Irish Republic, Italy, the Netherlands, Norway, Poland, Portugal, Romania, Sweden, Switzerland, Turkey, the United Kingdom, the United States, and Yugoslavia. *See also* INTERNATIONAL BANK FOR RECONSTRUCTION AND DEVELOPMENT (IBRD); INTERNATIONAL MONETARY FUND (IMF).

Significance   The Bank for International Settlements was to carry out banking functions in connection with the annual reparation payments to be made by Germany in such a way as to stimulate German exports and thereby its ability to pay. However, BIS soon ceased to be concerned mainly with reparations and assumed the more general function of providing facilities hitherto lacking in carrying out international settlements. Although the first proposal to institutionalize cooperation among central banks dates back to the nineteenth century, the creation of BIS resulted from conferences held at The

23

Hague in 1929 and 1930 to settle the question of German reparations. In the 1980s, the bank granted large-scale loans to the central banks of Latin American countries (Argentina, Brazil, and Mexico) in an effort to avoid their defaulting on international loans, and to the International Monetary Fund (IMF) to lend support to its Third World loan operations.

Benelux Economic Union   A customs union ensuring the free movement of persons, goods, capital, and services among Belgium, Luxembourg, and the Netherlands. The agreement establishing the union was reached in The Hague, the Netherlands, in 1958 and came into force in 1960. The political initiative to bring together the economies of the Netherlands, Belgium, and Luxembourg, taken during World War II, and which eventually led to the economic integration of these countries, had been started with the adoption of the Customs Union Treaty in 1944. The main purpose of the Benelux Economic Union was to follow a coordinated policy in economic, financial, and social fields in order to reach an optimum level of employment and the highest standard of life compatible with monetary stability, as well as to follow a common policy with regard to foreign trade. Nationals of the member countries may travel freely to one another's territories and are entitled to the same privileges as citizens of those nations. The Benelux Economic Union has abolished internal tariffs and greatly reduced trade quotas and other trade restrictions. The acronym "Benelux" is formed by the first syllables of Belgium, the Netherlands, and Luxembourg. Its members are also members of the European Economic Community (EEC). *See also* EUROPEAN ECONOMIC COMMUNITY (EEC).

Significance   The Benelux Economic Union has helped bring substantial benefits to the economies of its member countries without jeopardizing their full participation in the European Community (EC) or their efforts at closer economic and political integration with other arrangements. One of the major problems that stood in the way of achieving full integration among contracting parties was harmonizing the domestic policies of a laissez-faire economy like that of Belgium and those of a more tightly controlled economic system like the Netherlands. Yet Benelux has succeeded in bringing about an extensive coordination of financial and social policies and has developed a common system of excise taxes and a uniform tariff on non–European Economic Community imports. The 1958 Hague Treaty stipulated that the three Benelux countries should eventually merge their fiscal and monetary systems, but this and other integrative goals are in the process of being implemented through the larger EC system.

Bloc Politics in the United Nations   A group of states that adopt a similar position on certain types of issues, usually as a result of a caucus decision, in their voting as members of the United Nations General Assembly. Politics in the United Nations is often organized around caucusing groups, geographical groups, regional groups, common interest groups, and other special interest groups.[11] A caucus such as the Asian-African group, for example, has some degree of formal organization and holds fairly regular meetings. A geographical group, like the Latin American group, works on the basis of informal consensus among the members. A regional group, such as the Arab League, is bound together by certain common factors on issues before the General Assembly. A common interest group, such as one comprised of developing nations, although not bound by any formal arrangement, may have a certain mutuality of outlook regarding issues before the United Nations. The phenomenon of bloc politics was evident before the United Nations was formally organized. Some of the caucusing groups, for example the Latin American and Arab groups, were lobbying actively for their interests in 1945 at the San Francisco Conference, where the United Nations was formed. Over the years, bloc politics developed in other international organizations. *See also* GROUP OF SEVENTY-SEVEN; NONALIGNED MOVEMENT (NAM)

Significance   The device of bloc politics is not an entirely unmixed blessing. As the United Nations has grown, its membership has increased to 166 countries. These nations often are divided into various interest groups, and they create a potential for manipulative dealing in voting—to the detriment of universal consideration of issues and ultimate consensus of the world body. Thus, instead of becoming a united organization, the UN is divided into literally hundreds of groups and subgroups. Dealing with the narrow parochial interests of member nations has become the necessary mode for effective negotiation. There is considerable overlap of membership between the various blocs in the United Nations, which actually makes some of these groups superfluous. Yet a nation that does not belong to a caucusing group at the United Nations "is forced to rely upon more subtle political and economic pressures for gaining support for its point of view and consequently must risk individual moves which may have lasting unfavorable effects."[12]

Bretton Woods System   A global management of international monetary affairs that emerged as part of World War II planning. The Bretton Woods System established two international organizations— the International Bank for Reconstruction and Development (IBRD) and the International Monetary Fund (IMF)—to undertake international central banking functions. An international Monetary and Financial Conference was held in Bretton Woods, New Hampshire, in 1944 to draft the Articles of Agreement for these two international financial institutions. Called at the initiative of President Franklin Roosevelt, the conference was attended by 44 countries. A major role in creating the system was played by world-renowned economist John Maynard Keynes, who saw economic and financial cooperation as the only means for avoiding another world depression after the war. Under the Bretton Woods System, all participating nations agreed to establish the value of their currencies in terms of gold and to maintain that exchange rate within a plus or minus of one percentage range. The General Agreement on Tariffs and Trade (GATT) was not a part of the Bretton Woods negotiations; rather it evolved from the 1934 Reciprocal Trade Program and from the wreckage of the International Trade Organization (ITO), which failed to be ratified because of U.S. opposition; by default GATT became a permanent part of the Bretton Woods System. Under the system, the problem of maintaining world monetary stability became the responsibility of the IMF, the problem of encouraging reconstruction and development was assigned to the IBRD, and the problem of encouraging international trade was given to GATT. *See also* INTERNATIONAL BANK FOR RECONSTRUCTION AND DEVELOPMENT (IBRD); INTERNATIONAL MONETARY FUND (IMF).

Significance   The Bretton Woods System represented an initial international effort to reconstruct the post–World War II economy of the world. It hammered out the rules of the international economic game in the noncommunist world (the communist nations refused to join the Western capitalist system sponsored by the United States). As the world's strongest economic power in the mid-1940s, the United States exercised the preponderance of influence within the IMF and IBRD. Although the IMF credits were an innovation in international economics, the Bretton Woods System placed primary emphasis on national solutions to monetary problems. As noted by Walter Jones, "The Bretton Woods System was a response to the dual needs of a standardized code of behavior for international trade, finance, and payments, and a source of borrowing for nations with temporary balance-of-payments deficits."[13] The Bretton Woods System continues to function effectively despite some major changes in IMF and IBRD operations. In 1971 the initial modus operandi of the Bretton

Woods System collapsed when the United States was forced by a run on gold to discontinue its practice of allowing foreign countries to convert dollars into gold at a fixed rate. Since then the international monetary system has operated on the basis of floating or flexible, rather than fixed, exchange rates, with the relationship between different currencies determined mostly by their open market values.

C

Caribbean Basin Initiative (CBI)   A U.S. effort to aid economic development in Central America and the Caribbean area. The Caribbean Basin Initiative is based on increased foreign aid, tax incentives to stimulate investment by U.S. firms in the Caribbean Basin, and lowering of tariffs against imports from the Caribbean Basin into the United States (free-trade clauses were stripped away by the U.S. Congress). President Ronald Reagan announced the Initiative at a meeting of the Organization of American States (OAS) in 1982 and it went into effect in 1984 for an agreed-upon period of 12 years. The Caribbean members are Antigua, Aruba, the Bahamas, Barbados, Belize, British Virgin Islands, Dominica, Dominican Republic, Grenada, Haiti, Jamaica, Montserrat, Netherland Antilles, St. Kitts-Nevis, St. Lucia, St. Vincent, and Trinidad and Tobago. The five Central American countries are: Costa Rica, El Salvador, Guatemala, Guyana, and Honduras. *See also* CARIBBEAN COMMUNITY AND COMMON MARKET (CARICOM).

Significance   The Caribbean Basin Initiative was designed to promote the development of Latin America by giving special treatment to the countries of Central America and the Caribbean. But it was not entirely an altruistic venture on the part of the United States since the initiative was supposed to develop stable democratic values and free market economies open to U.S. trade in the region. The CBI was also meant to deal with the threat of Cuban and Nicaraguan revolutions. Nevertheless, the CBI provided opportunity, incentives, and promotional value. A number of countries have taken advantage of it; several have not. In Latin America, largely because of the debt crisis, there has emerged a trend toward greater free market orientation of the economies. In the Caribbean region, a similar orientation has also begun. Political and economic development in the Caribbean Basin region is crucial for the United States for at least two reasons: first, economic opportunities and creation of jobs in the region may help slow down illegal immigration into the United States, and second, they may offer uninterrupted passage through the Caribbean shipping lanes for 50 percent of all U.S. trade, including oil imports.

Caribbean Community and Common Market (CARICOM)   A customs union providing for elimination of trade barriers among members, a common external tariff, and the harmonization of certain domestic economic policies. The Caribbean Community and Common Market was created by the 1973 Treaty of Chaguaramas, Trinidad, entered into by Barbados, Guyana, Jamaica, and Trinidad and Tobago. Eight other Commonwealth Caribbean countries acceded to full membership in 1974. In 1976, the treaty was amended to facilitate the admission of the Bahamas as a member of the Caribbean Community without being required to join the Common Market. Some of the regional countries have observer status in CARICOM. The basic purpose of the Caribbean Community is to foster unity among peoples of the Caribbean through coordinated regional actions in such areas as health, education, labor, transport, economics, trade, and foreign policies. The Common Market was established to activate the Caribbean Community objectives for economic integration. CARICOM emerged as a successor to the Caribbean Free Trade Association (CARIFTA). *See also* ANDEAN COMMON MARKET; COMMON-WEALTH OF NATIONS.

Significance   The Caribbean Community and Common Market has proved an excellent example of cooperation in promoting broader understanding and increased trade and economic relations in its region. It inherited a free trade pattern from CARIFTA, which it has followed successfully except in some instances where complete elimination of old patterns has been necessary but difficult. Unlike CARIFTA, CARICOM continues to make slow but steady progress toward a higher level of economic and political integration even though no possible future merger into a single political unit is envisaged. However, the major difficulty in the way of a rapid transition toward unity is the conflict between divergent interests among member nations. Members with stronger economies tend to strive for free trade and unity, whereas those countries with weaker economies are reluctant to give up protection under national and international programs. There are also differing positions on the role of foreign investments in their respective countries.

Caribbean Development Bank (CDB)   A regional financial body designed to contribute to the economic growth and development of member countries. The Caribbean Development Bank aims to foster cooperation and integration by financing investment projects and programs of its less-developed members. CDB membership includes Anguilla, the Cayman Islands, the Turks and Caicos Islands and the British Virgin Islands, Canada, Colombia, France, Mexico, the United Kingdom, and Venezuela. Established in 1969, Caribank operates with its ordinary capital resources, partly supported by funds from the International Bank for Reconstruction and Development (IBRD) and other international financial institutions. Additional contributions are made largely by the member countries, as well as by the United States, Sweden, Germany, and New Zealand. A special development fund has been set up for specific purposes, such as development of small farming, livestock production, technical assistance, and housing. *See also* CARIBBEAN COMMUNITY AND COMMON MARKET (CARICOM); INTERNATIONAL BANK FOR RECONSTRUCTION AND DEVELOPMENT (IBRD).

Significance   The Caribbean Development Bank helps finance capital infrastructures and investment projects, both large and small, public and private. It is one of the few regional banks in the Third World that are sources of development capital for countries in the region; but it is hindered by low levels of funding. Inflation, recession, and the world debt crisis have had an unfavorable impact on the Caribbean people's search for upward mobility in a region of the world where the economies are suffering from a weakness in commodity prices. However, CDB has effectively operated as a corrective mechanism in favor of the less-developed members. Because of its close working relations with the Caribbean Community and Common Market (CARICOM), CDB has achieved considerable success in undertaking concerted economic policies that demonstrate that weak and poor countries can overcome regional and local problems.

Central American Common Market (CACM)   A regional organization to promote economic development through a customs union and an industrial integration program. The Central American Common Market aims to achieve full liberalization of existing trade between member countries. The members of CACM are Costa Rica, El Salvador, Guatemala, Honduras, and Nicaragua. Established in Managua, Nicaragua, in 1960, the organization's operations are based mainly upon two instruments: the General Treaty of Central American Economic Integration and the Convention Chartering the Central Bank for Economic Integration. The treaty was to expire in 1981, but the contracting parties declared in 1980 that it will be operative until agreement is reached on a new integration plan. The structure of the organization includes a tripartite commission of ministers and deputy ministers of finance and the governors of central banks. CACM decisions are made by (1) the Economic Council, (2) the Executive Council, and (3) the Permanent Secretariat. *See also* CARIBBEAN COMMUNITY AND COMMON MARKET (CARICOM); EUROPEAN ECONOMIC COMMUNITY (EEC).

Significance   The Central American Common Market aims at assisting in the processes of industrialization and economic integration, based on the model of the European Economic Community, by attracting foreign investment; however, its future cannot be described as bright. CACM was created after a decade of careful preparation, but political and social conflicts among member countries—aggravated by severe economic recessions—have on many occasions torn the organization apart. Despite some initial progress, war between El Salvador and Honduras in 1969, revolution in Nicaragua in the 1980s, serious unrest in El Salvador, and long-standing domestic problems in Guatemala and Honduras have made integration a low-priority concern in member states. Despite these problems and the nationalist rivalries, CACM represents the highest level of integration—an ideal not common in Latin America.

Central Treaty Organization (CENTO)   A former regional defense alliance against communist aggression in the Middle East aimed at the provision of security as well as encouragement of economic and social cooperation. The Central Treaty Organization, formerly the Baghdad Pact, was established in 1955 when Turkey and Iraq signed the Treaty of Mutual Cooperation, renewable at five-year intervals. Britain, Pakistan, and Iran joined the organization later in the year (1955). The United States (which initiated CENTO) never formally joined the organization as a member. CENTO was known as the Baghdad Pact until Iraq withdrew from it in 1959 following a revolution; the headquarters of the organization was then transferred from Baghdad, Iraq, to Ankara, Turkey. (Outside CENTO, bilateral agreements of cooperation for mutual security and defense were signed between the United States and Iran, and Pakistan and Turkey.) Combined CENTO ground, air, and naval exercises were undertaken until the 1979 revolution that toppled the shah of Iran, after which the organization ceased to function. *See also* REGIONAL COOPERATION FOR DEVELOPMENT (RCD); SOUTHEAST ASIA TREATY ORGANIZATION (SEATO).

Significance   The Central Treaty Organization's inability to attract Arab countries, as well as to solve domestic and international problems, weakened the organization from its inception. The number of Western ties accumulated by the member nations caused them to strain relations with Third World neighbors, who were mostly nonaligned. CENTO was also a weak organization from its beginning because the United States had not joined due to its own concerns about Arab repercussions (the regional members were three non-Arab countries). The three regional members were unhappy about Washington's lukewarm attitude toward them on issues of vital concern. (Pakistan suffered a humiliating defeat in a war with India in 1971 when Bangladesh was created and the United States was of no help to Pakistan; Washington had failed to support the Turks in their attempt to prevent Cyprus from being united with Greece and to insulate the Turkish population on the island from Greek attack; the United States also abandoned the shah of Iran.) However, CENTO achieved some successes in economic development projects. A 3,000-mile telecommunication service linking Turkey to Iran and Pakistan and several other communication and transportation links among the regional members were established by CENTO.

Charter of the United Nations   The international treaty that serves as the constitution of the United Nations. The Charter of the United Nations outlines the rules and regulations governing the organization. The preamble to the charter begins with the declaration that the peoples of the United Nations are determined "to save succeeding generations from the scourge of war," and Article I places the maintenance of international peace and security first among the purposes of the organization, followed by the development of "friendly relations among nations" and the achievement of "international cooperation in solving international problems of an economic, social, cultural, or humanitarian character." The charter has 19 chapters, containing 111 articles. They are organized as follows: Purposes and Principles; Membership; Organs; the General Assembly; the Security Council; Pacific Settlement of Disputes; Action with Respect to Threats to the Peace, Breaches of the Peace, and Acts of Aggression; Regional Arrangements; International Economic and Social Cooperation; the Economic and Social Council; Declaration Regarding Non-Self-Governing Territories; International Trusteeship System; the Trusteeship Council; the International Court of Justice; the Secretariat; Miscellaneous Provisions; Transitional Security Arrangements; Amendments; and Ratification and Signature. *See also* COVENANT OF THE LEAGUE OF NATIONS.

Significance The Charter of the United Nations is essentially an expression of Anglo-American approaches to international organization and world order. The charter was drawn by the representatives of 50 countries at the United Nations Conference on International Organization, which met at San Francisco from April 25 to June 26, 1945. The conference adopted the dominant American intellectual influence affecting the role of the United Nations. Comparing the principles of American government and the UN system, Riggs and Plano observe that "most of these principles are also found, explicitly or implicitly, in the UN system, supplemented by others that are germane to an international body."[14] However, the United Nations by no means represents a federal type of government like the United States. The charter does not confer upon the United Nations the authority to tax, nor does it have power to enforce its decisions upon individuals. It is apparent that with the increase in UN membership from the Third World and the Communist bloc, American and Western ascendancy has been diminished.

Civil War Violent conflict between organized political forces within a state. Civil (internal) war is a bloody struggle between different areas, ideologies, or political divisions of a country; it may also involve government and antigovernment forces. The fighting that took place in England during 1642–1651 between supporters of the king and parliamentarians is called the Civil War, or sometimes the Great Rebellion. The American Civil War was ignited when 11 Southern states asserted their right to leave the Union. It began when the South fired on the federal Fort Sumter on April 12, 1861, and ended with the surrender of General Robert E. Lee in Virginia on April 9, 1865, and of General Joseph Johnston in North Carolina on April 26, 1865. A century later, the Chinese Civil War of the late 1940s pitted Chiang Kai-shek's troops against Mao Zedong's Communist forces. Mao fielded an army of one million and eventually won victory on mainland China. Civil wars have occurred in almost all countries of Africa, Asia, Latin America, and Europe. *See also* GUERRILLA WAR.

Significance Civil wars, in some cases, have produced greater death tolls than other wars. For example, the Chinese Civil War between 1850 and 1864 is estimated to have cost as many as 30 million lives. The American Civil War is probably the most tragic in American history—costing 600,000 lives—and continues to be one of the most written- and talked-about grim experiences. Although civil wars are not a new phenomenon in the world arena, they have been especially frequent since the end of World War II in 1945. The birth of new nations in Asia, Africa, and Latin America, where ethnic conflicts and other divisive situations exist, continues to produce violence and civil wars. There are numerous examples of the incapacity of many of these governments to guarantee domestic tranquility, especially in the Third World, where outpourings of civil disturbances and civil wars have been and continue to be a familiar phenomenon. These may occur more often in the Third World because their political systems are not well established and various groups in such societies contend for control of the government. Furthermore, perennial political, ethnic, religious, tribal, linguistic, cultural, and economic problems contribute to unrest, sometimes resulting in civil wars.

Cold War   The political, diplomatic, economic, and military power struggle that characterized U.S. and Soviet relations in the post–World War II period from 1945 to 1990. The cold war period has been marked by fierce rivalry and tensions between Western nations and communist countries, in which hostile propaganda, diplomatic maneuvering, and military buildup were used by both sides. The tenure of the cold war is considered to be the period from 1945 to the emergence of the new Soviet administration of President Mikhail Gorbachev in the late 1980s. The cold war was caused by a number of developments. Central among these were the partition of Germany, the communization of Eastern Europe and the proliferation of military alliances and counteralliances, and competition in the Third World. Such events created a climate of fear and suspicion between the superpowers. In addition, the cold war was intensified by the very natures of the two diametrically opposed political and economic systems of the West and the Communist bloc. *See also* NORTH ATLANTIC TREATY ORGANIZATION (NATO); WARSAW TREATY ORGANIZATION (WTO).

Significance   The term *cold war* is used loosely to describe the varying states of tension between the Western nations and the communist countries over four decades. But with the beginning of President Ronald Reagan's second term (1984–1988) and the ascendancy of Gorbachev to power in the Soviet Union, winds of change began to sweep the horizon, ushering in what John Stoessinger calls "a new detente between the superpowers that went far beyond that of the Nixon-Brezhnev years. It led to five summits . . . the first arms reduction treaty in history; a Soviet pullout from Afghanistan;"[15] unification of Germany; and Soviet pullout from Central Europe. While misunderstandings might have played a part in superpower relations in the past, the situation is quite different today. Both superpowers are sophisticated in the art of contemporary diplomacy, and despite the continued pressure of many international problems, the frequency of communications and other contacts between them have increased the degree of understanding, further reducing world tensions.

Collective Security   A means of restraining aggression and ending breaches of peace by agreement of a body of nations to take common action. Collective security is based on the principle that one of the effective ways to deter aggression is to deal with it by joint confrontation by a pact among nations. As Stephen Goodspeed emphasizes, collective security "depends for its success upon the willingness of all states to recognize that an act of aggression against one state must be considered an act of aggression against all members of the organization."[16] Following World War I, President Woodrow Wilson insisted on formalizing the notion of collective security in the League of Nations. The league died, but the concept of collective security lives on. This system is centralized in the United Nations Security Council, which may call upon all members to impose sanctions under Chapter VII of the charter. Since 1950 the UN General Assembly, under its Uniting for Peace Resolution, has been empowered to authorize collective action against an aggressor if the Security Council is deadlocked. Enforcement action requires (1) measures against the delinquent nation not involving the use of force (Article 41) or (2) military measures (Article 42). *See also* PACIFIC SETTLEMENT OF DISPUTES.

Significance   The concept of universal collective security is codified within the UN charter. The United Nations has had many successes in dealing with threats to international peace and security. It is claimed that the United Nations decision to intervene when North Korea invaded South Korea in 1950 is the first example of collective security action within the limits of the charter (actually the United States decided to intervene before the United Nations acted). The essential element of an effective collective system is consensus. The 1990 Iraqi invasion of Kuwait resulted in a common vote of censure by the UN Security Council. The Security Council adopted more than 12 resolutions, mostly by unanimous consent of the five permanent members of the Council (China, France, Britain, the Soviet Union, and the United States), and most of the nonpermanent members also supported these resolutions. The Security Council imposed a comprehensive air and trade embargo against Iraq, banned financial dealings by the international community, and authorized use of force after January 15, 1991. This collective military action by 28 members of the United Nations, led by the

United States, forced Iraq to withdraw from Kuwait and accept all the relevant UN resolutions.

Colombo Plan   A regional cooperative effort to encourage and to coordinate economic aid programs. The Colombo Plan, established in 1950 in Colombo, Sri Lanka, is intended to enhance economic development in South Asia and the Pacific. It had its origin in a meeting of the Commonwealth foreign ministers, who set up the Consultative Committee to survey the needs of the area, assess its available resources in capital and technical manpower, and determine what additional resources were required. The ministers also sought to focus world attention on problems of development in their region and to provide a framework within which an international cooperative effort could be undertaken to assist the member countries. Both the Consultative Committee, which is concerned with economic development in general, and the Council for Technical Cooperation, which is concerned with the narrower field of technical assistance, are consultative conferences of governments. These governments are now no longer confined to members of the Commonwealth but include, among other nations, the United States, Japan, the Philippines, Thailand, and Nepal. *See also* COMMONWEALTH OF NATIONS.

Significance   The Colombo Plan is primarily an instrument for the promotion of interregional economic and social cooperation and development, rather than an operating agency. From the organizational point of view it represents governmental cooperation at the most elementary level. Although it began as a Commonwealth venture, the Colombo Plan now has many other noncommunist Asian nations as participants and recipients of aid. The majority of the development programs are in the region and are financed internally. The member countries also help one another with technical assistance as well as with provision of some capital. Members outside the region offer aid in the form of outright grants, intergovernmental loans, and loans by private institutions. In about 40 years regional members have been provided with about $30 billion in loans and grants by outside members. Under the technical assistance programs, hundreds and thousands of Asians have received training in one another's countries (including Japan) and in Western nations.

Commonwealth of Nations   A voluntary association of independent nations in which members cooperate and assist each other without formal agreement. The Commonwealth of Nations, formerly known as the British Commonwealth of Nations, grew out of the vast British Empire of the nineteenth and early twentieth centuries; members of this organization are former British colonies. They include 50 European, African, Asian, Western Hemispheric, and Pacific countries; the newest member is Namibia, which achieved independence on March 21, 1990. All member countries recognize the British monarch as the symbolic head of the Commonwealth. It meets and consults on a regular basis to foster common links, to coordinate mutual assistance for economic and social development, and to contribute to the restructuring of international economic relations and the achievement of a more equitable world community. Consultations are carried at many levels, with meetings of the Commonwealth heads of government held as frequently as needed. The Commonwealth unites some of the world's richest and poorest countries. *See also* COLOMBO PLAN.

Significance   The Commonwealth of Nations is a unique system of informal cooperation, making it difficult to draw up a precise list of functions it performs. However, certain advantages for its members are evident. For them, the Commonwealth serves the purpose of articulating whatever common objectives they may identify. The continued support of member governments for the maintenance of Commonwealth connections is clear enough and reflects more than force of habit. Another evidence of continuing relevance of membership in the Commonwealth can be found in the return of Pakistan after a 17-year absence and the joining of Namibia—not a recent British colony but a colony of South Africa, which was earlier ruled by Great Britain. Similarly, in the economic and social fields, the Commonwealth shows no sign of diminishing its presence. It has survived many predictions of inevitable collapse, and the value of its noncoercive, welfare-oriented multilateral policies can hardly be questioned. The members find the modern Commonwealth not only a source of pride but also the source of a unique set of connections offering trade, development, and security benefits that greatly outweigh the costs.

Concert of Europe   An understanding between great powers of the nineteenth century designed to resolve international problems wherever a dispute threatened to involve them or threatened the peace of Europe. The Concert of Europe grew out of the Quadruple Alliance of Britain, Russia, Austria, and Prussia in 1815. It was in effect a declaration of intent to support a new instrument of international law, the understanding created by the final session of the Congress of Vienna (1815). The concept of the Concert of Europe persisted through a series of nineteenth-century congresses until the

Congress of Berlin in 1878. The first congress after Vienna, held at Aix-la-Chapelle in 1818, actually registered changes: France was admitted to the status of a great power, and the Quadruple became the Quintuple Alliance. The Napoleonic Wars revealed the scope, intensity, and dynamism that conflict could attain when based on mobilization of manpower and popular will. This revelation forced the European powers to form a coalition to defeat Napoleon; thereafter the victors established the Concert of Europe, which combined the eighteenth-century concept of balance of power with a new concept of states pledged to concert their power and to consult among themselves in order to maintain international peace and order. *See also* CONGRESS OF VIENNA.

Significance   The Concert of Europe was a monarchistic body that protected the legitimacy of the state and royal rule between 1815 and 1870. However, it was also the first modern experiment to form an organization for international order—a forerunner of the League of Nations and the United Nations. The Concert of Europe system developed a multilateral diplomacy from its various conferences, a distinct departure from the earlier conduct of international affairs, which had been essentially a bilateral phenomenon. The purposes of great-power consultation, and the subject matter of international discussions, became more varied. "More than anything else, possibly," says Stephen Goodspeed, "the Concert system laid the groundwork for the creation of the executive organ of an international organization which was to come in the form of the League Council and the Security Council of the United Nations."[17] War-torn Europe needed—and the state of international relations of the nineteenth century demanded—that some institutions for multilateral diplomacy be developed. These exigencies found expression in the Concert of Europe system.

Congress of Vienna   The 1815 peace conference following the Napoleonic Wars, at which the Concert of Europe was created. The Congress of Vienna dealt with several unsettled problems and agreed to periodic consultations, which then became known as the Concert of Europe. The main preoccupation of the Congress of Vienna was the nature of boundaries and regimes in Europe and the disposition of colonies. It created the German Confederation, including Austria and Prussia, restored legitimate dynasties to thrones, and established a balance-of-power system intended to preserve peace. The peace was guaranteed by the preponderant might of the Concert of Powers: Britain, Russia, Austria, and Prussia. The Congress of Vienna also drafted a constitution for Switzerland and assured its neutrality, adopted a declaration for the abolition of the slave trade, and agreed upon rules for diplomatic procedures. It also established the diplomatic classification of heads of missions, other diplomatic ranks, and precedences. *See also* CONCERT OF EUROPE.

Significance   The Congress of Vienna produced one of the first sets of rules governing the exchange of ambassadors and the shaping of diplomatic relations among states. By establishing the Rhine River Commission, the congress created an international governmental organization (IGO) to regulate international traffic and trade. The decisions were made by the Committee of Five, which consisted of representatives from Austria, Britain, France, Prussia, and Russia. They did not threaten one another's existence as a nation. More than a century later, Henry Kissinger, a student of history and secretary of state in the Nixon administration, gained valuable insights from the Congress of Vienna. He wrote, "Since absolute security for one power means absolute insecurity for all others, it is obtainable only through conquest, never as part of a legitimate settlement. An international settlement which is accepted and not imposed will therefore always appear somewhat unjust to any one of its components."[18]

Council of Europe   A regional organization to promote economic, social, and political cooperation and unity among its members. The Council of Europe was proposed at the Congress of Europe in 1948, under the auspices of the International Committee of Movements for European Unity. It was then established in London in 1949 by Belgium, Denmark, France, Britain, Ireland, Italy, Luxembourg, the Netherlands, Norway, and Sweden. Since then, eight more nations have joined the organization: Austria, Cyprus, Germany, Greece, Iceland, Malta, Switzerland, and Turkey. In addition, Hungary was admitted in 1990 as the first member from the former Communist East bloc. The principal arms of the council are the Committee of Ministers, representing the governments of member countries; the Consultative Assembly, whose members come from the national parliaments; the Joint Committee; and the Secretariat. The Council of Europe functions by making recommendations to member states and by approving treaties that are submitted for ratification. In 1953, the Council of Europe adopted the European Convention of Human Rights and established a special commission and court to carry out its provisions. *See also* EUROPEAN COMMUNITY (EC); EUROPEAN CONVENTION ON HUMAN RIGHTS.

Significance   The Council of Europe represents one of the contemporary steps toward an eventual European federation. The idea of political unification of Europe is by no means of recent origin; in the immediate past it manifested itself in numerous national and international organizations, such as the United Europe movement, the European Union of Federalists, and the Economic League for European Cooperation. But the Council of Europe has been unique in its espousal of many new conventions (treaties) on a wide variety of matters, including human rights and social security. Some of these conventions have been ratified by the members in order to promote cooperation and further advances in the protection of human rights and democratic reforms. In social matters, for example, the council has ensured that citizens of one nation who are resident in another receive, so far as possible, the same social benefits as the nationals of the country in which they reside. Slowly but steadily, the Council of Europe is moving toward a united Europe.

Council of Mutual Economic Assistance (CMEA or COMECON)
A Soviet-bloc regional organization to encourage trade and economic integration in Eastern Europe. The Council of Mutual Economic Assistance was set up in Moscow in 1949 by the Soviet Union, Bulgaria, Czechoslovakia, Hungary, Poland, and Romania; later East Germany, Cuba, Mongolia, and Vietnam joined the organization. The purpose of the council is to promote, by uniting and coordinating the efforts of member countries, cooperation and development of socialist economic integration, planned growth of the national economies, acceleration of economic and technical progress, and greater industrialization in less industrialized member countries. A permanent executive committee implements policy decisions, a secretariat operates under council direction, and nearly two dozen standing commissions carry out planning and operations. Major economic policies are decided outside the CMEA structure at conferences of the first secretaries of the national Communist parties. *See also* EUROPEAN ECONOMIC COMMUNITY (EEC); WARSAW TREATY ORGANIZATION (WTO).

Significance   The Council of Mutual Economic Assistance, better known in the West as COMECON, is a major regional body of the socialist bloc of nations, headed by the Soviet Union. According to the charter of the organization, economic, technical, and scientific cooperation among member countries is to be carried out in conformity with the guiding principle of socialist internationalism. However, CMEA has been developing cooperative relations with third countries and with other international economic organizations within and outside the socialist bloc. It was established to emulate the European Economic Community's (EEC) integration concept, but it has been troubled and disadvantaged by the dominating economic and political strength of one member—the Soviet Union. The organization operates chiefly at the dictate of the Soviet Union; trade conditions and other agreements are sometimes imposed by Moscow. Recently the growing movement toward democracy and independence in Eastern Europe and in the Soviet Union itself has further weakened the organization's ability to function smoothly. Weaknesses in the Soviet economy have reduced that nation's ability to provide leadership and apply economic pressures on other CMEA members, and the organization has practically ceased to operate.

Covenant of the League of Nations   A document of 26 articles that served as the constitution of the League of Nations. The Covenant of the League of Nations was included in the Treaty of Versailles, which formally ended World War I. Part one of the Treaty of Versailles is the Covenant of the League of Nations, the basis of which was a draft presented by President Woodrow Wilson. This draft was made public in order that discussion of its terms might be facilitated. A great deal of criticism followed, and further suggestions resulted from hearings of representatives of 13 neutral states on March 20–21, 1919. The final draft was presented at the plenary session on April 28, adopted by unanimous decision of the conference, and thereupon assumed its formal role on January 10, 1920. The first seven articles established the constitutional basis of the League of Nations. Article I designated the membership: the original members were, first, all the Allied signatories of the peace treaties, and then 13 neutral states that chose to join the league without reservation. Others could be admitted by a two-thirds majority of the league's General Assembly. *See also* LEAGUE OF NATIONS; TREATY OF VERSAILLES.

Significance   The Covenant of the League of Nations was the work of a special committee established by the Paris Peace Conference of 1919. The committee consisted of the five great powers—Britain, France, the United States, Italy, and Japan—and nine smaller states. President Wilson served as chairman and the Great Powers dominated the proceedings. The world had become weary of large-scale global war, such as the one (World War I) just ended; therefore, the league's objective was to promote international cooperation and to achieve international peace and security. The system of collective security envisaged in the covenant rested on the notion of disarmament, pacific settlement of disputes and renunciation of war, as well as a collective guarantee of one another's independence and sanctions. The covenant did not satisfy the "doves," who rejected all use of force, or the "hawks," who wished the league to have its own armed forces and to impose all its decisions by its own military authority. But in the main, the failure of the League of Nations to maintain world peace resulted not from constitutional weaknesses, but rather from the inability of key members to support the covenant and from the devastating refusal of the U.S. Senate to ratify the treaty, thus preventing one of the leading nations from joining the first world body.

D

Danube River Commission A body commissioned to regulate various aspects of navigation on the Danube and to ensure the application of uniform rules. The original Danube River Commission was created in 1856 to control and improve conditions of navigation on the "maritime" Danube. Today's Danube River Commission, constituted in Belgrade, Yugoslavia, in 1948, was founded by Bulgaria, Czechoslovakia, Hungary, Romania, the Ukraine, and Yugoslavia; Austria joined in 1960. Since 1957, at the invitation of the commission, (West) Germany has taken part in the work of the organization. The commission supervises implementation of the decisions of the international conference that set up the Danube River Commission concerning the regulation of navigation on the Danube; draws up and carries out general plans (including obtaining cost estimates for consultation and repairs); establishes a uniform system of traffic regulation on the maritime portion of the river; unifies regulation of the Danube system; supervises the sanitary technology; and coordinates hydrometeorological services. The Danube River flows from its head springs in western Germany through Austria, Czechoslovakia, Hungary, Yugoslavia, Bulgaria, and Romania, touching Soviet soil as it empties into the Black Sea. The Danube River Commission has its own flag and enjoys diplomatic immunity. *See also* RHINE RIVER COMMISSION.

Significance The Danube River, like the Rhine, served as a border for the Roman Empire, and to guarantee its security, Romans crossed the river often, establishing colonies to the north. Several times before World War II, problems arose in the region that called for its reorganization. Navigation, flood control, water power, and irrigation all have created the need for an international authority—like the Danube River Commission—to supervise the waterway. It was not only the riparian countries that participated, but also others having

43

special interests in Danubian commerce and navigation, particularly France and Britain. The Danubian nations do not lack resources or technology, but they have not been able to take full advantage of their potential. All riparian states have been polluting the Danube, and the commission is getting more involved in cleaning up pollution.

Under Soviet domination, much of the overall economic planning of the Danubian countries has been directed to the attendant needs and policies of Moscow. The Danubian countries still possess a promising potential for development, but progress has been slow under Soviet auspices. The new movement toward democracy and independence in Eastern Europe will possibly help the region establish a more stable political and economic system, and as a result the ever-present and inhibiting shadow of its giant neighbor to the east may diminish.

Diplomacy   The art and practice of negotiation in the conduct of relations among nations. Diplomacy requires a measure of sophisticated interactive tact to be effective in the official intercourse between governments. The basic functions of diplomacy are (1) protection, (2) representation, (3) observation and reporting, and (4) negotiation. These functions range from routine activities to difficult decision making during crises, usually with minimal instructions. Most nations carry on their diplomacy through their foreign service departments. There are two types of diplomacy—open and secret. Open diplomacy takes place in public conferences, discussions, and debates; secret diplomacy is cloaked in confidential or secret negotiations and exchanges of information. Other forms of diplomacy are bilateral or multilateral, and ministerial or summit. Diplomacy is carried out by special representatives called "diplomats"; the highest-ranking representative to a foreign government is known as "ambassador." *See also* AMBASSADOR; CONGRESS OF VIENNA.

Significance   Diplomacy is an instrument of foreign policy closely identified with bargaining and may involve policy formulation and execution. It is an ancient institution, a modus operandi originating in relations between such powerful political entities as Egypt, China, India, Greece, and Rome; the latter two countries used it extensively. Following the transportation, communications, and technological revolution in the twentieth century, diplomacy became markedly different from that practiced in the earliest period. Among other elements, modern diplomacy is characterized by the loss of confidentiality as more open societies have emerged. Television, the telephone, the fax machine, the hot line, and convenient data bases—all have formed a communication network that drastically affects the role of diplomacy in explaining national and international policies. Many observers argue that effective diplomacy is not always possible under instant news coverage and in open settings such as the United Nations forum. Nevertheless, this type of conference diplomacy, which may influence public opinion, sometimes can encourage the solution of problems. In highly sensitive and delicate negotiations, however, there may be legitimate reasons for keeping the diplomatic process insulated from public scrutiny.

Dumbarton Oaks Conference   A meeting of the major powers to develop specific proposals for creating a new post–World War II international organization to replace the League of Nations. The Dumbarton Oaks (an estate in Washington, D.C.) Conference was held in 1944, in two separate phases. As a first step, conversations were held among the American, Soviet, and British delegations; and second, among the American, British, and Chinese delegations. The conference adopted the following proposals: *Purposes*—The primary function of the new organization was to maintain international peace and security, encourage friendly relations among nations, and achieve international cooperation. *Nature*—The new organization was to be based upon the sovereign equality of its members. *Membership*—All peace-loving states were to be eligible for membership. New members would be admitted through action by the Security Council and the General Assembly. *Organs*—Five major bodies were suggested for the new organization (plus such subsidiary agencies as might be necessary): the Security Council, the General Assembly, the Secretariat, the Court, and the Economic and Social Council. *Competence*—The Security Council would have the primary responsibility to maintain peace and security. *See also* CHARTER OF THE UNITED NATIONS; YALTA CONFERENCE.

Significance   With some changes, the proposals of the Dumbarton Oaks Conference became the United Nations charter. Key modifications in the proposals were agreed to by the Big Three leaders (President Franklin Roosevelt, Prime Minister Winston Churchill, and Premier Josef Stalin) at the Yalta Conference in 1945. These proposals provided the basis for writing the Charter of the United Nations and represented the views of the participants. The Dumbarton Oaks proposals, with requests for comments, were circulated among those states that had declared war on the Axis Powers and had agreed to the Declaration of the United Nations. Initial reactions from the Latin American countries were unfavorable, but after two months of negotiation, agreement was reached at San Francisco in 1945 by the representatives of 50 nations. The Charter of the United Nations was written and accepted unanimously. All five major powers—the United States, the Soviet Union, Britain, France, and China—joined the United Nations, and the U.S. Senate, which had rejected the League of Nations treaty earlier, gave its consent to ratification of the UN treaty by a vote of 89 to 2. American interest in establishing the United Nations was demonstrated by its sponsorship of the Dumbarton Oaks Conference.

E

East African Economic Community (EAEC)   A former regional
organization composed of Kenya, Uganda, and Tanzania that sought
to guarantee free movement of goods in the area. The East African
Economic Community was established in 1967 for a 15-year period to
coordinate communications, finance, commerce, industry, and social
and research services. The possibility of membership for Zambia and
other central African countries was left open. EAEC was intended not
only to create conditions in which trade would be as free as possible,
but also to equalize opportunities for commerce between the contracting parties. It also provided for the reorganization of the East African
Common Services Organization, the setting up of an East African
Bank, and the establishment of a Common Market as the EAEC's
main organ. Before the achievement of independence from Britain by
the member countries, those services were performed by the East
African Common Services Organization. Despite the considerable
contribution of existing cooperative arrangements to the economic
growth of the East African region, independence brought about serious frictions regarding distribution of the benefits of economic integration. *See also* WEST AFRICAN ECONOMIC COMMUNITY (CEAO).

Significance   The East African Economic Community's ultimate
failure dramatizes the problem that the newly independent African
nations have been facing. Each contracting party was competing for
political and economic benefits. Economic planning, implemented by
controls of various kinds over allocation of resources, commodities,
and foreign exchange, was characteristic of these countries. These
policies were influenced by the new nation's own political preferences
and pressures exerted by the former colonial powers, from which the
East African countries received substantial aid. Kenya followed capitalistic methods to increase the rate of "Kenyanization" in commerce
and industry; Tanzania adopted socialism; and Uganda's economy

47

was in complete chaos. Added to this discord were obvious personality clashes among the leaders of the three countries, resulting in a total impasse that brought about the demise of the EAEC in 1977.

Economic and Social Commission for Asia and the Pacific (ESCAP)
An economic organization that assists in formulating and implementing coordinated policies for promoting economic and technological development of the region. The Economic and Social Commission for Asia and the Pacific is the new title, adopted in 1974, of the Economic Commission for Asia and the Far East (ECAFE), which was founded in 1947. It is one of five regional economic commissions set up by the United Nations Economic and Social Council; the other four are the Economic Commission for Africa, the Economic Commission for Europe, the Economic Commission for Latin America and the Caribbean, and the Economic and Social Commission for Western Asia. Thirty-eight Asian and Pacific countries, including France, the Netherlands, the United States, the United Kingdom, and the USSR, are participants in ESCAP. The primary purpose of the commission is to initiate and participate in measures for facilitating concerted action for the economic development of Asia and the Pacific by raising the level of economic activity in the region and maintaining and strengthening economic relations among both the regional countries and outside nations. ESCAP also sponsors investigations and studies of economic and technological problems and developments in the region. *See also* ECONOMIC AND SOCIAL COMMISSION FOR WESTERN ASIA (ESCWA).

Significance   The Economic and Social Commission for Asia and the Pacific provides a good example of how a diverse group of developing states can, through regional economic cooperation, achieve mutual benefits that move them toward their goals of modernization. Besides furthering the objectives of economic integration, the commission pays increasing attention to the relationship between economic and social factors. Initially involved in helping to solve the problems of war-devastated economies in Asia, the commission later had its task expanded to include promotion of the general welfare of the people of Asia and subsequently the Pacific region. With this broader objective in mind, the commission has set up a number of specialized bodies: the Asian Free Trade Zone, the Asian Pacific Coconut Community, the International Pepper Community, the Asian Clearing Union, the Asian Reinsurance Corporation, the Asian Development Bank, the Regional Mineral Resources Development Center, and the South East Asia Tin Research and Development Center.

Economic and Social Commission for Western Asia (ESCWA)   A regional organization to promote economic and social development in the Middle East. The Economic and Social Commission for Western Asia was established in 1973 as a United Nations Economic and Social Council (ECOSOC) body for western Asia. It included Egypt and the Arab countries of southwestern Asia and excluded the remaining countries of the Middle East—Israel, Turkey, and Iran. Beirut, Lebanon, was chosen as the seat of the commission, but in 1979 the headquarters was moved to Baghdad, Iraq. This is the newest of the five ECOSOC regional commissions; the other four are the Economic Commission for Africa, the Economic Commission for Europe, the Economic Commission for Latin America and the Caribbean, and the Economic and Social Commission for Asia and the Pacific. The purpose of the ESCWA is to initiate and participate in measures facilitating concerted action for the economic development of western Asia. It is charged with raising the level of economic activity in the region. The commission sponsors research on economic and technological problems and advances, emphasizing issues such as food security, integrated rural development, transfer of appropriate technology, and transport and communications. *See also* ECONOMIC AND SOCIAL COMMISSION FOR ASIA AND THE PACIFIC (ESCAP); ECONOMIC COMMISSION FOR AFRICA (ECA).

Significance   The Economic and Social Commission for Western Asia has met with considerable difficulties of a political, rather than an economic, nature. Lack of regional harmony caused earlier plans for a Middle East Economic Commission to be abandoned. There are many extant problems between the Arabs and Israelis and between the Arabs, Turks, and Iranians that prevented these countries from joining the Arab-dominated organization. In response to the Camp David Accords between Egypt and Israel in 1979, the commission recommended that the United Nations Economic and Social Council (ECOSOC) suspend Egypt from ESCWA, even though under the terms of reference set by ECOSOC, the commission must deal with social aspects of economic development. In the economic field, it has played an active role in fostering intersectoral coordination at the regional level, despite economic disparities among members. Most of the oil-rich Arab countries obviously are more affluent than some of their oil-poor neighbors. Nevertheless, under the commission's mandate, an integrated approach is being worked out with regard to industrial and agricultural development, science and technology, and human resources development.

Economic Commission for Africa (ECA)   A United Nations regional organization to encourage cooperative economic experiments in Africa. The Economic Commission for Africa was founded in 1958 when eight independent African nations became members. Between 1958 and 1982, 41 other African countries became independent and subsequently joined the commission. Other African countries that have since achieved independence have also become members of the ECA. South Africa was suspended from the commission in 1963. The major purpose of the ECA is to promote and facilitate concerted action toward the economic and social development of Africa and to maintain and strengthen economic relations between African nations. In addition, the commission assists in formulating and developing coordinated policies as a basis for practical action in promoting economic and technological development in the region. This commission is one of five regional commissions operating within the United Nations system; the other four are the Economic Commission for Europe, the Economic Commission for Latin America and the Caribbean, the Economic and Social Commission for Western Asia, and the Economic and Social Commission for Asia and the Pacific. *See also* ECONOMIC AND SOCIAL COMMISSION FOR ASIA AND THE PACIFIC (ESCAP); ECONOMIC COMMISSION FOR LATIN AMERICA AND THE CARIBBEAN (ECLAC).

Significance   The Economic Commission for Africa is primarily an operational organization (serves a variety of functions), as distinguished from a functional body (devoted to a specific function), and can deal directly with governments and subsequently report to the United Nations Economic and Social Council (ECOSOC). It has helped establish many banking, trade, resource utilization, and other organizations in Africa, but a lack of resources and political problems have limited the ECA's success. The ECA acts within the framework of the policies of the United Nations and, subject to the general supervision of ECOSOC, takes no action against any country without the latter's consent. The commission is empowered, however, to draw up its own rules and procedures and to create the necessary subsidiary organizations. Decisions and resolutions are normally adopted by consensus. African issues have been addressed by the ECA within the overall context of North-South relations; it was in conformity with these concepts regarding the political policy of apartheid that ECOSOC suspended South Africa from membership in the ECA.

Economic Commission for Europe (ECE)   A regional United Nations body concerned with the promotion of concerted action to raise the levels of economic activity and expand trade and economic relations among member countries and nonmembers. The Economic Commission for Europe is also charged, under the Economic and Social Council, with carrying out investigations of economic and technological developments within the region. The commission, established in 1947, operates through an annual plenary session and through meetings of its subsidiary bodies dealing with specific sectors of the economy. The ECE, with the consent of the country involved, performs the following main functions: (1) initiates and participates in measures to facilitate concerted action for raising the level of European economic activity; maintains and strengthens the economic relations of the European countries, both among themselves and with other countries of the world; and concerns itself with European economic reconstruction; (2) investigates and studies economic and technological problems and developments within countries of the commission and within Europe generally; and (3) collects, evaluates, and disseminates economic, technological, and statistical information. *See also* ECONOMIC AND SOCIAL COMMISSION FOR ASIA AND THE PACIFIC (ESCAP); ECONOMIC AND SOCIAL COMMISSION FOR WESTERN ASIA (ESCWA); ECONOMIC COMMISSION FOR AFRICA (ECA); ECONOMIC COMMISSION FOR LATIN AMERICA AND THE CARIBBEAN (ECLAC).

Significance Initially, the Economic Commission for Europe was concerned with reconstruction of war-shattered Europe, but in recent years it has concentrated on European economic development. Normally it holds its annual session in Geneva with participation of all the members. The ECE cooperates with the relevant specialized agencies of the United Nations and other international organizations. Effective cooperation exists between the ECE and the United Nations Conference on Trade and Development (UNCTAD), the UN Environment Program (UNEP), and the UN Development Program (UNDP). Although obviously affected by the political climate prevailing in the world, the commission has placed a strong emphasis on the expansion of trade between the free market in Western Europe and the centrally planned economy in Eastern Europe. Still, East-West problems remain the priority agenda of the ECE, which has developed programs of special interest to the less-developed countries.

Economic Commission for Latin America and the Caribbean (ECLAC) A regional economic body that coordinates policies aimed at promoting development of Latin America and the Caribbean. The Economic Commission for Latin America was established in 1948 by the United Nations Economic and Social Council (ECOSOC); "and the Caribbean" was added to the title in 1984. Membership includes the countries of Latin America and the Caribbean, Canada, France, the Netherlands, Portugal, Spain, the United Kingdom, and the United States. It is one of the five regional commissions of the United Nations; the others are the Economic Commission for Africa, the Economic Commission for Europe, the Economic and Social Commission for Asia and the Pacific, and the Economic and Social Commission for Western Asia. The commission's main function is to promote economic development through concerted actions, including technical cooperation. International and interregional trade is constantly under review, with the primary objective of expanding markets for the area's goods. Headquartered in Santiago, Chile, the commission conducts research on economic and social problems, advises the United Nations, and makes recommendations to member countries. Like other United Nations commissions, ECLAC's recommendations require approval of the countries concerned before implementation. *See also* ECONOMIC COMMISSION FOR AFRICA (ECA); ECONOMIC COMMISSION FOR EUROPE (ECE).

Significance   The Economic Commission for Latin America and the Caribbean initially considered measures for dealing with the basic problems of the post–World War II economy that faced the region. Subsequently, the emphasis shifted toward improvement of planning, machinery and techniques, management of environmental and water resources, and strengthening of regional economic integration. With these objectives in mind, the commission invites representatives of the United Nations' specialized agencies and other experts as consultants. The commission has created the Latin American Institute for Economic and Social Planning and has assisted in the formation of the Latin American Free Trade Area (LAFTA), the Central American Common Market, and other regional groups. ECLAC approaches most regional issues within the broader frameworks of both the North-South conflict and the Latin American and Caribbean dissatisfaction with U.S. policies toward its southern neighbors. The commission considers the Latin American debt crisis a responsibility to be shared by the debtors and creditors, taking into account the economic implications for the region.

Economic Community of West African States (ECOWAS)   A regional economic organization that promotes trade, self-reliance, and cooperation in the West African region. The Economic Community of West African States seeks wide-ranging economic integration aimed at establishing a customs union and ensuring free movement of capital, services, and people. The ECOWAS treaty was signed in Lagos, Nigeria, in 1975; its aims are not only the establishment of a customs union, but also the creation of a common commercial policy and the harmonization of economic and industrial policies of the members. Membership includes Benin, Cape Verde, Gambia, Ghana, Guinea, Guinea-Bissau, the Ivory Coast, Liberia, Mali, Mauritania, Niger, Nigeria, Senegal, Sierra Leone, Togo, and Burkina Faso. The community is responsible for (1) eliminating customs duties and restrictions on trade between members; (2) establishing a common tariff and common commercial policy; (3) coordinating policies in the fields of transport, communications, energy, and infrastructural projects; and (4) creating a "Fund for Cooperation, Compensation and Development." *See also* ECO-NOMIC AND SOCIAL COMMISSION FOR ASIA AND THE PACIFIC (ESCAP).

Significance   The Economic Community of West African States emerged when the contracting parties felt that some kind of cooperation among West African countries could be mutually beneficial. Although its organizational structure appears to be adequate to carry out ECOWAS's assigned tasks, a number of factors cast doubt that it will be able to manage its mission successfully. The main difficulties are that half of the people of the 16-member states live in Nigeria, a feared and distrusted giant. It controls 60 percent of ECOWAS's trade and one-third of its budget. The community involves English, French, Portuguese, and Arabic-speaking countries with wide-ranging perceptions of economic integration. The technocrats who forged cooperation in the formative stage of the organization have not been able to emerge as the decision makers, due to the fact that weak and insecure political leaders have retained their prominence in those areas that control formulation and implementation of policy. Further, due to abject poverty in the West African region, many issues have become points of contention between the have and have-not members, and consensus is often unreachable.

European Atomic Energy Community (EURATOM)   An organization that seeks to establish a common market among European Community members for nuclear raw materials and equipment, form a technical pool, and coordinate research. The European Atomic Energy Community lists the following as objectives of the community: (a) to promote research and ensure dissemination of technical information, (b) to establish uniform safety standards, (c) to facilitate investment and ensure the establishment of necessary basic installations, (d) to ensure a regular and equitable supply of ores and nuclear fuels, (e) to prevent diversion and improper use of fissile materials, (f) to exercise the right of ownership over fissile materials (mainly uranium and plutonium), (g) to ensure wide commercial outlets, and (h) to establish such relations as will foster progress in the peaceful uses of nuclear energy. The body was created in 1958, and the original members were Belgium, France, West Germany, Italy, Luxembourg, and the Netherlands; in 1973, Denmark, Ireland, and the United Kingdom joined. Subsequently, Greece, Portugal, and Spain have become members. *See also* EUROPEAN COAL AND STEEL COMMUNITY (ECSC); EUROPEAN ECONOMIC COMMUNITY (EEC).

Significance   The institutional framework hammered out in the negotiations to establish the European Atomic Energy Community was similar to that of the European Coal and Steel Community (ECSC) in many respects. EURATOM introduced a common market for nuclear products, set up common nuclear research centers, and signed agreements with the United States and Canada providing for joint work programs. Indeed, considerable progress has been made toward the economic integration of Europe due to the efforts of the ECSC and the European Economic Community (EEC). However, achievement of a greater degree of unification has probably been impeded by the failure of the EEC, ECSC, and EURATOM communities to settle their policy differences. In spite of the various divisive elements that are still present, the evolution of a supranational body in Western Europe has been remarkable. The advanced nuclear members of EURATOM— Britain and France—are unhappy because, as Marvin Soroos comments, "the United States would decide to curtail the flow of spent fuel from other countries, thereby undermining the profitability of the large investments made by France and the United Kingdom in commercial reprocessing facilities."[19]

European Coal and Steel Community (ECSC)   A regional organization for cooperation that deals with the coal and steel sectors of the member states. The European Coal and Steel Community, formed in 1952, placed under a single, supranational authority the coal and steel production facilities of (West) Germany and France and removed distributive restrictions among the six member countries. The original members of the ECSC were France, Belgium, (West) Germany, Italy, Luxembourg, and the Netherlands. Denmark, Ireland, and the United Kingdom became members in 1973; Greece joined in 1981; and Portugal and Spain entered the ECSC in 1986, bringing the total membership of the organization to 12. The aims of the ECSC are to contribute to the expansion of the economy, development of employment, and improvement of the living standard in the participating nations through the creation of a common market for coal and steel.

ECSC was the brainchild of French Foreign Minister Robert Schuman, who proposed the concept in 1950; the Treaty of Paris in 1951 outlined the purposes of the organization. ECSC is to assure the most rational distribution of production at the highest possible level of productivity, while avoiding the creation of persistent disturbances in the economies of member states. The six original members of ECSC brought into force two other communities in 1958—the European Economic Community and the European Atomic Energy Community. *See also* EUROPEAN ATOMIC ENERGY COMMUNITY (EURATOM); EUROPEAN ECONOMIC COMMUNITY (EEC).

Significance   The European Coal and Steel Community is an experiment not only in economic cooperation and integration but also in the political unification of Western Europe. While the early euphoria over the formation of the ECSC still exists, Western Europe is slowly moving toward closer cooperation and harmonization by 1992. Clearly, the member states have transferred some governmental powers to this and other supranational institutions. The ECSC is the first major successful international organization working toward political integration of a large and diverse region. The need to facilitate the free movement of goods and services and people between members has contributed decisively toward Western European integration, but political integration has also been urged in recent years. The plans for political union, at least until recently, go beyond the sporadic coordination of foreign policies, and broad institutional changes are always possible. However, there is still considerable opposition to supranational authority.

European Community (EC)   The common political organization created to make decisions concerning essential economic interests for three operating units: the European Economic Community (EEC), the European Coal and Steel Community (ECSC), and the European Atomic Energy Community (EURATOM). The EC is the overarching organization with six original members: Belgium, France, (West) Germany, Italy, Luxembourg, and the Netherlands. Since its formation six other nations—Denmark, Ireland, the United Kingdom, Portugal, Spain, and Greece have joined. The basic purpose of the EC is to establish a common market, a common external tariff, free flow of capital, and free migration of workers. The major institutions of the EC are: (1) the Council of Ministers, (2) the Commission, (3) the European Parliament, (4) the Court of Justice, and (5) the Court of Auditors. The Council of Ministers and the Commission constitute a dual executive, with the former directly representing the views of the member countries. The Commission's primary function is to initiate EC policy; decisions require approval by the Council of Ministers. The European Parliament serves as a deliberative body. The Court of Justice functions as the common court that interprets EC treaties and resolves disputes, and the Court of Auditors supervises audits and financial investigations. See also EUROPEAN ATOMIC ENERGY COMMUNITY (EURATOM); EUROPEAN COAL AND STEEL COMMUNITY (ECSC); EUROPEAN ECONOMIC COMMUNITY (EEC).

Significance   The European Community has a relatively high level of economic integration and it is now taking steps toward further integration, particularly toward a single market. The potential broadening of the EC membership by admitting East European states has raised new goals and directions, and these may have complex implications for the EC, both internally and externally. The road to 1992 and beyond will be both rocky and smooth for the EC. "Rocky" because the British government has been showing increasing resistance to the unification plan. There is skepticism outside Western Europe, especially in the United States and Japan, that the plan will ultimately be anything but a form of regional protectionism. If so, the question is, Will Western Europe emerge as a unified federation to threaten American and Japanese trade interests? This question, and many more, will be answered soon.

European Convention on Human Rights   A treaty establishing machinery for safeguarding human rights in Europe. The European Convention on Human Rights, adopted by the Council of Europe in 1953, set up a special commission and court to carry out its provisions. Twenty-three members of the Council of Europe have accepted the convention: Austria, Belgium, Cyprus, Denmark, France, Finland, Germany, Greece, Iceland, Ireland, Italy, Liechtenstein, Luxembourg, Malta, the Netherlands, Norway, Portugal, San Marino, Spain, Sweden, Switzerland, Turkey, and the United Kingdom. The Council of Europe proposed the European Convention on Human Rights in 1950, which then established machinery to investigate alleged violations of human rights in Europe. By accepting the convention, the contracting parties agreed to submit certain types of human rights violations and controversies to the binding decision of an international organization. Appeal can be made to the European Court of Human Rights; enforcement of the court decision is voluntary. See also COUNCIL OF EUROPE; EUROPEAN COURT OF HUMAN RIGHTS.

Significance   The European Convention on Human Rights is a most ambitious experiment by a large number of countries (23) to deal collectively with protection of human rights. It is also considered to be the most extensive international machinery devoted to dealing with human rights in the entire history of civilization. This convention—the first of its kind—has been emulated by the Organization of American States (OAS), which created the American Convention of Human Rights, to take effect in 1978. The Organization of African Unity (OAU) adopted a Charter of Human and People's Rights in 1982. To a limited extent, Amnesty International, the International Committee of the Red Cross, and the International Labor Organization (ILO) also have been actively involved in following rules to safeguard human rights on a worldwide scale. The United Nations itself and the Helsinki Accord (1975) provide many standards for protection of global human rights. The European Convention on Human Rights may increasingly serve as a model in many parts of the Third World and Communist bloc countries where human rights violation is a routine occurrence.

European Council   The summit meeting of the member states of the European Community (EC). The European Council was added to the formal European Community structure in 1974 in Paris. It discusses affairs of the European Community at the highest ministerial level, including substantive questions of foreign policy. The European Council meets three times a year in the capital of the country of the current president of the European Community. It has overall responsibility for comprehensive European cooperation and goal setting. The European Council has spelled out objectives for completion of a European internal market and creation of an area without national frontiers by 1992. In addition, the European Council is involved in technical development, progress toward economic and monetary union; strengthening of economic and social cohesion, improvement of the environment, measures to make the European Community more effective and democratic, and institutionalization of foreign policy cooperation. Members are the heads of state or government of the twelve countries represented at the European Community: Belgium, Denmark, France, Germany, Greece, Ireland, Italy, Luxembourg, the Netherlands, Portugal, Spain, and the United Kingdom. *See also* EUROPEAN COMMUNITY (EC).

Significance   The European Council—not to be confused with the Council of Europe—establishes general guidelines that are implemented by the Council of Ministers. The executive functions of the European Community are shared by the EC Commission, the EC Council of Ministers, and the European Council. In matters of internal community policy, the European Council receives proposals from the EC Commission and instructs it to implement its decisions. Both the EC Commission and the Council of Ministers have, in recent years, been involved in suggesting potentially critical steps toward supranationality. In 1985, the EC Commission called for 300 measures to remove physical, technical, and fiscal barriers to economic integration. The European Council approved the commission's recommendation, called the Act of European Unity, which intends to establish a single European market by 1992.

European Court of Human Rights   The judicial body of the European Convention on Human Rights. The European Court of Human Rights was established in 1959 by a protocol to the European Convention on Human Rights. The convention defined a wide range of civil, political, economic, and social rights and set up a mechanism for states and individuals to file complaints. As provided by the European Convention on Human Rights, the following human rights are to be guaranteed by the Court: security of persons; exemption from slavery and servitude; freedom from arbitrary arrest, detention, or exile; freedom from arbitrary interference in private and family life, home, and correspondence; freedom of thought, conscience, and religion; freedom of opinion and expression; freedom of assembly; freedom of association; freedom to unite in trade unions; the right to marry and found a family. The court consists of one judge from each of the member states of the Council of Europe (currently 23). No two judges may be nationals of the same state. The judges are elected by the Consultative Assembly for nine years; they may be reelected. The judges work in their individual capacities and they enjoy full independence in the discharge of their duties. The court is empowered not only to determine violations of the European Convention on Human Rights but also to rule on damages; its decisions are legally binding upon the parties concerned. *See also* EUROPEAN CONVENTION ON HUMAN RIGHTS.

Significance   The European Court of Human Rights has gone far beyond the purely hortatory Universal Declaration of Human Rights by the United Nations. This is due partly to the regional character of the experiment—one that deals mostly with developed nations. But, as Daniel Papp says, "Here Europe again leads the way with its European Court of Human Rights."[20] The implication of the legally binding decisions of the Court of Human Rights depends on the voluntary compliance of the government concerned in the case. A government has the right to denounce the court's decision, as the military government of Greece once did. In that instance negative publicity caused the military dictatorship in Greece to collapse and it was replaced by a more humane administration. The court's impact lies primarily in the public attention its decisions bring to governments charged with violation of human rights.

European Court of Justice   The judicial court of the European Community (EC). The European Court of Justice interprets treaties, settles disputes, and assesses penalties. It is composed of 13 judges— assisted by 6 advocates-general—appointed jointly by all member governments. They serve for renewable six-year terms, by common agreement between member states. The president of the court, who is selected by its full membership, directs the work of the court. Created in 1952 and located in Luxembourg, the Court of Justice is the final authority on all legal matters falling within the domain of the European Community. Its decisions are binding on member nations, European Community (EC) institutions, corporations, and all individuals. National courts can appeal to it for rulings on how to interpret EC law. For example, if one member country imposes tariffs on another member, complaints against the tariffs by the affected party may be made to the court, which then will rule on the legality of such tariffs. The court may also review the validity of measures taken by the EC Commission or the EC Council of Ministers and is authorized to judge on actions by a member country. *See also* EUROPEAN COMMUNITY (EC); EUROPEAN PARLIAMENT.

Significance   The European Court of Justice is one of the most obscure institutions in the European Community, but it has acquired a supranational character of its own. Ordinarily, any international court, including the International Court of Justice (ICJ), hears cases from member states, but the European Court of Justice is empowered to admit complaints from individuals, corporations, and other legal entities. "The European Court of Justice, for example, fulfills a community role that is somewhat like that of the U.S. Supreme Court in the United States."[21] Due to the unique nature of the EC as an international organization, its court not only has some features similar to an international tribunal, but also performs constitutional, administrative, and appellate functions. Like the ICJ, the European Court of Justice can, in certain instances, deliver advisory opinions.

European Economic Community (EEC)   One of the principal organizations of the European Community (EC) to bring about the creation of a common market and economic integration among member nations. The European Economic Community was established in 1958 by the Treaty of Rome to provide for free movement of goods, services, labor, and capital among its members and to adopt common economic, social, and political policies for the community. The other two organizations of the European Community are the European Coal and Steel Community (ECSC) and the European Atomic Energy Community (EURATOM). The original membership of the EEC was composed of Belgium, France, (West) Germany, Italy, Luxembourg, and the Netherlands. Since the founding of the EEC, six more members have joined it: Denmark, Ireland, the United Kingdom, Greece, Portugal, and Spain. The chief aims of the organization are to promote throughout the community a harmonious development of economic activities, a continuous and balanced expansion, an increase in stability, an acceleration in the rise of the standard of living, and closer relations between member states. These goals are to be sought through a common market and coordination of the economic policies of member states. *See also* EUROPEAN ATOMIC ENERGY COMMUNITY (EURATOM); EUROPEAN COAL AND STEEL COMMUNITY (ECSC); EUROPEAN COMMUNITY (EC).

Significance   The European Economic Community, or Common Market, is perhaps the most ambitious and pragmatic approach to interregional economic cooperation of our time. The EEC has shown remarkable success in eliminating trade barriers among rival countries and adopting common policies to create a common market. The Common Market has promised to yield economic benefits for the member states that could not be gained by their national economies operating as separate units. Larger enterprises have been able to take advantage of the economies of scale in goods production that a market of over 320 million consumers offers. Undoubtedly, Western Europe is the most successful region in the world in development of regional international organizations; the EEC is a prime example of its achievements. Implementation of plans for further political integration in 1992 will depend upon the collective will of member countries to promote policies that will be cooperative rather than competitive.

European Free Trade Association (EFTA)   A regional organization set up to eliminate tariffs and other trade barriers on industrial goods among its members. The European Free Trade Association, often dubbed the "Outer Seven" because its original members—

Britain, Norway, Sweden, Denmark, Switzerland, Austria, and Portugal—is distributed around the bloc of the European Economic Community's (EEC) "Inner Six." Established by the Stockholm Convention of 1959, EFTA has since been joined by Iceland as a full member and Finland as an associate, and Britain has dropped its membership. According to the convention, the objectives of EFTA are: (1) to promote within the area of the association and in each member country sustained expansion of economic activity, full employment, increased productivity and the rational use of resources, financial stability, and continuous improvement in living standards; (2) to ensure that trade between member countries takes place in conditions of fair competition; (3) to avoid disparity between member countries in the conditions of supply of raw materials produced within the area of the association; and (4) to contribute to the harmonious development and expansion of world trade and to the progressive removal of barriers to it. *See also* EUROPEAN COMMUNITY (EC).

Significance   The European Free Trade Association is a modest venture compared to the European Community (EC). Initially, Britain was refused membership in the EC; thus, in self-defense, it assumed the leadership of the rival scheme: the EFTA. But Britain and Denmark eventually withdrew from it the day before they became members of the European Coal and Steel Community (ECSC), the European Economic Community (EEC), and the European Atomic Energy Community (EURATOM) (in tandem these three organizations form the EC). With Britain's withdrawal from the EFTA, it went into eclipse. It is an ironic fact that the EFTA, whose goals clearly conflicted with nationalism, was forced to retreat, while there is now much optimism about the success of similar supranational objectives of the EC. On the positive side, the EFTA achieved its goals of eliminating tariffs and quotas on industrial goods among its members. The deepening of cooperation with the European Community in several areas led to the EFTA-EC Luxembourg Declaration of 1984, which stressed the common goal of creating a dynamic economy for all of Western Europe.

European Organization for Nuclear Research   A regional body of European countries constituted to encourage and facilitate collaborative efforts in fundamental nuclear research. The European Organization for Nuclear Research (usually known as CERN, from the French title of the interim body) was founded in 1954 in Paris. CERN is not concerned with work for direct military requirements; all of its experimental and theoretical findings are published or made public.

The members of the CERN are Austria, Belgium, Denmark, France, Germany, Greece, Italy, the Netherlands, Norway, Portugal, Spain, Sweden, Switzerland, and the United Kingdom. The main structure of the organization is its council, which meets once a year and is composed of not more than two delegates from each member country. The council has three principal committees: the Committee of Council, the Scientific Policy Committee, and the Finance Committee. Officials of these bodies have international responsibilities but they are not permitted to seek or receive instructions from any authority external to CERN. *See also* EUROPEAN ATOMIC ENERGY COMMUNITY (EURATOM); INTERNATIONAL ATOMIC ENERGY AGENCY (IAEA).

Significance   The European Organization for Nuclear Research has some of the world's largest accelerators and has attracted the interest of the leading nuclear physicists from many countries. Teams of research workers from CERN member countries and a number of Ford Foundation fellows are working cooperatively with CERN in subnuclear research of a purely scientific and fundamental character. The members of CERN are at comparable stages of nuclear research development. Its counterpart in Eastern Europe, the Joint Institute for Nuclear Research, consists of eleven countries from the former Communist bloc. John Stoessinger comments that "both these organizations are based on the common experiences and goals of the countries comprising their respective regions and, undoubtedly, derive considerable scientific and technological benefits from this fact."[22] They are the leading regional organizations in the world to conduct theoretical and experimental research in peaceful uses of nuclear physics.

European Parliament   The legislative institution of the European Community (EC). The European Parliament exercises democratic control over the European Community and over the legislative process. The composition of the European Parliament derives from the following nations: Belgium, Denmark, France, Germany, Greece, Ireland, Italy, Luxembourg, the Netherlands, Portugal, Spain, and the United Kingdom. The parliament consists of 518 representatives directly elected by the member countries, apportioned as follows: France, Germany, Italy, and the United Kingdom 81 each; Denmark 16; Ireland 15; Luxembourg 6; Belgium, Greece, and Portugal 24 each; Spain 60; and the Netherlands 25. The parliament holds consultations, hearings, and an annual deliberative session. It is consulted concerning the annual budget of the European Community, advises on legislation, and exercises democratic control over the EC Commission and the EC Council of Ministers. The parliament can adopt resolutions on its own initiative—not only on internal EC matters but also on international issues. The parliamentarians and the interest groups they form are supported by research, language, and secretarial services. Members sit in the parliament in political, not national, groups; sessions are held in either Strasbourg, France, or Luxembourg and the parliamentary committees normally meet in Brussels. *See also* UNITED NATIONS GENERAL ASSEMBLY.

Significance   The European Parliament is a part of the European Community's institutional framework for the promotion of national interests of EC member states. Although the EC Commission has clearly allied itself with the European Parliament, the main channel for the exertion of influence on EC decisions remains the EC Council of Ministers. Thus, in spite of wide-ranging transnational possibilities of coalition among the parliamentarians, the European Parliament is nothing but a weak link in the EC decision-making apparatus. The European Parliament has many wasteful procedures, including carting some 50 tons of documents back and forth. However, the parliament serves as a forum for general discussion and criticism, and the commissioners appear before it to answer questions and defend their policy. The most remarkable single political step in recent years occurred in 1979 when the first direct elections for the European Parliament were held. Ultimately, the parliament may pass laws that could be effective within the member states and thereby form the basis of a kind of "European government."

F

Falkland Islands War   A limited war between Argentina and Britain in 1982. The Falkland Islands War lasted for only 74 days; thereafter Britain recovered the Falklands from an initial Argentinian takeover. Called the Malvinas by Argentina, the Falklands lie 8,000 miles from Britain in the South Atlantic, and 400 miles off the Argentine coast. The islands were invaded and quickly captured by Argentina. Britain retaliated by imposing a sea blockade within 200 miles of the islands. The British response to the Argentinian invasion of the Falklands was the result of a long-standing commitment to hold the islands; they have been a British dependency since 1833, and 1,900 inhabitants there, mainly of British origin, demonstrated a preference for continuing the British connection. Argentina, on the other hand, based its claim to this approximately 4,700 square miles of territory on having wrested it from Spain following Argentina's independence in 1816. The Falklands War resulted in the loss of 255 British lives and 712 Argentines dead and injured; Britain lost 2 destroyers, 2 frigates, 2 other ships, and 34 aircraft; Argentina lost 1 cruiser, 1 submarine, 3 other ships, and 100 aircraft. *See also* IRAN-IRAQ WAR.

Significance   In the Falkland Islands War, British loss was clearly considerably more than the islands could be worth. The islands themselves have had no strategic or economic value for Britain, yet a military expedition was mounted to recapture the islands. This decision was probably based on the British government's concern that if Argentina's takeover was allowed to go unchallenged, other states in dispute with Britain would be tempted to take similar actions. Another reason might have been that British Prime Minister Margaret Thatcher wanted to build her national popularity prior to approaching elections by demonstrating her leadership and also enhancing Britain's prestige and standing in the world. President Ronald Reagan broke the position of neutrality in

Latin American disputes and decided to assist Britain with nonmilitary and diplomatic support. Now, the British government maintains a garrison of 3,000 troops in the Falklands, has built a strategic airport, and has developed a small number of industries there.

Food and Agricultural Organization (FAO)   A specialized agency of the United Nations charged with raising the levels of nutrition and the efficiency of production and distribution of food and other agricultural products in the world. The Food and Agricultural Organization also aims at improving national standards of living and contributing to the expansion of the world economy. Established in Quebec, Canada, in 1945 and headquartered in Rome, FAO is empowered to promote (1) scientific, technological, social, and economic research relating to nutrition, food, and agriculture; (2) the improvement of appropriate education and relevant administrative practices and the spread of public knowledge of nutritional and agricultural sciences; (3) the conservation of natural resources and the adoption of improved methods of agricultural production; (4) the improvement of the processing, marketing, and distribution of food and agricultural products; (5) the adoption of policies for the promotion of adequate agricultural credit; and (6) the adoption of international policies with respect to agricultural commodities. The 1974 FAO World Food Conference, held in Rome, made several recommendations to increase grain reserves as part of a world disaster stockpile. *See also* SPECIALIZED AGENCIES OF THE UNITED NATIONS.

Significance   The Food and Agricultural Organization has been subject to criticism for a variety of reasons, including putting too much emphasis on short-term food aid and not enough effort into long-term agricultural growth to cope with the serious food crises already ravaging the world. With the support of the United States, a World Food Council was created in 1974 consisting of 36 members who are responsible to the United Nations Economic and Social Council (ECOSOC). This move was greeted with some skepticism by the FAO. Another organization, called the International Fund for Agricultural Development, arose, also over the objection of FAO, from the Rome Convention; the charge here was to develop agricultural projects in the Third World. The FAO began its operations by responding to the immediate problem of feeding the starving millions in the post–World War II period; even today the same tremendous problem of food shortages exists. Clearly the international system of food production and distribution is in a period of profound transformation. One of the symptoms of that transformation is the perception that international governmental organizations that remain rooted in the world of the 1940s no longer work. However, a lasting contribution that FAO and a few early international organizations have made is that their internal structures (conference, council, and secretariat) have been adopted by other, and more contemporary, world bodies.

Functionalism   The theory that international economic and social cooperation is a prerequisite for the ultimate solution of conflicts and elimination of war. Functionalism is based on the premise that socio-economic problems tend to be universal and a coherent attack upon them must elicit action from the world community. The assumptions of functionalism may be divided into three segments: First, war is regarded as the product of the objective conditions of human society. Functionalism is postulated as a way to extirpate the roots of war by eliminating the objective conditions of society. Second, functionalists attribute the phenomenon of war to the institutional inadequacy of the nation-state system; the state system is incapable of coping with the problems of vast economic and social development. The theory of functionalism proposes to make peace attainable by organizing hu-man social life according to its requirements. Finally, functionalists believe that war is caused by the attitudes, habits of thought and feeling, and national outlook that are fostered by the state system. To functionalists, politics is the root of all evil, so they want to separate it from economics and provide an international organization that will build habits of cooperation at the economic and technical levels. The assumption is that people will slowly shed their narrow national out-looks and that common solidarity will be deepended. *See also* REGIONAL ECONOMIC GROUPS; REGIONAL POLITICAL GROUPS; UNITED NATIONS: REGIONALISM.

Significance   Functionalism is the hypothesis that, having learned the usefulness of international cooperation at the technical and eco-nomic levels, nations thereafter will be agreeable to transfer their habits of mind to collaborative solutions at the political level. Accord-ing to David Mitrany, "the problem of our time is not how to keep the nations peacefully apart but to bring them actively together."[23] The theory itself is subject to criticism on several counts. First, the func-tionalist analysis of the causes of war is inadequate. A necessary con-nection between war and economic and social inequity has not been established empirically. Second, separability of politics from econom-ics seems to be at variance with demonstrated reality. Third, although functional cooperation in the world has increased, conflict does not appear to have undergone any corresponding decrease. Finally, the assumption that loyalties are created by functions, and can be transferred, is subject to question. Despite its visible weaknesses, functionalism provides an alternative scheme that holds more promise than current grandiose world government proposals.

G

General Agreement on Tariffs and Trade (GATT)   An international organization to promote trade among members by liberalizing and reducing tariffs. The General Agreement on Tariffs and Trade consists of an international set of bilateral trade agreements that are multilateralized through GATT's application of most-favored-nation (MFN) clauses in all agreements. It is aimed at the abolition of trade restrictions among the contracting parties. GATT was signed in Geneva in 1947 by 23 countries as a preliminary document pending the establishment of an International Trade Organization (ITO). The United States rejected the ITO, which would have been a specialized agency of the United Nations. GATT, based on executive agreements, gradually developed as the main instrument for the encouragement of foreign trade. It is designed to achieve the objectives set forth in the preamble to the agreement: the contracting parties recognize that their relations in the field of trade and economic endeavor should be conducted with a view to raising standards of living, ensuring full employment, developing the maximum use of the resources of the world, and expanding the production and exchange of goods. The 96-member GATT's current functions are: (a) negotiating the reduction of tariffs and other impediments to trade, (b) developing new trade policies, (c) adjusting trade disputes, and (d) establishing rates to govern the trade policies of its members. *See also* GROUP OF SEVENTY-SEVEN.

Significance   Trade restrictions under the General Agreement on Tariffs and Trade cover hundreds of thousands of commodities. Tariff concessions are applied to more than two-thirds of the total imports of all GATT members. From the Third World perspective, the entire trend toward free trade not only places them in jeopardy, but is also being promulgated by the developed nations in violation of the principles that these countries themselves enunciated through

68

GATT. There is growing tension between the so-called rich and poor nations, as the latter attempt to induce changes in the international economic system that will favor their economic and social interests. Although 96 (actually there are over 108 GATT members, if associate members are included) of the 166 members of the United Nations are members, many Third World nations do not belong to GATT. Third World nations favor the United Nations Conference on Trade and Development (UNCTAD) to GATT as a forum for discussing trade with developed nations. East European states, including the Soviet Union, have begun to solicit membership, as they try to change over from a directed (state-controlled) to an open-market economy.

Genocide   The killing or destruction of a population solely because of its racial, religious, national, tribal, or ethnic origin. The term "genocide" is derived from the Greek *genos,* meaning race, nation, or tribe, and the Latin suffix *cide,* meaning killing. In 1948 the United Nations General Assembly adopted an International Convention on the Prevention and Punishment of the Crime of Genocide; this went into effect in 1951. Responding to the horrors of Nazi atrocities against the Jews, the Convention sought to make genocide an international crime. The Convention defines genocide as participation in the following acts, committed with the intent to destroy, in whole or in part, a national, ethnic, racial, or religious group as such: (1) killing members of the group, (2) causing serious bodily or mental harm to members of the group, (3) deliberately inflicting on the group conditions of life calculated to bring about its physical destruction in whole or in part, (4) imposing measures intended to prevent births within the group, and (5) forcibly transferring children of the group to another group. *See also* WAR CRIMES.

Significance   Genocide occupies a prominent place in the history of civilization; the Genocide Convention is a response to the brutality of the period prior to and during World War II by Nazi Germany, especially against persons of Jewish origin. The Convention includes as punishable: conspiracy, incitement, directing and planning, attempts, and complicity to commit genocide, as well as overt acts of genocide. The contracting parties agreed that genocide, whether committed in time of peace or in time of war, is a punishable crime under international law. International public opinion has traditionally opposed genocide, but many dictators ignore international law and public opinion, killing thousands of their countrymen. Originally the convention was partly a post hoc justification for aspects of the international trial of war criminals in Nuremberg, but since its adoption by the United Nations, it has become a basis for prosecuting contemporary violators of the convention. Although the United States was a leader in drafting this convention, the U.S. Senate did not ratify it until 1986.

Good Offices   The services rendered by an impartial third party in a dispute. The good offices of a third state involve communication between two other parties without suggesting any form of settlement or compromise. In mediation, the third party participates in the negotiation process itself. But a state is said to offer good offices when it tries to induce the parties to negotiate between themselves. The disputing parties are free to construct their own solution to the problem while the state offering good offices merely acts as a conduit for communication or a catalyst for action. Often, when a dispute seems at a stalemate, further negotiation is stimulated by an influential state coming forward to offer good offices. In a strict sense, the third party does not act as an arbitrator, but, as with most political processes, the practical execution of good offices is not so clearly defined. Good offices frequently blend with mediation and vice versa. *See also* MEDIATION; PACIFIC SETTLEMENT OF DISPUTES.

Significance   Early formalization of good offices into a viable diplomatic tool to avert war was demonstrated by the Hague Conventions for the Pacific Settlement of Disputes (1899 and 1907). The Hague Conventions declared it desirable for third parties to offer their good offices to a dispute, and stated that such an offer should not be regarded as an unfriendly act. The activities of the secretary general of the United Nations are often referred to as "mediation"—particularly in the media, as well as by many political scientists and even by some international lawyers. This has, in effect, led to the creation of a new tool for the promotion of peaceful solutions—the Commissions of Inquiry. Upon the agreement of both parties, a commission would be formed to address a particular dispute. That commission's function would be to investigate the facts of the disagreement and to report them. The report would not be in the nature of an award to either side but, in the spirit of good offices, would provide information for the disputing parties to utilize or disregard as they pleased. The underlying idea of the formalization of good offices into the Commissions of Inquiry was that if war could be postponed, the facts clarified and presented, then war might be avoided altogether.

Great Powers   States that possess exceptional military and economic strength and consequently play a major and often decisive role in international affairs. States are frequently categorized as (1) great powers, (2) intermediate powers, and (3) smaller nation-states. The great powers reside at the summit of the world pecking-order hierarchy. Left unchecked, a great power could easily overcome any military resistance that could be summoned by the intermediate or smaller nation-states. Although the great powers remain at the summit of a bargaining position, the balance-of-power system makes peaceful negotiation more palatable than risking war. The fundamental principle of the balance-of-power is that once an equilibrium is reached (often satisfactory to the great powers, and to a lesser degree the other states), then the status quo is maintained. This has been characterized as the halfway point between world order and world chaos. *See also* UNITED NATIONS SECURITY COUNCIL.

Significance   Great powers have the potential to gobble up the lesser actors, but the balance-of-power system keeps them in check. The first large-scale attempt at a balance-of-power system followed the Peace of Westphalia in 1648. But the great power of Napoleon and his armies upset the tenuous balance and threatened world domination. France violated the balance-of-power system but subsequently pointed out the value in its maintenance. With the proliferation of nuclear technology, it is only a matter of time before the United States, the Soviet Union, Britain, France, China, and India lose their monopoly on nuclear power to other nations. Yet, the five permanent members of the Security Council (Britain, China, France, the Soviet Union, and the United States) that possess the veto power—a positive indication of great-power status—remain after almost 50 years the militarily most powerful nations in the global state system.

Group of Seventy-Seven (G-77)   A conglomerate of Third World countries focused on developing unified solutions to economic issues by effective use of caucuses. Originally, the Group of Seventy-Seven (G-77), composed of African, Asian, and Latin American nations, gathered to intensify their involvement in international conferences and to bring Third World concerns to the fore. By 1964, their persistence had paid off and their members (77 at that time) participated in the first United Nations Conference on Trade and Development (UNCTAD). Their aim was to balance the scales vis-à-vis the great powers and create viable economic and trade policies that were mutually beneficial to the great powers and the G-77 members. As their successes grew, so did their ranks. The original 77 grew to 130 members in the 1980s. *See also* NONALIGNED MOVEMENT (NAM); UNITED NATIONS CONFERENCE ON TRADE AND DEVELOPMENT (UNCTAD).

Significance   The Group of Seventy-Seven has been playing a major role in promoting the interests of the Third World by pressing upon the developed countries the need for attention to foreign aid, technical cooperation, and better trade policies. While their primary focus has been in the area of economics and trade, they have also solicited humanitarian and technological aid packages from the more developed countries. With such a large number of members, achieving a consensus on agenda, issues, tactics, and solutions has been difficult for G-77. They frequently have fallen short of their goals due to internal conflict and lack of power to build a winning coalition. Because there were originally 77 states, the caucus is known as the Group of Seventy-Seven, despite the numerical increase. Universal membership organizations, like the United Nations, spurred by the Group of Seventy-Seven, have endorsed the less-developed countries' (LDCs) position on a variety of issues by means of hortatory resolutions. Since the G-77 states gained a demographically dominant position in these organizations, their activities have increasingly reflected the priorities that these states give to the struggle against colonialism and racial discrimination and to the promotion of economic and social development of the Third World.

Guerrilla War   Warlike acts by individuals or groups not immediately under the orders of responsible military authorities. Guerrilla forces are not always accorded the rights enjoyed by regular armed forces of a belligerent. Because guerrillas are usually grossly outnumbered by regular armed forces, tactics include surprise raids and attacks on communication and supply lines. Guerrilla warfare is an efficient style of combat because it requires few resources. Factors affecting the viability of guerrilla operations are popular support, ideologically committed personnel, adequate supplies, and favorable terrain. The aims of guerrilla war are not always to win a military victory, but often to win a political victory through prolonged resistance. It has developed as the leading instrument of revolutionaries in their fight against what they perceive as world imperialism. *See also* CIVIL WAR; INSURGENCY.

Significance   Traditionally, the success of guerrilla war has depended largely on the support accorded to it by the local population in supplying food and havens. However, it brings armed conflict back into the political process. One of the earliest guerrilla wars was the

Boer War (1899–1902) in South Africa, in which the Dutch-descended Boers and the British fought and won an uneasy partnership. In 1968, the North Vietnamese Tet offensive utilized guerrilla forces. Although the offensive was not a military success for the North Vietnamese, its demoralizing effect on the already reluctant American public was a major political victory for North Vietnam. Guerrilla strategists took advantage of American discord over the Vietnam War, knowing that the United States would not continue prosecuting a protracted war. Another major victory for guerrillas was the fall of the Somoza regime in Nicaragua. It should be noted that most guerrilla campaigns fail to achieve any considerable military victories, but the prolonged engagement of guerrilla forces can undermine the willingness of a larger but less committed force to continue. Currently, groups utilizing guerrilla warfare tactics on a limited scale include the Irish Republican Army (IRA), the African National Congress (ANC), and the Palestine Liberation Organization (PLO).

Gulf Cooperation Council (GCC)   A regional grouping of six Arab states in the Persian Gulf. The Gulf Cooperation Council was formed in 1981 by Bahrain, Kuwait, Oman, Qatar, Saudi Arabia, and the United Arab Emirates (UAE). The contracting parties seek to ensure security and stability of the region through economic and political cooperation and to promote, expand, and enhance economic ties on solid foundations and for the best interests of the people; to coordinate and unify economic, financial, and monetary policies, as well as commercial and industrial legislation and customs regulations; and to achieve self-sufficiency in basic foodstuffs. The GCC emphasizes stability based on traditional political systems, self-reliance, and a collective approach. Although GCC's Conciliation Commission is responsible for resolving disputes among members, it is not a vehicle for political and economic integration. All members of the GCC are oil-producing states and have special ties and common systems of government, which helps them to agree upon a coordinated approach in politics and economic and cultural fields. *See also* LEAGUE OF ARAB STATES.

Significance   The Gulf Cooperation Council restored a feeling of unity to its member states, and its constant endeavor is now to maintain and uphold identifiable views on common problems, to project a unified front against external threats (for example, from Iran and then recently Iraq), and to accelerate coordination in the diverse areas influencing their day-to-day lives. Within the first decade since the inception of the GCC, it has emerged as a dynamic force, providing stability not only to the region but also to the Arab world as a whole.

Divisions, backwardness, and isolation were the results of European rule, which ended in 1971 when Britain pulled out of the Gulf region. Throughout the 1970s and the 1980s the Gulf achieved tremendous advances in all spheres of activity, aided by its new-found oil wealth and its strategic position. Caught in the whirlwind of development and modernization, the Gulf countries have grown closer together and have ways to cooperate as members of one family in tackling regional problems and planning for the future. This cooperation was demonstrated in 1990 when Iraq occupied Kuwait, a GCC member, and the Emirates and other members joined an international coalition led by the United States to liberate Kuwait. The GCC showed maximum solidarity and with the help of the international coalition, Kuwait was liberated on February 27, 1991.

H

Hague Peace Conferences   The two international conferences held at the Hague in the Netherlands in 1899 and 1907. The Hague Peace Conferences, called by Tsar Nicholas II of Russia, were notable as major diplomatic gatherings—assembled in a time of peace—designed to deal with a number of subjects relating to international relations. The first Hague Conference, attended by 26 states, concluded an agreement on arms control and other measures for maintaining peace; the second conference, in which 44 countries participated, sought conventions on the pacific settlement of disputes and other related issues of war and peace. The first Hague Peace Conference codified international arbitration procedures in its Convention for the Pacific Settlement of Disputes (later revised by the second Hague Conference) and established the Permanent Court of Arbitration. It was an attempt to establish a permanent machinery and procedures for the peaceful resolution of disputes. The two Hague conferences were precursors for such modern universal international organizations as the League of Nations and the United Nations. *See also* PERMANENT COURT OF ARBITRATION.

Significance   The Hague Peace Conferences were meant to deal more directly with the threat of war by decreasing armament levels; they failed to attain their chief objective. However, the conferences represented further development toward international organization. "For the first time," says Stephen Goodspeed, "virtually all states in the world met on equal terms to consult together on mutual problems of international concern."[24] Another leading feature of the Hague conferences was that small states and great powers, European and non-European, all met on equal terms. The most lasting contribution of the Hague conferences was the creation of the Permanent Court of Arbitration. The final act of the conference proclaimed the unanimity of the delegates in admitting the principle of compulsory arbitration.

75

The Permanent Court (which still exists) is not a court in the common sense of the term, but consists of a panel of persons (nominated by the signatories) from which judges can be selected to arbitrate a dispute. The Hague Convention of 1899 codified many of the accepted practices of land warfare, and the Hague Convention of 1907 revised the 1899 convention concerning the rights and duties of belligerents and of neutral states and persons.

Helsinki Accord   An agreement signed in 1975 aimed at providing peace and stability in Europe between the West and the East. The Helsinki Accord, also known as the Final Act, entered into by the United States, Canada, the Soviet Union, and 32 European countries at the end of the Conference on Security and Cooperation (1973–1975) was concluded in Helsinki, Finland. Although the Helsinki Accord did not carry the full force and effect of a binding treaty, it did ameliorate the postwar dispute over the German peace settlement and establish a status quo for Europe. The Helsinki Accord was more a firm "declaration of policy intent" than a treaty. The agreement declared inviolable the frontiers of all the signatory nations, thus legitimizing the Soviet Union's World War II territorial gains; provided for scientific, technological, and cultural exchanges; and pledged the signatories to respect human rights, including "freedom of thought, conscience, religion, or belief." All parties to the agreement have interpreted the individual components of the accord in their own way, and Western critics and Soviet dissidents have frequently accused the Soviet government of violating the Helsinki human rights declaration. *See also* CONCERT OF EUROPE.

Significance   The full impact of the Helsinki Accord has only been felt recently, during the dramatic changes occurring in the Soviet Union. Even though the Soviet Union has made great technological and scientific strides since World War II, it lags sorely behind the Western world in these areas. To be sure, the considerable technological and scientific exchange that has taken place since the accord has substantially benefited the Soviet Union while yielding little benefit to the Western participants. But increased cultural contacts, travel between East and West, and proliferation of press coverage have nevertheless transformed the once debatable concept of "détente" into a reality. Closer communication between East and West has gradually brought about political and philosophical changes within the Soviet Union. It may well be said that the 16-year-old accord has played no small part in effecting the democratization and secession of some of the Soviet republics, German unification, and the fall of the Communist party, the monopoly organization that had controlled the Soviet Union since 1917 and all of the East European socialist bloc states since World War II.

Holy Alliance   A compact signed in 1815 by Alexander I of Russia, Francis I of Austria, and Frederick III of Prussia. The Holy Alliance was the brainchild of Tsar Alexander, and the other two monarchs also agreed to join with him in invoking the name of "the very holy and indivisible Trinity." These monarchs further agreed that they would be guided in their mutual relations by the "sublime truths taught by the eternal religion of God, our Savior." The alliance was to further Christian ideals of justice, charity, and peace in government, in the relations of rulers, and between rulers and their subjects. The declaration was subsequently signed by all but three of the European rulers (the British prince regent, the pope, and the Ottoman sultan). *See also* CONGRESS OF VIENNA.

Significance   Although the Holy Alliance became associated with repression, it nevertheless was a landmark in international relations. The alliance was perceived by liberals as a tool to maintain the reactionary political settlement of the post-Napoleonic peace treaties, including the plan to reconquest those Spanish colonies in the New World that had achieved independence; they of course were not reconquered. The great powers had seen the horrors of war in the previous twenty years and were thus not eager to risk another. The Holy Alliance, born of the religious emotionalism of the tsar, has no parallel. However, nobody was serious about the treaty except the tsar himself. It was considered a dead document from the moment of issue and did not influence the policy—either domestic or foreign—of any state. Despite its drawbacks, the Holy Alliance marked the arrival of a new age of international unity and cooperation and would serve as a future model for similar attempts.

I

Independence   Freedom from subjection to the influence or control of others. Independence movements are encouraged by principles enunciated in the Declaration Regarding Non–Self Governing Territories of the United Nations Charter and served to legitimate their aspirations for nationhood. By 1990, the emergence of new nations had more than tripled the membership of the UN. In the nineteenth and twentieth centuries, much of Latin America and almost the whole of Africa had been colonized by Britain, France, Spain, Belgium, Portugal, Germany, Italy, and the Netherlands. In 1960, the UN General Assembly adopted the historic declaration Granting of Independence to Colonial Countries and Peoples, and the last wave of independence and statehood swept through Africa. *See also* UNITED NATIONS: MEMBERSHIP.

Significance   Independence is not so much a right as it is a condition, status, or quality of a state. It is a condition in which a state assumes the freedom to manage its own domestic and international affairs without external interference. This includes the power to establish its own constitution, to create and enforce its own laws, and to exercise exclusive jurisdiction over all persons and property within its territory. Also, independence implies the right of a state to conduct foreign relations without interference or control from other states. This includes the right to enter into treaties and alliances, to acquire territory, and to make war and create peace. But independence does not mean freedom from law—merely the freedom from control by other nations. No state is truly independent of others; being a part of the international community requires contact, whether direct or indirect. States may coexist as sovereign nations, but they are required to interact with one another out of necessity. For example, territorial boundary disputes must be settled through negotiation, and, likewise, fishing limits must be determined. While independence means

78

freedom from another state's authority, it also carries the burden of international responsibility.

India-Pakistan Wars   Three armed conflicts between India and Pakistan that have occurred since the independence of India and the creation of Pakistan in 1947. The first limited armed confrontation between the two neighbors occurred in 1948 in Kashmir—a disputed territory. (Muslim Kashmiris have never felt fully a part of India. They were split off from fellow Muslims in the northern half of the state and delivered to India in 1947 by their Hindu maharaja). Since then there have been sporadic clashes between the armies of the two neighboring countries. In 1965 Pakistani troops, supported by 90 Patton tanks, crossed the cease-fire line into southern Kashmir and advanced so rapidly that they threatened the vital road over the mountains linking Srinagar, the capital of Kashmir, with the plains of India. India opened a new front and invaded West Pakistan in a massive attack. This round of Indian-Pakistani confrontation ended through the diplomatic efforts of the Soviet Union. The third round of the India-Pakistan wars was fought in East Pakistan when India intervened in the 1971 Pakistani civil war, which resulted in the formation of Bangladesh. *See also* PEACEKEEPING FORCES: UNITED NATIONS MILITARY OBSERVER GROUP IN INDIA AND PAKISTAN (UNMOGIP).

Significance   The three India-Pakistan wars were the outgrowth of religious conflict between the two countries. As John Stoessinger postulates, "The most savage religious war in history was neither the Christian Crusades against Islam nor the Thirty Years' War that pitted Catholic against Protestant. It was the war of Hindu against Moslem in the twentieth century."[25] This Hindu-Muslim antagonism in the Indian subcontinent is deep-rooted and goes back to around A.D. 1000 when Islam came to India. The only attribute Islam shared with Hinduism was its emphasis on the hereafter; there the similarity ended. Primarily, the religious conflict between Hinduism and Islam was at the root of the past struggles for independence between India and Pakistan and remains the chief cause of contention today. Prospects for peace and stability in the Asian subcontinent do not seem so bright in the 1990s because the dispute has surfaced again and the armies of the two countries are positioned for confrontation.

Institute of International Law   A nongovernmental society of international law specialists devoted to the development of the law of nations. Founded in 1873 in Ghent, Belgium, the Institute of

International Law undertakes the clarification of general principles and their codification into international law. Membership is restricted to 60 specialists in theory or practice of international law and to 72 associates. The Institute of International Law promotes the progress of international law by giving assistance to all genuine attempts at gradual and progressive codification of international law; contributing both to maintenance of peace and observance of the legalities of war; and assisting in bringing about the triumph of those principles of justice and humanity that should regulate international relations. Institute proceedings are conducted in French. Its headquarters, first in Ghent and later in Geneva, are now in Paris. *See also* INTERNATIONAL LAW; INTERNATIONAL LAW COMMISSION.

Significance   The Institute of International Law drew on the greatest minds in international law. One such international law scholar was Louis Renault, cowinner of the 1907 Nobel Peace Prize. An early member of the Institute of International Law, Renault defined its task as the judicial organization of international life. As a nongovernmental organization the institute is free to pursue potential solutions without governmental restraint. During the critical formative years of international law, in the nineteenth and early twentieth centuries, the institute's goal was to create a viable system of international law that would encourage better international relations and eventually replace war as an ongoing mechanism for resolving conflicts. The Institute of International Law was awarded the 1904 Nobel Peace Prize.

Insurgency   A rebellion against a government that does not reach the magnitude of an all-out revolution. In most cases the insurgents do not receive recognized status as belligerents; when they do it is very limited. After World War II, communist regimes found insurgency to be a vehicle with which to advance their nationalistic and economic goals. Clearly, the threat to use nuclear arms was not a viable option in dealing with insurgencies. Another option had to be devised. President John Kennedy developed a strategy known as "flexible response" to counter Soviet-backed insurgencies. This policy was one of reaction to every Soviet probe with equal response, thereby negating any gain that was made. As a result the United States and other Western countries have formed counterinsurgency units. Units such as the Green Berets, the Delta Force, the Seals, and the Rapid Deployment Force have almost continually engaged insurgencies of communist origin or support. Vietnam, Angola, Mozambique, Namibia, El Salvador,

Nicaragua, and Afghanistan are recent examples of long-duration insurgencies. *See also* CIVIL WAR; GUERRILLA WAR.

Significance   Although insurgency is sometimes recognized in the Western Hemisphere, it does not have universal application. If the magnitude, effectiveness, and duration of the insurgency is great, then some measure of diplomatic recognition from foreign states and limited belligerency rights are granted. The United States extended such recognition to the Cuban insurgents in their rebellion against Spain in the 1890s. In the 1980s the United States officially supported the Afghan insurgency against the Soviet-backed communist regime in Afghanistan. Since the end of World War II, insurgencies increasingly have been ascribed to the use by communist forces of certain nationalistic aspirations to challenge established authority in many Third World countries.

Inter-American Commission on Human Rights   An organization that promotes the establishment and observance of standards for human rights by members of the Organization of American States (OAS). The Inter-American Commission on Human Rights was established in 1959 and has functioned since then as a collateral body supporting the aims of the OAS. The commission makes recommendations on human rights issues to members of the OAS, performs studies, investigates allegations of human rights violations, and encourages members to provide information on their human rights activities. The commission is the primary implementation mechanism of the American Convention on Human Rights, entered into by most American states in 1969. The American Convention on Human Rights guarantees 22 basic political and civil rights—including the right to life, humane treatment, personal freedom, fair trial, privacy, compensation, equal protection, freedom from slavery, and others. The commission is composed of seven individuals nominated by member governments and selected by the Permanent Council. Following the model for safeguarding human rights in Europe, a court has been set up in Costa Rica to apply and interpret the American Convention on Human Rights. *See also* EUROPEAN CONVENTION ON HUMAN RIGHTS.

Significance   The Inter-American Commission on Human Rights acts as a mediatory body, using its power to issue reports that could be regarded as sanctions against malefactors and thereby induce compliance. The Commission may investigate complaints, conduct on-site inspections with the consent of the state involved, and make recommendations. The Inter-American Commission on Human Rights receives hundreds of complaints every year, although very few cases have resulted in public debate. Through quiet persuasion, it has been a positive influence on a number of states that have furnished information to the commission; others have refused to provide any data. The commission has been ineffective in influencing the conduct of the Cuban, Brazilian, and Chilean governments in recent years. It has no authority to force members to respond to its requests or to enforce its decisions.

Inter-American Development Bank (IDB)   A regional financial institution for promoting the economic and social development of Latin America. The Inter-American Development Bank's basic goal is to contribute to the acceleration of development in member countries—individually and collectively—through the financing of economic and social projects. Its current membership includes Latin American countries (except Cuba), the United States, Canada, Austria, Belgium, Denmark, France, the United Kingdom, Japan, Israel, the Netherlands, Spain, Switzerland, Germany, and Yugoslavia. The bank operates with ordinary capital resources and a Fund for Special Operations, both contributed by all member countries. Besides these capital funds, a number of other funds placed under its administration enable the IDB to extend additional financial assistance to developing nations. Established in 1959, the bank began operation the following year with an authorized capital of $1 billion, of which 55 percent was provided by its Latin American members. *See also* INTERNATIONAL BANK FOR RECONSTRUCTION AND DEVELOPMENT (IBRD); ISLAMIC DEVELOPMENT BANK (IDB).

Significance   The Inter-American Development Bank is the oldest regional institution in the world in the field of development finance. It has had a remarkable impact on Latin American economic and social development despite the inadequacy of its resources. By the end of the 1980s, the bank had provided cumulative loans totaling nearly $25 billion in support of 2,000 development projects, with much of this funding provided by the United States. The bank has also been successful in securing financing in private capital markets in Europe and Japan. As is often the case with Third World countries, the Latin American members of IDB, uneasy about the dominant role of the United States in the bank, have welcomed European and Japanese infusion of capital. IDB maintains close ties with the International Bank for Reconstruction and Development (IBRD) and other international financial agencies in order to ensure effective coordination of technical and financial development strategies for its members.

Inter-American Treaty of Reciprocal Assistance   A regional alliance formed to safeguard the Western Hemisphere from aggression. Adopted in 1947 in Rio de Janeiro, the Inter-American Treaty of Reciprocal Assistance, also known as the Rio Treaty, was signed by 19 of the 21 American republics; only Ecuador and Nicaragua withheld their signatures. Cuba withdrew from the treaty in 1960. The region covered by the Inter-American Treaty of Reciprocal Assistance extends from the North Pole to the South Pole and includes Canada, Alaska, the Aleutians, Greenland, the Falklands, the South Orkneys, and Antarctica. The signatories condemned war and agreed not to resort to the threat or the use of force in any manner inconsistent with the United Nations Charter or this treaty. They sought to resolve all possible controversies that might arise by peaceful settlement. The contracting parties also wanted to settle controversies among themselves—within the Inter-American system—before referring disagreements to the United Nations. *See also* ORGANIZATION OF AMERICAN STATES (OAS).

Significance   The Inter-American Treaty of Reciprocal Assistance is the military wing of the Organization of American States (OAS). It provides a security system to ward off any direct or indirect aggression committed in the Western Hemisphere. In the case of direct attack, the signatories would undertake appropriate action against the aggressor. Indirect aggression calls for consultation among member countries. The treaty supports American opposition to foreign intervention in the Western Hemisphere, which was originally proclaimed in the Monroe Doctrine in 1823. Thus the Treaty constituted the first general security pact entered into by the United States. The Inter-American Treaty of Reciprocal Assistance provides that an armed attack by any state against an American state would be considered an attack against all American states; each of the signatories would meet as quickly as possible and agree upon collective measures against the aggressor. Appropriate measures of self-defense would be undertaken until such time as the United Nations Security Council could impose measures necessary to maintain peace. The treaty served as a model for the North Atlantic Treaty Organization (NATO) and other post–World War II defense alliances. Jurisdictional conflicts between the OAS and the United Nations have arisen since 1947 in several cases involving questions of aggression and dispute settlement.

International Air Transportation Association (IATA)   A nongovernmental organization that regulates the fares that member airlines may charge on international routes. The International Air

Transportation Association draws its legal basis from a special act of the Canadian Parliament, given royal assent in 1945; the association was founded in Havana, Cuba, that year. Headquartered in Montreal, Canada, the IATA promotes safe, regular, and economical air transport. It provides the means for collaboration among air transport enterprises engaged directly or indirectly in international air transport service. The association is made up of voluntary members of airline companies. Their membership is composed of 128 scheduled airlines, flying flags of over 100 countries. Any airline is eligible to join the IATA if it operates scheduled air services between two or more countries. The governing body of the IATA convenes at an annual general meeting, where each member has one vote. At these meetings, rates and fares, schedules, tariffs, condition of carriage, and other agency matters are discussed. IATA resolutions must have the approval of interested governments before they can become effective. *See also* INTERNATIONAL CIVIL AVIATION ORGANIZATION (ICAO).

Significance   Most members of the International Air Transportation Association are state-owned airlines and other similar organizations. The IATA decides the fares to be charged in international routes, and member airlines must follow its decisions. When the IATA was established, the airlines preferred renouncing their rate-setting autonomy and moving to a system of unrestricted price competition. The association is active in the fields of traffic, finance, legal, and technical knowledge for member airlines. The IATA is one of the few international nongovernmental organizations prominently involved in creating air transport rules. It acts as an agency from which member airlines may seek solutions for those problems they cannot handle individually.

International Alliance of Women   A multilateral organization for the improvement of the status of women and the creation of conditions of gender equality. The International Alliance of Women was founded in Berlin, Germany, in 1904 under the title of the International Women's Suffrage Alliance. The inception of the international movement for women's suffrage (voting rights for women) in Washington in 1902 was the beginning of cooperation among women for that purpose. But by the end of World War I (1914–1918), the battle was half won and the activities of the organization were gradually extended to secure equality in all fields. Its statutes were revised in 1960, and the original title of International Women's Suffrage Alliance was changed to International Alliance of Women. This was done because enfranchisement had been secured for women in many countries; thus the original name was considered superfluous. Membership in the International Alliance of Women includes nationally affiliated societies in 53 countries and associated societies in 10 others. *See also* UNIVERSAL DECLARATION OF HUMAN RIGHTS.

Significance   The International Alliance of Women has been successful in securing many reforms to establish equality of liberties, status, and opportunities between men and women in all spheres of life. The first intergovernmental efforts for the improvement of the status of women, which took place in the late 1920s in Latin America, were a result of pressures exercised by the International Alliance of Women in that region. Before the outbreak of World War II in 1939, in nearly all countries where agitation was permitted, most of what the suffrage movement had struggled for had been won. When the United Nations Commission on the Status of Women was established in 1946, many nongovernmental women's organizations, including the International Alliance of Women, began to participate in its activities as observers. On the whole, it can be said that such inequalities as then existed sprang from social and economic conditions—enforced not by law, but rather by customs and prejudice. Thus the International Alliance of Women found itself in a peculiar position: where its works were most needed, it was not permitted to function, and where it was permitted, relatively little remained to be done.

International Atomic Energy Agency (IAEA)   An autonomous body of the United Nations that seeks to accelerate and expand the societal contributions of atomic energy for peaceful purposes. The International Atomic Energy Agency, proposed by President Dwight Eisenhower in 1953, was established in 1957 and is headquartered in Vienna, Austria. According to its statute, the agency is authorized: (1) to encourage and assist atomic energy research and development as well as its practical application; (2) to make provision for materials, services, equipment, and facilities to meet the needs of research and pragmatics; (3) to foster the shaping of scientific and technical information on peaceful uses of atomic energy; (4) to encourage exchange and training of scientists and other experts; (5) to establish and administer safeguards to ensure that special fissionable and other materials, services, equipment, facilities, and information made available are not diverted to military use; (6) to establish, in consultation or collaboration with specialized and competent agencies of the United Nations, the optimum standards of safety for protection of health and the minimization of danger to life and property; and (7) to acquire or establish facilities, plants, and equipment that are deemed useful for the implementation of its tasks. See also NUCLEAR PROLIFERATION.

Significance   The International Atomic Energy Agency has made a substantial contribution to the development of the peaceful uses of atomic energy on a worldwide scale. It teaches modern technology to scientists of many developing nations and seeks to raise the living standards of the people by developing cheap energy sources. The agency conducts 1,800 on-site inspections annually, at 520 locations around the globe. The IAEA has formulated basic safety standards for radiation protection and issued regulations and codes of practice for specific types of operations, including the safe transport of radioactive materials. Further, it plays a pivotal role in the effort to reduce the threat of war by encouraging cooperation—especially between the atomic powers and developing nations.

International Bank for Economic Cooperation (IBEC)   A multilateral system of payments arranged between ten socialist countries on the basis of "collective currency," that is, a transferable ruble (TR). The International Bank for Economic Cooperation advances credits for financing foreign trade and other transactions. The origin of IBEC dates back to the late 1950s, when the first steps toward multilateralization of payments between Eastern European countries were taken within the framework of the Council of Mutual Economic Assistance (CMEA). The basic principle regulating IBEC's activity is the full equality of member countries, under which they enjoy similar rights regardless of the size of their individual contributions to IBEC's capital fund. The administrative arms of IBEC are its Council and Board. The council is its chief organ, charged with the general direction of activities, and is composed of representatives of all member countries. Each country casts one vote. See also COUNCIL OF MUTUAL ECONOMIC ASSISTANCE (CMEA or COMECON); INTERNATIONAL INVESTMENT BANK (IIB).

Significance   The International Bank for Economic Cooperation provided a sound financial basis for an integrated economic system based on the principles of socialist international cooperation and in accordance with the goals set by the Council of Mutual Economic Assistance (CMEA). It sought to harmonize financial and currency relations among member states by effecting bilateral and multilateral settlements (and other financial transactions) on the basis of the transferable ruble—a unit of account that had the same gold content as the Soviet ruble. IBEC offered credits to member states with a view to satisfying their financial needs in areas such as international trade, industrial production, economic planning, and financial organization. It cooperates with the United Nations Conference on Trade and Development (UNCTAD) and the Economic Commission for Europe (ECE). Its future, however, is questionable given the demise of socialism and socialist cooperation in an Eastern Europe formerly dominated by the Soviet Union but in a state of flux today, both politically and economically.

International Bank for Reconstruction and Development (IBRD)
A specialized agency of the United Nations created to provide capital for rebuilding those countries devastated by World War II and for the development program of underdeveloped societies. The International Bank for Reconstruction and Development, commonly known as the World Bank, was established by the Bretton Woods agreement of 1944, began operations in 1946, and currently has 155 members. It makes loans for projects and relies for its funding on its ability to borrow in the international capital markets and to secure substantial contributions from members. Voting power of member nations is proportionate to their capital subscriptions, known as weighted voting. The IBRD has made 3,000 loans, totaling over $150 billion. Interest rates vary, depending on the international cost of borrowing hard currency, since the lending funds of the IBRD come mainly from private world capital markets. Headquartered in Washington, D.C., the IBRD is the second pillar of the Bretton Woods System concerned with international financial and trade management—the first and the third, respectively, are the International Monetary Fund (IMF) and the General Agreement on Tariffs and Trade (GATT). *See also* BRETTON WOODS SYSTEM; GENERAL AGREEMENT ON TARIFFS AND TRADE (GATT); INTERNATIONAL DEVELOPMENT ASSOCIATION (IDA); INTERNATIONAL FINANCE CORPORATION (IFC); INTERNATIONAL MONETARY FUND (IMF).

Significance   The International Bank for Reconstruction and Development is the leading organization in the field of multilateral financing of investment and technical assistance. Initially concerned mainly with the reconstruction of Europe after World War II, the bank since then has been providing funds and technical assistance to developing countries. The World Bank makes loans on terms that are fair but sufficient to earn a profit in the form of interest and commission fees; it has instituted assumable interest rates that fluctuate according to the rates of world inflation. The bank's affiliate, the IDA, operates the "soft loan" window (soft loan features include the low cost of a loan—no interest [but a small annual service charge], a long repayment period, a slow amortization rate, and several other easy terms). The IBRD's decision to lend is supposed to be based only on economic considerations, but critics have accused the organization of allowing politics, corruption, favoritism, incompetent consultancy, and inefficient bureaucracy to dominate the evaluation process and financing of projects. The bank is the world's biggest source of aid to developing countries, and although it has progressively increased the scope of its lending programs, it is unable to respond to the capital needs of debt-ridden Third World nations.

International Chamber of Commerce (ICC)   An organization that represents all the economic factors of international business, including commerce, industry, finance, and transportation. The International Chamber of Commerce was chartered by a decision taken at the International Trade Conference held in Atlantic City, New Jersey, in 1919, and founded in Paris in 1920. It is a professional organization that seeks to further the interests of its members. Fifty-eight National Committees are members of the ICC and serve as the major components of the organization. These committees gather in Council meetings, which take place twice a year. The council is the supreme governing body of the ICC; its executive board consists of 15 members appointed by the council upon the recommendation of the president. The ICC promotes trade and investment according to the concepts of free and fair competition. It harmonizes trade practices and terminology and secures effective and consistent action for the improvement of business conditions among nations as well as for the solution of international economic problems. *See also* INTERNATIONAL CONFEDERATION OF FREE TRADE UNIONS (ICFTU).

Significance   The International Chamber of Commerce vocalizes the considered judgments of a worldwide business membership in developed and developing countries. The ICC's lobbying efforts are aimed at contributing to international stability and amicable exchange by formulating norms of international business relations. Its agenda includes backing the expansion of international trade and examining—jointly with the major international governmental organizations (IGOs)—any measures that might help the liberalization of international trade and promote world prosperity. Furthermore, by encouraging closer professional relationships and greater cultural understanding among business leaders and business organizations of various countries, the ICC promotes peace and friendship in the world community. The variety of objectives pursued by the ICC as an international nongovernmental organization are both extensive and important in a world so dominated by private business operations.

International Civil Aviation Organization (ICAO)   A specialized agency of the United Nations charged with the development and regulation of international air traffic. The International Civil Aviation Organization was established in 1947 at a convention chartered by the International Civil Aviation Conference held in Chicago the same year. The Convention on International Civil Aviation superseded the Paris Convention of 1919, which had established the International Commission for Air Navigation, as well as the Pan American Convention of Air Navigation at Havana in 1928. With headquarters in Montreal, Canada, the ICAO was set up to study and report on customs facilities, traffic control, aircraft maintenance, and the need for standardization. Some of its additional functions include safeguarding the rights of the member countries to operate international airlines, preventing discrimination practices, promoting simpler formalities at international borders, developing regional plans for ground facilities and services, and fostering development of air law conventions. *See also* INTERNATIONAL AIR TRANSPORTATION ASSOCIATION (IATA).

Significance   The International Civil Aviation Organization is a leading contributor of technical assistance to states seeking to develop their civil aviation programs. All members of the United Nations may subscribe to it, and any sovereign country not a member of the United Nations may seek admission; there are more than 150 members. In electing these states, the ICAO Assembly must give equal representation to (1) states of major consequence in air transport, (2) states that make the largest contribution to the provision of facilities for the international civil air navigation, and (3) states not otherwise included whose election would ensure that all major geographical areas of the world are represented. The ICAO has provided efficient machinery for the achievement of international cooperation in the air, improving safety and regularity, and promoting the use of technical methods and equipment. In view of the rapid expansion of air transportation, the ICAO has been active and effective in the area of air safety; it conducted an outstanding investigation of the 1983 downing of a Korean airliner by the Soviet air force.

International Civil Service Commission (ICSC)   An international organization that reviews and reports on UN administrative and budget matters. The International Civil Service Commission, established by United Nations General Assembly Resolution 3357 (XXIX), 1974, regulates and coordinates the conditions of service in the UN system. It reviews the UN salary schedule and periodically submits progress reports to the General Assembly. The General Assembly appoints 15 members of the commission, two of whom—the chairman and the vice chairman—serve full time; others have four years in their personal capacities as individuals of recognized competence. The doctrine of the international civil service, which has been articulated by officials and legal writers, is based upon an understanding of the British civil service code. Like the British civil service, which loyally and impartially serves the government of the day, the international civil service is also expected to fashion the secretariats of international organizations as a body above national self-interest. *See also* INTERNATIONAL ORGANIZATIONS (IOS).

Significance   The International Civil Service Commission serves to ensure proper management and employee practices within the UN system. It deals with questions concerning management improvement, staff composition, career development, personnel policies, staff rules, field staff, and privileges and immunities. It functions as an agency concerned with the improvement of the civil service and the employee work situation. The commission has been instrumental in fighting to maintain a balance of nationalities and women within the UN Secretariat. The traditional concept of a truly effective civil service is that it must serve the interests of the organization as a whole. According to Graham and Jordan, this concept can be said to consist of four basic principles: loyalty, impartiality, independence, and fair recruitment.[26] Although the United Nations and other international organizations attempt to follow these apolitical principles of administration, it is not always possible to do so since many of these organizations are political in nature.

International Coffee Organization   An organization seeking to achieve a reasonable balance between coffee supply and demand while assuring that adequate supplies are available at fair prices. The International Coffee Organization furthers international cooperation in connection with world coffee problems. Established in 1963 under the International Coffee Agreement, with headquarters in London, the organization has 51 coffee-exporting members and 24 importing countries. Most of the countries of Africa, South America, and the Caribbean are coffee-exporting members. The importing countries are Canada, the United States, Japan, Singapore, Australia, Fiji,

Austria, Belgium, Denmark, Finland, France, Germany, Greece, Ireland, Italy, Luxembourg, the Netherlands, Norway, Portugal, Spain, Sweden, Switzerland, the United Kingdom, and Yugoslavia. The structure of the International Coffee Organization includes the International Council, consisting of representatives of all member countries, and the Executive Board, composed of eight members from importing countries and eight from exporting nations. *See also* INTERNATIONAL TIN COUNCIL (ITC).

Significance   The International Coffee Organization periodically reviews the problems concerning world demand and supply of coffee and establishes export quotas accordingly. It attempts to foster economic diversification and development of coffee-producing countries to improve political and economic relations between producers and consumers and to increase the consumption of coffee, as well as to avoid excessive fluctuations in prices. The 51 exporting countries account for over 99 percent of world coffee exports, Brazil being the largest supplier; the 24 importing countries use 90 percent of the coffee supply. Following the lead in oil price increases in the 1970s, the coffee-exporting countries also demanded a higher price for coffee. Even though the price subsequently went up, exporters were unsuccessful in the global market generally.

International Commission of Jurists   An organization that monitors worldwide observance of the rule of law and due process. The International Commission of Jurists documents systematic violations of human rights and seeks to mobilize public opinion against such violations. Founded in 1952 in Geneva, it supports and advances those principles of justice that constitute the basis of the rule of law, and it mobilizes the jurists of the world in support of the rule of law through public meetings, conferences, publications, and other appropriate actions. The commission gives aid and encouragement to those who are denied the rule of law. The International Commission of Jurists receives financial contributions from lawyers, law firms, individuals, foundations, and governments. It includes 40 members, elected in personal capacities from 40 countries. The commission has no member from the former Communist bloc countries, but several are considering membership. The Executive Committee consists of seven members elected by the commission. *See also* AMNESTY INTERNATIONAL; UNIVERSAL DECLARATION OF HUMAN RIGHTS.

Significance   The International Commission of Jurists conducts worldwide inquiry into the definition and applications of the rule of law, observes trials, and reports on situations in various countries. It regularly issues judgments on cases in violation of the rule of law and human rights issues. Like Amnesty International, the International Commission of Jurists is highly respected for its work and enjoys a reputation for thoroughness and impartiality in researching complaints. It is one of the international nongovernmental organizations (INGOs) in the forefront of monitoring the status of human rights. Although the United Nations itself is involved in protecting human rights worldwide, many INGOs, such as this commission, are also dedicated to the promotion and protection of universally recognized human rights.

International Confederation of Free Trade Unions (ICFTU)   An international organization promoting the interests of the working people of the world. The International Confederation of Free Trade Unions works in the interests of constantly rising living standards, full employment, social security, and reductions in the gap between the rich and the poor. The ICFTU was founded in 1949 in London by 70 trade unions from 53 countries, with a total membership of 50 million. Today it has 141 affiliated organizations, totaling 87 million individual members in 96 countries and territories. The ICFTU is a member of the Conference on Non-Governmental Organizations in a consultative status with the United Nations Economic and Social Council (ECO-SOC). In the immediate post–World War II period, many new international nongovernmental organizations (INGOs) were founded. Some were being torn apart by the East-West conflict of that time. The Americans, the British, and others, for example, left the World Federation of Free Trade Unions (WFTU), and a rival organization, the ICFTU, was formed. Its governing structure is the Congress, which meets every four years; the headquarters of the organization is in Brussels. *See also* INTERNATIONAL LABOR ORGANIZATION (ILO).

Significance   The International Confederation of Free Trade Unions could be viewed as an incipient global labor movement. Since its inception, the ICFTU has been fighting for adequate aid for economically developing areas of the world. In defense of freedom—not only trade union rights but also the right of every nation to self-determination—the ICFTU has taken action in various countries. It has given active assistance to union movements through the offer of solidarity funding and the assistance of experienced trade union representatives. The ICFTU also has been working to promote international understanding for disarmament and for the establishment of peace. By condemning dictatorships and trying to alleviate the grievances of oppressed people, the ICFTU has gained the attention of workers all over the world. It frequently takes vocal policy positions, especially when it feels that the rights of affiliated trade unions and their members have been violated.

International Council of Scientific Unions (ICSU)   An international forum for maintaining contact among the members. The International Council of Scientific Unions provides opportunities for its members to engage in scholarly activities such as public presentations, collegial stimulation of research, and dissemination of findings. It is a forum for planning and organizing cooperative international research projects, such as the International Geophysical Year (IGY). Founded in Brussels in 1919 as the International Research Council, its present title was adopted in 1931. The ICSU maintains special cooperative relations with the United Nations and its various agencies and with international nongovernmental organizations. The council has set up the following committees to facilitate scientific activity on an international level: Committee on Space Research, Scientific Committee on Antarctic Research, Committee on Data for Science and Technology, and Joint Committee with the World Meteorological Organization (WMO) for the Global Atmosphere Research Program. *See also* WORLD METEOROLOGICAL ORGANIZATION (WMO).

Significance   The International Council of Scientific Unions is a center for the aggregation and articulation of interest in particular disciplines, and as such it lobbies at both national and international levels. The council is used by the international scientific community as a repository where highly technical advice may be sought and data within particular fields compared. It is also used as a forum in which compromise solutions to problems can be explored and in which mutual understanding can be reached. The council encourages international scientific activity with a view to promoting research and scientific education. The ICSU has been able to recruit and organize the support services of governments of diverse political persuasions in furthering its programs on a global basis. It has vigorously pursued research in the field of natural resource development so that renewable energy resources can be harnessed for the benefit of humankind.

International Criminal Police Organization   A nongovernmental organization through which police departments around the world cooperate to help prevent and suppress international crime in the world. The International Criminal Police Organization, known as

INTERPOL, was established in Vienna in 1923 under the name International Criminal Police Commission and is composed of a government-related membership. It was reconstituted in 1946 and its headquarters were transferred from Vienna to Paris. The police agencies of 146 countries are currently members. According to its statutes, the purpose of INTERPOL is to ensure and promote the widest possible mutual assistance network among criminal police authorities, within the limits of laws existing in individual states. Further, it undertakes to establish and develop diverse institutions capable of contributing to an efficient repression of common law crimes. Its parameters, however, exclude all matters having a political, military, religious, or racial character. *See also* INTERNATIONAL NONGOVERNMENTAL ORGANIZATIONS (INGOS).

Significance   The International Criminal Police Organization is not an international police force with agents around the globe. Rather, it serves as a clearinghouse for the exchange of information and requests for assistance from member police agencies. It furnishes members with studies and reports on individuals and groups engaged in international crimes. INTERPOL uses an extensive radio network and circulars to provide members with information on wanted criminals, missing persons, unidentified bodies, and stolen properties. The principal crimes of interest to INTERPOL are narcotics traffic and counterfeiting operations in Europe. The presence of such criminal activity is not surprising, since so many countries on that continent have common frontiers and malefactors can easily travel to a neighboring country to escape punishment.

International Development Association (IDA)   An affiliate of the International Bank for Reconstruction and Development (IBRD) that makes "soft loans" to developing countries. The International Development Association, technically a separate institution, is in fact a subsidiary of the IBRD, or World Bank. The IDA was created in 1960 and has a separate pool of funds drawn from member contributions. It has 139 members and it focuses on making soft loans to the poorest countries, usually at no interest and only a small service charge. The IDA has extended over $15 billion in credit, to more than 50 countries. It promotes economic development by providing more flexible financial terms that bear less heavily on the balance of payments of the recipient countries. The membership of the IDA is open to member countries of the World Bank. IDA subscriptions are roughly proportionate to subscriptions to the World Bank's capital; thus the United States is the largest shareholder. As in the World Bank, voting rights in the IDA are proportionate to subscriptions. *See also* INTERNATIONAL BANK FOR RECONSTRUCTION AND DEVELOPMENT (IBRD); INTERNATIONAL FINANCE CORPORATION (IFC).

Significance   The International Development Association is a "soft money" window of the World Bank; it provides capital on exceptionally favorable terms for less developed countries. This is done because of criticism of the World Bank's conservative lending practices. Soft loan features of the IDA include low cost (no interest, but a small annual service charge) and a convenient policy of 50 years for full repayment of the principal, with a ten-year grace period before any payments are due, then 1 percent payable annually for the next ten years, and 3 percent annually for the next thirty years. Judging from the poor record of debt payment by many impoverished nations of the world, it is doubtful whether a majority will ever repay IDA loans. Another unique feature of the IDA is that member countries are organized into two groups for purposes of subscription of funds; different provisions are made for the two groups. Subscriptions are payable over a five-year period, and countries in both groups subscribe 10 percent of their initial subscriptions in gold or freely convertible currencies; the remaining 90 percent is paid in five equal installments in gold or convertible currencies by the industrialized and developed nations and in national currencies by the less developed nations.

International Energy Agency (IEA)   An organization formed in 1974 by the industrialized Western nations, Japan, and Turkey to counter the bargaining power of the Organization of Petroleum Exporting Countries (OPEC). The International Energy Agency was created as a reaction to the 1973–1974 Arab oil embargo and the dramatic increase in oil prices by OPEC. The Agency was established as an operating body within the framework of the Organization for Economic Cooperation and Development (OECD) when the energy problem of the industrialized nations had become acute. The IEA fosters cooperation among major oil-importing nations, promotes stability in world energy markets, provides a bargaining mechanism for confronting OPEC, and ensures the security of energy supplies. The United States, Canada, Japan, Turkey, and 12 European countries formally created the IEA in Paris. France, Greece, and Finland abstained from voting for the establishment of the IEA; five other members of the 24-nation OECD voted favorably but did not join it. Current members are Canada, the United States, Australia, New Zealand, Japan, Austria, Belgium, Denmark, Germany, Greece, Ireland, Italy,

Luxembourg, the Netherlands, Norway, Portugal, Spain, Sweden, Switzerland, Turkey, and the United Kingdom. The agency has an executive committee composed of representatives from its member countries; its decisions are binding upon its members except for the priority of contrary arrangements. *See also* ORGANIZATION FOR ECO-NOMIC COOPERATION AND DEVELOPMENT (OECD); ORGANIZATION OF PETROLEUM EXPORTING COUNTRIES (OPEC).

Significance   The International Energy Agency has adopted an emergency oil-sharing plan to be put into operation in the event of a reduction in oil supplies to member countries. The formation of the IEA and its oil-sharing policy in case of another crisis demonstrates that the major oil consumers wish to be prepared in advance for any emergency situation. However, the agenda has not yet been put into operation as no oil crisis has occurred since the inception of the IEA. Nevertheless, an extensive system of reviews is conducted in order to assess the effectiveness of programs by member nations in the fields of energy conservation, research, stockpiling, energy sharing, and use of alternative sources of oil. Most of these measures are in operation in the IEA countries and have helped to reduce the demand for oil, thereby lowering its price. The main weakness of the IEA is that its influence is basically confined to industrialized noncommunist states, and consequently it cannot coordinate global energy resources.

International Finance Corporation (IFC)   A specialized agency of the United Nations responsible for furthering economic development through loans to private enterprises in less developed member countries. The International Finance Corporation invests—without government guarantees—in productive private enterprises in association with investors who can provide competent management. The corporation was established in 1956, and its basic function is to encourage investment in private enterprises in developing countries through both lending and equity participation. The origin of the IFC goes back to President Harry Truman's request in 1950 that the United States International Development Advisory Board recommend an appropriate policy toward economically backward regions of the world. Subsequently the board proposed the establishment of the IFC, and the United Nations set it up with a subscribed capital of $78,366,000. It has 155 members, and, as in the International Bank for Reconstruction and Development (IBRD) and the International Development Association (IDA), the voting power of member states is weighted according to their financial contributions. *See also* INTERNATIONAL

BANK FOR RECONSTRUCTION AND DEVELOPMENT (IBRD); INTERNATIONAL
DEVELOPMENT ASSOCIATION (IDA).

Significance The International Finance Corporation seeks to supplement, but not compete with, private capital sources. It looks to
other investors to provide part of the capital required for a project.
It is essentially an investing, rather than a lending, institution and
judges projects on the basis of their merits as investments for private
capital. In addition to capital subscriptions, the IFC also obtains funds
from repayments of investments, sales of equity and loan investments,
and net income. The corporation's overall goal is to make the greatest
possible use of private capital for economic development. Accordingly, it is empowered to undertake financing on terms that it considers appropriate, taking into consideration the requirements of the
borrowing firm and the risks to be assumed by the corporation. Along
with the International Bank for Reconstruction and Development
(IBRD), the International Development Association (IDA), the International Monetary Fund (IMF), and some of the regional financial
organizations, the IFC is one of the major institutional sources of
capital assistance to developing nations.

International Fund for Agricultural Development (IFAD) A specialized agency of the United Nations that offers grants and loans
to help increase food production in the Third World. The International Fund for Agricultural Development was established in 1977,
following a resolution adopted by the World Food Conference held
in Rome in 1974. The IFAD's purpose is to mobilize resources to
be made available on concessional terms for agricultural development
in Third World member countries. It provides financing for projects
and programs specifically designed to introduce, expand, or improve
food production, taking into consideration the need to increase production in the food-deficit countries. Funds for the IFAD come mainly
from the Organization of Petroleum Exporting Countries (OPEC) and
the Western nations. The Governing Council of the IFAD has three
kinds of representation: donor-developed countries, donor-develop-
ing countries, and recipient-developing nations. Membership in the
IFAD is divided into the following three categories: (1) developed
countries, 20; (2) developing non-exporting countries, 12; and (3)
other developing Third World countries, making a total of 143 countries. *See also* FOOD AND AGRICULTURAL ORGANIZATION (FAO); WORLD
FOOD COUNCIL (WFC).

Significance   The International Fund for Agricultural Development was designed to serve as a financial source for agricultural projects in the Third World. The oil-producing Third World countries donated 43 percent of the IFAD's initial three-year $1 billion capitalization. Their efforts were supplemented by the industrialized nations and several international organizations that participate in financing and are responsible for the administration of loans and supervision of project implementation. Initially the financing system worked well, but the collapse of the world oil prices in the 1980s led to the refusal of OPEC nations to contribute, and since then the IFAD has had serious problems in maintaining an optimum program. Consequently Third World per capita food production has barely raised the poverty level and there is constant threat of calamity.

International Governmental Organizations (IGOs)   Institutions in which various states are members by agreement among governments. This kind of organization provides the process by which states establish and develop formal institutional structures for the conduct of certain aspects of their relationships with each other. IGOs are also called public intergovernmental organizations. The evolution of the earliest international governmental model can be traced to the ancient Greek city-states and the Concert of Europe in 1815. The Rhine River Commission in Europe, established in 1815, is the oldest surviving international governmental regional organization. The International Telegraphic Union (now International Telecommunication Union), established in 1865, and the General Postal Union, founded in 1874 (since 1878, the Universal Postal Union), are the oldest extant global organizations. Two general global organizations—the League of Nations and the United Nations—were set up in 1919 and 1945, respectively. The United Nations with its many specialized agencies and conferences has the potential for increasing political and economic cooperation worldwide. *See also* LEAGUE OF NATIONS; RHINE RIVER COMMISSION; UNITED NATIONS (UN).

Significance   International governmental organizations are formed to deal with a variety of cross-national technical, political, economic, military, and cultural problems. The debate about how extensively and in what ways these organizations should involve themselves in world affairs remains controversial. Nonetheless, IGOs continue their diverse activities in various regional and global policy-making bodies. They take independent positions from member states on economic, social, and cultural global problems, and it is the newer states, and those most vulnerable politically and economically, that are most supportive of IGOs. Feld and Jordan opine that "Membership in IGOs broadens their [new nations'] range of national options—they can 'shop,' for instance, among various international technical cooperation programs . . . to get the best 'deal'."[27]

International Institute for Strategic Studies (IISS)   A center with headquarters in London formed to provide a foundation of accurate information and promote security and peace among the nations of the world. The International Institute for Strategic Studies assists in the public comprehension of key world security issues and promotes professional debates and scholarship on international security matters through provision of an open forum. Founded in 1958 by a group of British analysts, academics, politicians, journalists, and clergymen, the IISS as of 1989 had become fully international with 1,680 full members, 565 associate members, and 200 student members from 74 countries. Its financial support is mostly from the United States. The institute publishes *Strategic Survey*, an annual overview; *Survival*, a journal; and *The Military Balance*, an assessment of military strength and defense spending of every country in the world. It also publishes a series of monographs entitled the *Adelphi Papers*.

Significance   The International Institute for Strategic Studies is a nonpartisan soundingboard for the ideas, concerns, and desires of individuals from many different countries, all relating to arms control, disarmament, and the problems of survival in the nuclear age. The Institute is concerned with strategic questions—not just with the military aspects of security but also with the social and economic sources, and with the political and moral implications of the existence and use of armed force; in other words, with the basic problems of achieving peace. It is international in its council, has a staff independent of any government, and is not the advocate of any particular interest group. The IISS has become a most prestigious forum for discussion and debate for an international constituency concerned with security and peace. The reports and publications issued by the institute on strategic matters are taken very seriously by policymakers all over the world because of their objectivity and accuracy.

International Investment Bank (IIB)   A financial organization created within the framework of the Council of Mutual Economic Assistance (CMEA) to encourage trade and development of socialist nations. The International Investment Bank grants long-term and medium-term credit, primarily for carrying out projects connected with the international socialist division of labor. Established in 1970 in Moscow, the bank consists of ten nations belonging to the CMEA; it uses as a unit of account the transferable ruble (TR), having the same gold content as the Soviet ruble. The main functions of the bank include (1) forming reserve capital as well as creating special funds; (2) receiving funds in TR, convertible, and other currencies; (3) issuing interest-bearing bond loans for placement on international capital markets; (4) placing surplus funds with other banks and buying and selling currency, gold, and securities; and (5) making other business transactions within the limits of its competence. *See also* COUNCIL OF MUTUAL ECONOMIC ASSISTANCE (CMEA or COMECON); INTERNATIONAL BANK FOR ECONOMIC COOPERATION (IBEC).

Significance   The International Investment Bank, like other financial institutions in the socialist bloc, is state-run and state-controlled. The command economic system is essentially a developmental strategy that relies on administrative control and the mobilization of resources under state direction, as opposed to the Western market-oriented and private ownership enterprises. In practice, the problems connected with financing common investment projects are considered within the context of intra-CMEA cooperation. Recent attempts to reinvigorate coordination by the CMEA of Eastern bloc economic activity have run into serious obstacles. Economic managers in the IIB turn to world markets to satisfy, for example, their countries' needs for energy and raw materials. The IIB has established wide contacts with other international economic organizations, and mutually beneficial operations are carried out with banks of developed capitalist countries and even with banks of the developing nations. Dramatic developments in IIB operations have occurred in the late 1980s and early 1990s as a result of political, military, and economic changes, both internally and externally, in Eastern Europe.

International Labor Organization (ILO)   A specialized agency of the United Nations responsible for the improvement of working conditions in member countries. The International Labor Organization was created originally by the 1919 peace settlement but became a part of the United Nations system in 1945. The organization was established as an autonomous institution within the League of Nations; it now has over 150 members. The format includes the all-member International Labor Conference and the smaller Governing Body, both of which are represented by tripartite delegations: one worker, one employer, and two government delegates, each with a separate vote. The conference normally meets annually at the ILO's headquarters in Geneva to determine general policies. Major goals include full employment, raising the standard of living, ensuring proper earnings and working conditions, the provision of adequate training facilities, recognition of the right to collective bargaining, and social security measures.

Significance   The International Labor Organization is one of the oldest international organizations, and a unique one. It sits apart from other international governmental bodies because, although its members are nation-states, a tripartite system of national representation—including individuals—is provided. Members who persistently disregard ILO labor rules and principles are placed on a special "blacklist" until they improve their standards. Like any other international organization, the ILO is a politicized body. In the 1970s, it devoted so much time to resolutions dealing with the Arab-Israeli conflict and other disputes that the United States became disenchanted. In 1977, the United States decided to withdraw from the ILO, complaining that it ignored labor conditions in communist countries. As a result, the ILO finally addressed that issue to the satisfaction of the United States, and its membership was resumed in 1980. If American withdrawal had become permanent, and other developed nations had followed suit, the potential of this respected voice for the resolution of global labor problems would have been gravely diminished.

International Law   The body of rules, principles, and standards to which states are supposed to be bound by mutual consent. International law sets out rules explicating the rights and duties of states in their international relations. The origin of international law may be first traced to the fourth and third milliennia B.C., but the general body of modern law dates from the late sixteenth and early seventeenth centuries, when it was created to bring order to the relationship and conduct of sovereign nations in Europe. The Dutchman Hugo Grotius established himself as the "father of international law" with the publication of his book *De jure belli ac pacis* (*Law of War and Peace*) in 1625. The sources of international law include (1) treaties and agreements, (2) international custom and usage, (3) general principles of law, and (4) international judicial decisions. The International Court of Justice (ICJ) is responsible for interpreting international law. The subjects of international law are states, acting through their recognized governments. International law strives to ensure freedom of trade, communication, and conduct of international relations. *See also* CONGRESS OF VIENNA; UNITED NATIONS INTERNATIONAL COURT OF JUSTICE (ICJ); INTERNATIONAL LAW COMMISSION; INTERNATIONAL RELATIONS.

Significance   The conceptualization of international law is a noble one but its application often has been difficult and unsuccessful. The lack of coercive sanctions has influenced some to assume that international law has the character of moral imperative rather than legal agreement. The difficulty was compounded after World War II by the cold war between the superpowers. The contending nations strongly resisted measures supported by their opponents, thus hindering the United Nations in its progress toward formulating guidelines for international security. Nevertheless, the United Nations, through the International Law Commission, has continued to codify international law concerning the rights and duties of states, international crimes, the regime of the high seas, and the law of treaties. International law aspires to protect the civil rights of individuals, especially the right to enjoy freedom of thought, expression, and press. With the birth of many new nations in the Third World, demands were voiced for a new body of international law. Among other concerns, the emerging nations and the socialist bloc countries insisted upon guarantees of sovereign equality. Thus the new concept of international law is not that of a system imposed upon them by former colonial or other foreign powers, but one of consensual rules and regulations governing relations among equal nations.

International Law Commission   An agency of the United Nations General Assembly charged with initiating studies and making recommendations to encourage the development of international law and its codification. The International Law Commission was established by the General Assembly in 1947 and has 34 members, chosen for five-year terms, according to the following pattern: eight from Africa, seven from Asia, six from Latin America, three from Eastern Europe, eight from Western Europe and other states, an additional member from Africa or Eastern Europe in rotation, and one from Asia or Latin America in rotation. They represent the various geographical regions, political views, and legal traditions of UN members. Established under Article 13 of the United Nations charter, the International Law Commission has concerned itself with such subjects as recognition of states and governments, state succession, diplomatic immunity, the high seas, territorial waters, nationality, aliens, laws of treaties, asylum, and arbitral procedures, among many others. Headquartered in Geneva, the International Law Commission works in close cooperation with the Sixth Committee of the General Assembly. This committee has set up a variety of subsidiary organs, such as the Special Committee on the Principles of International Law concerning Friendly Relations and

Cooperation among States. *See also* UNITED NATIONS INTERNATIONAL COURT OF JUSTICE (ICJ); INTERNATIONAL LAW.

Significance   The International Law Commission spends most of its time on the problem of codification of certain aspects of international law rather than on progressive development. This is because present international law is largely a creation of the European colonial powers, who are reluctant to see rapid changes. The new nations' priority is a political one—to create a sense of confidence in international law and an appreciation that it is not an instrument of neocolonialism. Following decolonization of the world, it has become necessary to refashion the classic notions of international law and bring them into tune with the realities of today. The fundamental question to be asked is whether the International Law Commission—in its organizational context—is responsive to the expressed aspirations of the international community. The fact is, with all that has been accomplished to date, the International Law Commission still concentrates on the hard core of traditional international law.

International Literacy Year (ILY)   An observance in 1990 to help people in the world to read and write with understanding. Proclaimed by the UN General Assembly, the International Literacy Year attacked the problem of illiteracy throughout the world, including the developed countries. The United Nations Educational, Scientific and Cultural Organization (UNESCO) defines a literate person as one "who can both read with understanding and write a short simple statement on his everyday life." The International Literacy Year is intended to give a boost to the literacy work carried out around the world by governments, agencies, international and national nongovernmental organizations (NGOs), and, especially, groups working at the grassroots level. A major goal is to launch a decade-long Plan of Action to combat illiteracy. The United Nations is calling upon member states to consider new ways of attacking the problem of illiteracy in their own countries. Each year on September 8, International Literacy Day is observed throughout the world. *See also* UNITED NATIONS EDUCATIONAL, SCIENTIFIC AND CULTURAL ORGANIZATION (UNESCO).

Significance   The International Literacy Year provides an opportunity to direct world attention to a major problem that discourages and offends human dignity; it also challenges the world to redress the damage. The ILY is not a celebration, but a summons to action. It will be remembered not for what is said, but for what is done. The

International Literacy Year conveys two basic messages: (1) education matters because it plays a decisive role in shaping the world's as well as humanity's future, and (2) cooperation—a partnership among people and nations—will help to ensure that men, women, and children everywhere will be able to exercise their rights to adequate education against a backdrop of population growth, world financial crises, and austerity. All of these have an adverse impact on efforts to bridge the widening gap between educational needs and available resources, and all are in a race against time.

International Maritime Organization (IMO)   A specialized agency of the United Nations to facilitate cooperation on technical matters relating to shipping, safety, and passenger service on the oceans and other international waterways. The International Maritime Organization is also concerned with efficient navigation and protection of the marine environment from pollution. Its predecessor, the Inter-governmental Maritime Consultative Organization (IMCO), was established in 1948, but its convention was amended and supplemented on a number of occasions. In 1982, the organization had the words "Inter-governmental" and "Consultative" dropped from its name and adopted the present nomenclature. Members of the United Nations accede to the organization; its present membership includes 132 countries. With headquarters in London, the organization's structure consists of an assembly, a council, a maritime safety committee, a secretariat, and several subsidiary bodies. The IMO encourages the highest practicable standards for maritime safety and encourages the removal of discriminatory action and unnecessary restrictions affecting shipping.

Significance   The International Maritime Organization is endowed with consultative and advisory powers. It advises members on maritime issues, including the operation of oil tankers. The IMO has adopted numerous conventions on pollution of the oceans for the world's enormous fleet of oil tankers. In recent years, the IMO has expanded technical assistance in the Third World. Those countries obviously need more help in applying the international safety regime for shipping, training their nationals in manning the ships, and administering their merchant marines. Another important need is the development of harbor facilities that can meet international standards. In order to achieve its purposes, the organization considers and makes recommendations upon matters submitted by member countries, by any organ or specialized agency of the United Nations, or by any other intergovernmental institution. In recent years, because of tragic oil spills, much attention has been given to the possibility of requiring double-fueled tankers with a number of compartments so as to eliminate or reduce the spillage likely to occur.

International Monetary Fund (IMF)   A specialized agency of the United Nations designed to stabilize international monetary exchange rates. The International Monetary Fund was established by the Bretton Woods System to promote international monetary cooperation and the stabilization of currencies in order to facilitate the expansion and balanced growth of world trade. The IMF also helps member countries meet temporary difficulties encountered in foreign exchange payments. Together with the International Bank for Reconstruction and Development (IBRD), its articles of agreement were signed at Bretton Woods, New Hampshire, in 1944. Operating funds are subscribed by member governments. Each member has a quota related to its national income, monetary reserves, trade balance, and other economic indicators. A member's subscription is equal to its quota and is payable in special drawing rights (SDRs), in other members' currencies, or in its own. The quota approximately determines a member's voting power, the amount of foreign exchange it may purchase from the IMF, and its allocation of SDRs. There are 155 member countries; membership in the Washington-based fund is a prerequisite for joining the IBRD. *See also* BRETTON WOODS SYSTEM; INTERNATIONAL BANK FOR RECONSTRUCTION AND DEVELOPMENT (IBRD).

Significance   The International Monetary Fund has been the subject of severe criticism regarding the strict conditions attached to its loans, and the austerity that these conditions dictate has upon several occasions touched off political unrest and riots in the recipient countries. In order to benefit from the financial assistance of the IMF, a state must make a commitment toward monetary stability. A major reason that the IMF is afflicted with this type of problem is that the participating nations are politically independent but economically interdependent. The function of the fund is to reconcile the conflicting economic policies of its politically sensitive members. The IMF is like a savings and loan association in the United States, rather than a commercial bank. It can lend its funds but cannot create new funds in the way a bank can create deposits. Because of the Third World debt crisis in the 1980s, the IMF had to function as a "lender of last resort" and acted to avoid major economic catastrophe by providing new loans for debtor countries. These were to enable them to meet outstanding loan payments.

International Narcotics Control Board (INCB)   An organization to ensure the continuous evaluation and overall supervision of government implementation of drug control treaties as well as the availability of drugs for medical and research purposes. The International Narcotics Control Board was created by the 1961 Convention on Narcotic Drugs—a body consisting of eleven experts, three chosen from a list of World Health Organization (WHO) nominees and eight from a list of UN and other agency nominees. The INCB came into existence in 1965 and represents a merger of two League of Nations bodies—the Permanent Central Opium Board and the Drug Supervisory Body. Drafting of the 1961 Convention on Narcotic Drugs began in 1948, when the United Nations Economic and Social Council (ECOSOC) adopted a resolution inviting the secretary-general to initiate the design of a Single Convention. This convention was amended by a protocol signed in 1972 in Geneva and entered into force in 1975, considerably enlarging the function of the board and mandating its membership as thirteen representatives to be elected by ECOSOC. *See also* UNITED NATIONS ECONOMIC AND SOCIAL COUNCIL (ECOSOC); WORLD HEALTH ORGANIZATION (WHO).

Significance   The International Narcotics Control Board oversees governmental monitoring of the production and distribution of narcotic drugs so as to limit their use to medical and scientific purposes. The board visits individual countries for investigatory purposes, and it may direct recommendations to particular governments. Faced with increasing seriousness of the global drug problem, the United Nations General Assembly has called for an international campaign against traffic in drugs. However, drugs are increasingly abused by large numbers of persons in most parts of the world, thus making it more and more difficult for the board to exercise effective control. Because governments have a common interest in drug control, there are strong incentives toward international cooperation. To assist those countries experiencing difficulty in carrying out the regulations of the INCB, the United Nations Fund for Drug Abuse Control was established to encourage replacement of illicit opium cultivation and to advise on treatment and rehabilitation of drug addicts, as well as on the strengthening of governmental control.

International Nongovernmental Organizations (INGOs)   Associations of private individuals or groups formed to further international cooperation in the fields of their concerns. International nongovernmental organizations are heavily involved in the exchange of culture across international boundaries and help establish many of the international exchanges and competitions. The International Olympic Committee, for example, helps to operate the various forms of athletic competition and arrange guidelines and regulations to govern the games. The business community is also greatly aided and influenced by INGOs and their advisers. Technical experts of professional INGOs have helped establish international standards of measurement and exchange value that are crucial to the conduct of business and trade. INGOs assist medical organizations in exchanging information with international counterparts in cases where the respective governments involved are maintaining only minimal contact in official relations. International nongovernmental organizations include over 2,400 consumer and producer associations, religious groups, teacher organizations, professional and legal societies, relief societies, trade unions, and other groups. See also INTERNATIONAL GOVERNMENTAL ORGANIZATIONS (IGOs); INTERNATIONAL OLYMPIC COMMITTEE (IOC); INTERNATIONAL ORGANIZATIONS (IOs).

Significance   The distinction between international nongovernmental organizations and international governmental organizations is not always clear. For one thing, the United Nations—the most prominent IGO—and its various specialized agencies embrace many INGOs, each in a consultative status. Indeed various INGOs were present as observers at the United Nations Conference on International Organizations (San Francisco Conference, 1945) when the United Nations was established, and they played a major role in ensuring that the UN charter would make adequate provisions for social and human welfare. The relatively greater role in world affairs of IGOs, compared with INGOs, stems first from the fact that there is no more powerful organization in any society than its own government; therefore, authoritative policies and their implementation more frequently emanate from governmental bodies than from nongovernmental institutions. Governments are still the primary focal points of activity in the modern world; therefore, nongovernmental institutions interested in affecting policy are most likely to attempt to influence the national governments, which wield greater authority in their own right. However, many INGOs possess great financial and other resources that make it possible for them to influence the policy-making of both national governments and IGOs.

International Olympic Committee (IOC)   A worldwide organization for the development of sports and sports competition, guiding and maintaining sports within the Olympic ideal by promoting and strengthening friendship among sportsmen. The International

Olympic Committee ensures the direction of the Olympic movement and regulation of its games. The exact origin of the Olympic games is not known; the first celebration of the ancient games was in 776 B.C. Thereafter they were celebrated at four-year intervals until they were abolished by Roman conquest of Greece in A.D. 393. The modern Olympics began in 1896 when the French government organized the games to inspire the nation and mark its leadership, following the establishment of the IOC in 1894 in Paris. There are three tiers of governing bodies in the Olympic organization. First is the IOC; second, the international federations for various sports; and the third tier consists of the various national Olympic committees. With headquarters at Mon Repos, Lausanne, Switzerland, the IOC elects members for life. *See also* INTERNATIONAL NONGOVERNMENTAL ORGANIZATIONS (INGOS).

Significance   The International Olympic Committee is a unique body in that its members do not represent their countries but are delegates *from* the committee *to* their countries. Members are not permitted to receive from their own governments or from other organizations instructions that may interfere with their voting. The IOC's primary source of revenue derives from the sale of rights to televise the Olympic Games. For example, the IOC has awarded CBS television rights to the 1992 Olympics for the sum of $325 million. As a by-product of this commercialism of the Olympics, the games are not immune from politics. Boycotts are nothing new to the Olympics— the first one was imposed by Germany in 1920. The world did not really take note of boycotts, however, until the American boycott of the Moscow Olympics in 1980, called as a protest against the Soviet invasion of Afghanistan. Although the IOC maintains that politics should have no role in international sports, it has become entwined nevertheless in many political issues it would have preferred to avoid. The IOC has been forced, for example, to decide whether Taiwan, South Africa, and certain other nations should be permitted to participate in the Olympic Games in light of their controversial internal policies. It is clear, however, that as an international nongovernmental organization (INGO), the IOC plays no official or participatory role in North-South issues as such.

International Organizations (IOs)   Institutions that promote international cooperation and understanding. International organizations are of two types—governmental and nongovernmental. They are created to further political, economic, social, cultural, military, and other objectives of their members. The governmental or public

international organizations are established by states, and nongovernmental or private bodies by individuals or groups. In both categories,
global and regional international organizations also find membership.
Examples are the United Nations, which is a global international organization, and the Association of Southeast Asian Nations (ASEAN),
which is a regional organization. Couloumbis and Wolfe classify international governmental organizations by four major groupings: (1)
general membership and general-purpose organizations such as the
United Nations; (2) general membership and limited-purpose organizations such as the World Health Organization (WHO); (3) limited
membership and general-purpose organizations such as the Organization of African Unity (OAU); and (4) limited membership and limited-purpose organizations such as the North Atlantic Treaty
Organization (NATO).[28] *See also* INTERNATIONAL GOVERNMENTAL OR-
GANIZATIONS (IGOS); INTERNATIONAL NONGOVERNMENTAL ORGANIZA-
TIONS (INGOS).

Significance   In general, international organizations contribute to
world peace, international understanding, and human well-being. It is
unfortunate that contemporary research on international organizations has been focused upon the United Nations and regional institutions of Western Europe, leaving a need for systematic political
analysis of other institutions. A failure to fill this gap inhibits our
ability to understand the full range of the international organizational
system. As researchers provide analysis of the political process and the
effects of an increasing number of international agencies, it may become possible to develop a new field of comparative international
organizations. In any case, there is a steady growth in the number of
international organizations; currently there are over 300 international
governmental organizations and more than 2,000 active international
nongovernmental organizations, and the numbers are proliferating.
Whatever size and form international organizations may take, states,
individuals, and groups enter into membership because of certain
anticipated benefits.

International Refugee Organization (IRO)   A former specialized
agency of the United Nations created to assist persons uprooted and
displaced by the events of World War II and offering them needed
assistance in resettlement. The International Refugee Organization
was established by the General Assembly in 1946 to provide relief for
the homeless who, as a consequence of the war and postwar boundary
changes, found it impossible to return to their native countries. From
1947 to 1952 the IRO helped resettle more than a million, repatriated

73,000, and made arrangements for 31,000 who required institutional care. These refugees came mostly from Eastern Europe; the International Refugee Organization resettled them in the United States, Australia, Israel, Canada, and the United Kingdom. Besides legal and political protection, the IRO arranged relief in its own camps, as well as provided training, transportation, education, health care, employment, and other social resettlement programs. In 1952 the IRO closed operations and the remaining refugees were taken care of by the United Nations High Commissioner for Refugees; thenceforward resettlement was facilitated by the Intergovernmental Committee on European Migration. *See also* UNITED NATIONS: REFUGEE PROGRAMS; UNITED NATIONS HIGH COMMISSION FOR REFUGEES (UNHCR).

Significance   The International Refugee Organization was abolished when it became a victim of the cold war and the then-prevalent belief that refugee problems were temporary. The Soviet Union and other Eastern European countries were bitterly critical of the IRO. Although a number of countries urged that the IRO be continued, the United States—which underwrote more than half of the IRO budget—was not willing to continue the program. Eighteen governments participated in the International Refugee Organization and contributed to its expenditures: Australia, Belgium, Brazil, Canada, China, Denmark, the Dominican Republic, France, Guatemala, Iceland, Italy, Luxembourg, the Netherlands, New Zealand, Norway, the United Kingdom, the United States, and Venezuela. The IRO was based on the assumption that cooperative efforts by the democratic nations of the world could nurture the homeless refugees and repatriate them in humane and suitable environments, free from fear of persecution by the Nazis and the Communists.

International Relations   The interplay among nations as they conduct official business. International relations may include all kinds of relationships involving different countries and national groups. It is as old as the political history of the world, but as an academic discipline, international relations was developed primarily at American universities as a result of the United States' experience in World War I. Before that, the many concepts of international relations were covered under philosophy, international law, or military and diplomatic history. For example, through these disciplines we were able to understand the international relations of the Greek city-states that Thucydides describes and the international relations of the Indian states of the fourth century B.C., from which Kautilya derived his philosophy. In reaction to the horrors of World War I, in which over 20 million lives were lost, world conscience demanded the abolition of war and the establishment of a global system for collective security. Following the war and the emergence of the United States as a great power, scholars at American universities began teaching courses on international relations as part of the political science curriculum. After World War II, in which over 60 million people died worldwide, courses on international relations were offered all over the world as a separate discipline in many instances. *See also* INTERNATIONAL LAW; INTERNATIONAL ORGANIZATIONS (IOS).

Significance   The dynamic forces that mold international relations are determined chiefly by national governments, with varying influence exerted by such bodies as international organizations and nongovernmental institutions, as well as diplomats, scholars, and writers. Many analysts focus their work in the field of international relations by examining the circumstances of international relationships, which may be characterized by equality or inequality, hierarchy or dominance, alliance or enmity, and contact or estrangement. The subjects of such studies include diplomacy, world politics, economics, geography, international trade, foreign aid, military sanctions, alliances, international organizations, espionage, propaganda, influence, demography, national identity, ideology, and a host of other concerns. Some scholars and writers use international relations and international politics interchangeably and define them narrowly as "the study of who gets what, when, and how in the international arena."[29]

International Studies Association (ISA)   A professional group of scholars whose concerns extend beyond their own national perspective. The International Studies Association provides opportunities for educators, researchers, and practitioners to converse with specialists from all over the world. The ISA facilitates cultural and professional exchange and provides a channel of communication between academics and policymakers. By forging such linkages it is hoped that the production and utilization of research can be more effectively carried on, ensuring the improvement and dissemination of international studies, new ideas, and current information. Founded in 1959, the association has gained formal recognition as an international nongovernmental organization (INGO) by the United Nations. The ISA has a network of associated organizations in over 40 countries. Individual members, totaling 3,000, come from some 63 countries. Headquartered in the United States, the ISA holds annual conventions—international, national, and regional. It celebrated the 30th year of its founding in London in 1989, in collaboration with the

British International Studies Association (BISA). The ISA is one of 15 full members of the International Social Science Council and administers the World Assembly of International Studies Program. *See also* INTERNATIONAL INSTITUTE FOR STRATEGIC STUDIES (IISS).

Significance   Nearly all international scientific associations are characterized by a plurality—and in many cases, a majority—of members residing in North America. This will probably continue in the foreseeable future for the ISA. It is a multidisciplinary body, although the preponderance of political scientists is apparent; in recent years many economists and historians have joined. There may never have been a better time to study international affairs than during the last several years. The Soviet Union is being transformed. The Berlin Wall has been torn down and Germany reunited. Eastern Europe is democratizing. Western Europe stands poised for full economic integration. Prodemocracy movements are flourishing in the world. At the same time confrontation in the Persian Gulf ended in a war and poses a major challenge to UN peacekeeping. In the midst of all these and other significant international developments, there is great potential for the continuing growth of the ISA as it offers a podium to international scholars and practitioners.

International Telecommunication Union (ITU)   A specialized agency of the United Nations responsible for managing the flow of telegraph, radio, and television communications across the globe. The International Telecommunication Union was created to ensure that telecommunication services could be provided without undue interference among the contracting parties. Twenty states established the International Telegraph Union in 1865 in Paris, and its new title was assumed in 1932 to reflect contemporary advances in communications. The ITU now has 166 member states. It aims to maintain and extend cooperation among its members for the improvement and rational use of telecommunications of all kinds, as well as to promote and offer technical assistance to developing countries. The ITU seeks to fulfill these basic purposes through international conferences and meetings, publication of information, organization of world exhibitions, and technical cooperation. Some of the continuing functions of the union include allocation and recording of radio frequencies and establishing the lowest possible rates. The ITU operates mainly within the framework of the United Nations Development Program (UNDP) and administers funding by which telecommunications experts are sent to various countries to advise on telegraph, telephone, and radio systems; it cooperates with the Universal Postal Union (UPU). *See also* UNIVERSAL POSTAL UNION (UPU).

Significance   The International Telecommunication Union is the oldest intergovernmental international organization and is the nerve center of radio and other telecommunications systems throughout the world. ITU activities provide for the satisfactory operation of telecommunications services, both international and domestic; allow networks to interconnect and interoperate; establish international routing of telecommunications; set international tariffs and billing arrangements; and prevent harmful interference among radio stations engaged in scientific research. In reality, the ITU is a voluntary group of nations, acting in unison and recognizing that they have to make certain adjustments in their operations. Members do not give up the right to conduct and maintain telecommunications systems in their own national interests. The authority of the ITU is moral, not regulatory. The union provides an opportunity for systems operators and manufacturers from many nations to gather, exchange views, and agree upon an extremely broad range of multilateral arrangements.

International Tin Council (ITC)   An organization to promote the achievement of a long-term balance between world production and consumption of tin and to prevent excessive fluctuations in price. The International Tin Council, in pursuit of these objectives, creates and operates a buffer stock system, fixes floor and ceiling prices, and, when considered necessary, regulates exports. The council has seven subsidiary bodies: Economic and Price Review Panel, Administrative Committee, Buffer Finance Committee, Committee on Costs and Prices, Committee on Development, Credentials Committee, and Statistical Committee. The first international agreement for tin was initiated in 1921 by the governments of the Federated Malay States and the Netherlands East Indies. Its purpose was to buy up the accumulated surplus stocks to stop the decline of prices by holding supplies off the market. After the United Nations Conference on Trade and Employment held in Havana, Cuba, in 1947, the International Tin Study Group came into existence and surveyed the world supply and demand of tin. Following the work of the International Tin Study Group, the ITC was established in London in 1956. Mandatory contributions to buffer stocks are made by producing and consuming countries, as decided by the council. *See also* INTERNATIONAL WHEAT COUNCIL (IWC).

Significance   The International Tin Council is concerned primarily with export prices of tin. But the frequent changes in both floor and ceiling prices have adversely affected prospects of an effective price stabilization on the world market. Efforts to support prices in conditions of worldwide glut have caused difficulties in the pricing system, leading, in the past, to cessation of the trading in tin on buffer stock operations. To the extent that the Organization of Petroleum Exporting Countries (OPEC) as a cartel has not succeeded in controlling the price of oil, Walter Jones argues that such a commodity group as the International Tin Council has limited prospects for success.[30]

International Union of Students (IUS)   An international organization that defends the rights and the interests of students worldwide. The International Union of Students strives for peace and disarmament, solutions to world problems, the right of all people to enjoy primary, secondary, and higher education, and academic freedom. Its headquarters are located in Prague, Czechoslovakia. The question of defending the rights and interests of students is further identified by three main objectives: (1) to secure for all young people the right to education regardless of sex, economic circumstances, social standing, political conviction, religion, color, or race; (2) to represent the interests of students in international affairs, to bring before international organizations the problems of students, and to publicize in all spheres the most urgent needs of students; and (3) to assist the students of colonial, semicolonial, and dependent countries to attain full social, economic, and educational development. The IUS has consultative status with the United Nations Educational, Scientific and Cultural Organization (UNESCO). *See also* UNITED NATIONS EDUCATIONAL, SCIENTIFIC AND CULTURAL ORGANIZATION (UNESCO).

Significance   Arising from the struggle in which democratic youth and students fought against fascism and Nazism in Europe, the International Union of Students kept contacts alive between students of many countries during a time when it became almost impossible. As the struggle for independence intensified in the Third World countries in the late 1940s, 1950s, and 1960s, the IUS was successful in helping the youth and students of those decades understand that the fight for independence in the colonial and dependent territories was part of the general struggle for peace. When decolonization was followed by dictatorial regimes in many parts of the world, the IUS organized protests and demonstrations for democracy and democratization in the Third World. Continuing its leadership role, it organizes the International Students' Week in mid-November every year to promote international understanding.

International Wheat Council (IWC)   An organization to further international cooperation in all aspects of wheat trade and other grains. The International Wheat Council is entrusted with the administration of the Wheat Trade Convention (1986) and the provision of administrative services for the Food Aid Convention (1986). Established in 1949, the IWC divides voting powers between exporting and importing countries equally. Each group holds one thousand votes, distributed among the members in proportion to their respective guaranteed purchases or sales for a crop year. The major wheat-exporting countries are Argentina, Canada, the United States, Australia, France, and Germany. The main wheat importers are Third World and most European countries. *See also* INTERNATIONAL TIN COUNCIL (ITC).

Significance   The International Wheat Council keeps the world wheat situation under review, lays down the policies of the organization, and establishes rules of procedure. In promoting the expansion of international trade in grains, the IWC secures its freest possible flow in the interests of members—particularly developing countries—and contributes to the stability of international grain markets. Further, it enhances world food security and provides a forum for the exchange of information about and decisions of the membership's concerns regarding trade in grains. The council promotes international cooperation in connection with world wheat problems, recognizing the relationship of the wheat trade to the economic stability of markets for other agricultural products.

Interparliamentary Union (IPU)   A nongovernmental international organization to promote contacts among members of all national parliaments, which are formed into national groups. The Interparliamentary Union unites its members in common action to secure and maintain the full participation of their respective nations, urging them toward establishment and development of representative government and its institutions. The IPU was founded in 1888 in Paris, largely as a result of the efforts of a British Member of Parliament (MP), Randal Cremer, who was an internationalist and a believer in international arbitration. The First Interparliamentary Arbitration Conference was held in Paris the next year. The yearly plenary conference is the deliberative body of the IPU. The number of delegates representing each member group at the conference is determined on a mixed basis, the chief factor being population. The work of the IPU is directed by a council on which each group is represented by two delegates. The IPU's membership includes interparliamentary

national groups in 110 countries. *See also* INTERNATIONAL NONGOVERN-
MENTAL ORGANIZATIONS (INGOS).

Significance   The Interparliamentary Union studies and seeks solutions for all questions of an international character suitable for settlement by parliamentary means. Its work is essentially carried out in two
fields: action for peace, and the strengthening of parliamentary institutions. The IPU has adopted a "Procedure for the Examination and
Treatment of Communications Concerning Rights of Parliamentarians" that is applicable to any member of a parliament who is a victim
of arbitrary measures. In addition, the union examines international
security and disarmament and judicial, economic, social, cultural, and
environmental questions relating to the development of parliamentary institutions, with a view to improving the work of those institutions and increasing their prestige.

Intervention   Forcible overt or covert interference in the internal
or external affairs of one state by another. Intervention may be
brought about by military, economic, or diplomatic measures. Military
intervention may be achieved by sending troops across a border; economic intervention by extending financial assistance to an insurgent
group; and diplomatic intervention by advising a threatened government on how to deal with a rebellion. Some contemporary U.S. overt
interventions include Korea, 1950–1952; Lebanon, 1958; Vietnam,
1965–1973; the Dominican Republic, 1965–1966; Grenada, 1983;
Libya, 1986; and Panama, 1989. Some major U.S. covert interventions are Iran, 1953; Guatemala, 1954; Cuba, 1961; Chile,
1970–1973; and Nicaragua, 1981. The Soviet Union and other major
powers also intervene in the affairs of other nations. Major Soviet
interventions took place in Cuba, Angola, Ethiopia, (South) Yemen,
and Afghanistan. Historically, powerful states have often interfered
and resorted to armed intervention to protect their interests. *See also*
INSURGENCY; INTERNATIONAL LAW.

Significance   Although in principle intervention may be justified in
many instances, it is almost always considered to violate one of the
principles of international law—the principle of "nonintervention."
Charles Beitz says that nonintervention "is the most important embod-
iment of the modern idea that states should be treated as autonomous
entities; it is also the main structural principle of a conception of the
world, dominant since the mid-seventeenth century."[31] Clearly, the
norm suggested by Beitz, absolute nonintervention in the national
affairs of other states, is frequently violated. But it cannot be claimed

that every case of interference is unjustified; among the many justifications for intervention are self-defense, treaty obligations, and collective action by the international community against an aggressor state.

Iran-Iraq War   A military confrontation that started between the two major Persian Gulf states when Iraq attacked Iran in 1980. The Iran-Iraq War ended in 1988 after the United Nations Security Council called for a cease-fire. There were at least eight major reasons for the outbreak of this dangerous conflict: (1) the Shatt al-Arab waterway and other border disputes, (2) the issue of Iranian nationality in Iraq, (3) the Kurdish problem, (4) sectarian differences, (5) ideological contests, (6) linguistic chauvinism, (7) economic struggle, and (8) personal vendetta. Some of these issues, particularly the intractable Shatt al-Arab boundary question, have been a perennial source of conflict between the two Middle Eastern Muslim neighbors. The problem of personal vendetta, on the other hand, was considered temporary, arising when Ayatollah Khomeini became the supreme leader of Iran. The new Iranian revolutionary regime was seen by Iraqi President Saddam Hussein as a revisionist power, fomenting revolution and unrest and threatening to eliminate his military rule. *See also* AFGHAN CIVIL WAR, 1979–1989.

Significance   The Iran-Iraq War devastated the economies of the two oil-producing OPEC nations. The on-and-off war reverted to stalemate many times; it did not trigger a Shiite rebellion in Iraq, just as the Iraqi invasion of Khuzistan had failed to produce a liberation movement in Iran. In fact, the war seems to have had the unforeseen result of increasing national pride and support for both regimes among their respective populations. Death and destruction, however, were extensive; the limited confrontation between Iran and Iraq "took over one million lives and may thus claim the dubious distinction of being one of the most vicious wars of this century."[32] It is even more tragic that the war ended inconclusively. Finally, in the wake of the Iraqi invasion of Kuwait in 1990, Iraq decided to unilaterally withdraw its troops from the Iranian border, return Iranian territory occupied during the war, and exchange prisoners of war with Iran.

Iraqi Invasion of Kuwait   The blitzkrieg Iraqi invasion of Kuwait on August 2, 1990, and its subsequent annexation of the emirate as Iraq's nineteenth province. The immediate cause of the invasion of Kuwait by Iraq was a dispute over oil pricing, but the conflict has deeper roots as well. For just over 60 years (until its independence in

1961) Kuwait was a British protectorate. Before that, it had been under Turkish suzerainty. Shortly after independence Iraq laid claim to the whole of Kuwait, arguing that it had been an integral part of Basra province under Turkish rule and that Iraqi sovereignty had succeeded Turkish sovereignty at the end of World War I in 1918. Fearing an Iraqi invasion, Kuwait requested assistance from Britain, which sent troops in 1961. These were later withdrawn and replaced by troops from Arab League countries, who left the country in 1963 at the Kuwaiti government's request. In October 1973 Iraq recognized Kuwait as a sovereign state. Iraq, however, maintained its claims to certain parts of Kuwaiti territory, notably the islands of Warbah and Bubiyan in the Persian Gulf and the land border area incorporating the southern tip of the Rumaila oil field. In 1973 Iraqi forces occupied a border post, but later withdrew. In 1975 Iraq proposed that Kuwait lease to it parts of Bubiyan and cede Warbah in return for Iraqi recognition of Kuwaiti land borders. In response Kuwait stressed that the two islands belonged to it. In 1981, Iraq repeated its 1975 proposal, and in 1990 Iraq occupied the whole of Kuwait, including the two disputed islands. *See also* IRAN-IRAQ WAR.

Significance   The Iraqi invasion of Kuwait resulted in a common vote of censure by the UN Security Council. Within hours of the unprovoked Iraqi invasion of Kuwait, the Security Council adopted resolution 660 (1990) condemning the Iraqi invasion. The resolution was supported by the five permanent members of the Security Council (China, France, Britain, the Soviet Union, and the United States) and nine of the ten nonpermanent members; Yemen, the only Arab member of the Security Council, did not take part in the vote. The resolution called on the international community to support sanctions against Iraq until Kuwait's sovereignty and legitimate government were restored. The Security Council passed 12 resolutions condemning Iraq's invasion of Kuwait, imposed a comprehensive air and trade embargo against the aggressor, banned financial dealings by the world community with Iraq, and authorized use of force if Iraq did not withdraw its troops and release all hostages held by January 15, 1991. The use of force by 28 UN members, led by the United States, liberated Kuwait. The collective military action by the members of the United Nations against Iraq set in place a crucial model for maintaining order in the post–cold war world.

Islamic Development Bank (IDB)   A financial institution that assists Muslim nations and communities in economic development according to the Islamic principles. The Islamic Development Bank follows the *Shariah* (Islamic law) as far as practicable in borrowing, lending, and investment practices. It was established in Saudi Arabia in 1973 by a declaration issued by the Conference of Finance Ministers of the Muslim countries. The agreement creating the bank was signed under the auspices of the Organization of the Islamic Conference (OIC); the bank began functioning in 1975 in Jeddah, Saudi Arabia. Membership includes all the Muslim countries—numbering 44—and the Palestine Liberation Organization (PLO). The Board of Governors, consisting of a governor and an alternate governor for each member country, meets once each year. The authorized capital of the IDB is two billion dinars. *See also* ORGANIZATION OF THE ISLAMIC CONFERENCE (OIC).

Significance   The Islamic Development Bank is an Islamic financial body of the Muslims, by the Muslims, and for the Muslims. It follows Koranic principles forbidding usury; it does not extend loans or credits for interest and supports economic and social development by taking up equity participation in public and private enterprises. The IDB maintains cooperative links with various international financial institutions, both Islamic and non-Islamic. Emergency aid and other financial assistance is also extended to Islamic countries and to Muslims in non-Islamic nations. The concept of adapting modern banking and financial practices to Islamic beliefs is still in its infancy—even in the Middle East, where most of the population is Muslim and the region itself is the birthplace of Islam. However, the concept of Islamic banking appears to be gaining some momentum all over the world, even in the United States. *The Washington Post* reported August 6, 1989, that a half-dozen Islamic financial institutions have sprouted in the United States in the last two or three years.

K

Korean War   The 1950 military confrontation between North and South Korea involving active participation by the United Nations following its decision to defend South Korea. The Korean War was precipitated when North Korea invaded South Korea; China joined North Korea in the war. North Korea launched a massive assault on South Korea to oust the South Korean government then in power. The United States was the principal participant in the United Nations' command forces that came to the aid of South Korea. The causes of the Korean War can be traced to Japanese victories in the Chinese-Japanese War (1894–1895) and the Russo-Japanese War (1904–1905) and the Japanese annexation of Korea. Korea still belonged to Japan during World War II. In 1945, when Japan surrendered to the United States, the Allies partitioned Korea. The United States accepted the surrender of Japanese forces south of the 38th degree latitude (South Korea), while the Soviet Union accepted surrender north of the 38th parallel (North Korea). Following the invasion of South Korea by North Korea, President Harry Truman ordered American air and sea forces in the area to aid South Korea. Eventually, 16 members of the United Nations joined the UN command. A cease-fire was concluded in 1951, and an armistice agreement was signed in 1953. *See also* VIETNAM WAR (1945–1975).

Significance   The Korean War was an early example of military force under the auspices of an international governmental organization—the United Nations. The UN Security Council was able to make the decision to create a UN command because of the absence of the Soviet Union from the meeting, and at that time, the People's Republic of China did not hold a seat in the world body. However, the Soviet Union soon vetoed further action by the Security Council. In the face of this crisis, the General Assembly adopted the Uniting for Peace Resolution, which allowed it to make recommendations to member

120

nations with respect to the use of armed forces to restore international peace. The Uniting for Peace Resolution has since been used many times for setting in motion other global peacekeeping operations. The Korean War effort and the adoption of the Uniting for Peace Resolution were possible because the most powerful country (the United States) was willing to make major military and financial contributions and thus garner enough support from other members of the United Nations to pass enabling resolutions.

L

Latin American Economic System (SELA)   A regional arrangement intended to provide Latin American countries with institutional machinery for consultation and coordination in economic and social matters. The Latin American Economic System was created in 1975 to coordinate existing integration mechanisms, give new impetus to intraregional cooperation, organize producers of raw materials and basic agricultural products, and synthesize positions and strategies of member nations toward the outside world. SELA's operational goal is to establish a system for pooling resources and creating multilateral government-owned agencies to sell primary commodities on the world market. It has developed relations with the Group of 77 (a Third World caucusing group of more than 130 members), the United Nations Conference on Trade and Development (UNCTAD), the General Agreement on Tariffs and Trade (GATT), the United Nations Development Program (UNDP), the United Nations Industrial Development Organization (UNIDO), and the International Monetary Fund (IMF). SELA has 25 members in Latin America. *See also* GROUP OF SEVENTY-SEVEN; NEW INTERNATIONAL ECONOMIC ORDER (NIEO); ORGANIZATION OF PETROLEUM EXPORTING COUNTRIES (OPEC).

Significance   The Latin American Economic System has been making a notable effort to expedite regional cooperation and to build up Latin American solidarity on international economic issues. To examine the problems of Latin American external debt, SELA organized— in cooperation with the Economic Commission for Latin American Countries (ECLAC)—a Latin American Economic Conference. In many respects, SELA follows OPEC in tactics, goals, and mode of operations. The Latin American members of OPEC (Venezuela and Ecuador) have helped SELA toward cooperative efforts with the oil cartel. At the extraregional level, efforts are made to avoid competition with other Third World countries in the world market, so that they do not suffer from the consequences of producing and trading the same commodities. In addition to this South-South cordiality, SELA maintains substantially improved mutual relations with the European Economic Community (EEC).

Latin American Free Trade Association (LAFTA)   A defunct regional group formed to increase trade and foster economic development in Latin America. The Latin American Free Trade Association's constituent document, the Treaty of Montevideo, Uruguay, was signed in 1960, emulating the success of the European Community (EC). LAFTA's membership included Argentina, Bolivia, Brazil, Chile, Colombia, Ecuador, Mexico, Paraguay, Peru, Uruguay, and Venezuela. The United Nations Economic Commission for Latin America (UNECLA) and the Inter-American Economic and Social Council of the Organization of American States (OAS) were requested to act as technical advisers to the Association. The institutional framework of LAFTA was minimal, consisting mainly of the Conference of the Contracting Parties and the Permanent Executive Committee. The conference, a plenary organization, normally met once a year. It was responsible for engaging in periodic tariff-cutting negotiations as required under the agreement. *See also* EUROPEAN COAL AND STEEL COMMUNITY (ECSC); EUROPEAN COMMUNITY (EC); EUROPEAN ECONOMIC COMMUNITY (EEC).

Significance   The initial years of the Latin American Free Trade Association marked considerable progress in trade negotiations, which resulted in a rapid expansion of trade among the member nations. Other than that achievement, LAFTA's only other success during the first years of its brief existence was the mapping out of the area's resource complementarity and identification of the problems of development. Inspired by the studies of the UNECLAC, LAFTA's hopes were high that it could become a viable experiment in regional economic development. However, dismantling of tariff barriers—a cumbersome process under the Treaty of Montevideo—blocked real progress in fostering economic integration. In this regard, LAFTA's difficulties arose from (1) differences in the stages of economic development among member countries, (2) disagreements between the big and small states and relatively rich and poor nations, and (3) failure of members to implement policies formulated by LAFTA. Clearly, LAFTA's level of performance and management efficiency was too low to ensure its success.

Latin American Integration Association (LAIA)   A regional body that seeks to promote economic development through joint action. The Latin American Integration Association, established in 1980 at Montevideo, Uruguay, was signed by 11 Latin American countries. Its purpose was to create a Latin American Common Market, and member countries approved a regional tariff preference mechanism that entered into effect in 1984. In addition, regional agreements concern trade, economic complementation, agricultural and livestock trade promotion, scientific and technological cooperation, tourism, and preservation of the environment. LAIA supersedes the Latin American Free Trade Association (LAFTA) created by the 1960 Treaty of Montevideo. LAIA consists of the Council of Ministers and the Secretariat. LAIA's members include Argentina, Bolivia, Brazil, Chile, Colombia, Ecuador, Mexico, Paraguay, Peru, Uruguay, and Venezuela. *See also* LATIN AMERICAN ECONOMIC SYSTEM (SELA); LATIN AMERICAN FREE TRADE ASSOCIATION (LAFTA).

Significance   The Latin American Integration Association pursues a long-term goal of establishing a common market through the creation of an area of economic preference. In spite of the Latin American Free Trade Association's inability to become a viable organization, the same member countries formed its successor, LAIA. To avoid the mistakes of LAFTA, several new integrative efforts have been undertaken in the region. The LAIA seeks to reduce tariffs among its members with concessions based on each nation's level of development; the country classifications are (1) less developed (Bolivia, Ecuador, and Paraguay), (2) medium-developed (Chile, Colombia, Peru, Uruguay, Venezuela), and (3) more developed (Argentina, Brazil, and Mexico). More favorable terms are granted to intermediate countries, while additional and special benefits are provided for less-developed nations. Together, these countries comprise three-fourths of the Latin American population south of the United States.

League of Arab States   A regional organization designed to strengthen unity, coordinate political activities, and promote social, cultural, and economic cooperation among member states. The League of Arab States, often called the Arab League, was formed in 1945 as the first Pan-Arab organization to engage all Arab countries. The original members were Egypt, Iraq, Jordan, Lebanon, Saudi Arabia, Syria, and Yemen. Since then, each of the 20 Arab countries and the Palestine Liberation Organization (PLO) have joined the Arab League. Egypt, expelled in 1979 after it signed a peace treaty with Israel, has since been readmitted. The primary governing body is the

Majlis, or Council, composed of a representative from each member nation, which meets twice a year. Binding decisions require unanimous agreement, while majority rulings are nonobligatory. The organization is run by a secretary-general, and a secretariat has departments assigned to political, economic, legal, cultural, social, labor, petroleum, finance, health, information, communications, and Palestinian affairs. As a caucusing group, the Arab League works closely with the United Nations and has won acceptance of Arabic as one of the official languages of the United Nations. *See also* ARAB MONETARY FUND.

Significance   The League of Arab States is a loose-knit organization of sovereign states, with emphasis placed on voluntary cooperation. Member nations are bound by the pact to respect the forms of government existing in other member countries. They are pledged not to use force for the settlement of disputes among members. The league has often fallen short of its expectations and has not increased unity among its members. It has shown unity of interest, however, when it comes to Arab-Israeli conflict. The Arab League has several tangible accomplishments—establishment of the Arab Common Market, the Arab Development Bank, the Arab Press, and the Arab States Broadcasting Union. But the August 1990 Iraqi occupation of Kuwait completely destroyed the desired image of the Arab League. In this case it was very ineffective in bringing its members together. At an emergency summit meeting in Cairo on August 10, 1990, 12 of the 20 members present (Tunisia did not attend) approved a Pan-Arab force to defend Saudi Arabia against possible aggression by Iraq. At Saudi Arabia's request, the United States deployed a massive military force to defend that oil kingdom against a potential Iraqi attack.

League of Nations   The global organization established to maintain world peace and security by the victors of World War I. The League of Nations was formed in 1920, based on 26 articles included in the Treaty of Versailles, which served as the constitution of the organization. By the end of World War I, the principal allied powers were committed to establishing some form of world organization to preserve world peace. The principal architect of the league was President Woodrow Wilson, who insisted that the new organization do whatever would be necessary to ensure future peace. He was chairman of the committee that wrote the Covenant of the League of Nations, but despite his leading role in its formation, the United States did not join because its Senate refused to give its consent. The league had an assembly, a council, and a secretariat, which formed the central organs of the world body. The membership was divided into three categories: first, the original members who were signatories to the Treaty of Versailles; second, the neutral states—not parties to the Treaty of Versailles; and third, other self-governing states, dominions, or colonies. The latter were eligible for membership if accepted by two-thirds of the league assembly. The League of Nations had 63 members over the period of its existence, with 59 the maximum at any one time. *See also* COVENANT OF THE LEAGUE OF NATIONS; LEAGUE OF NATIONS ASSEMBLY; LEAGUE OF NATIONS COUNCIL; MANDATES SYSTEM OF THE LEAGUE OF NATIONS.

Significance   During its first decade the League of Nations demonstrated a successful record in resolving many dangerous disputes, but failed to act decisively when confronted with a series of violations of its covenant. These failures resulted ultimately in World War II. Situations that produced league failures included the bombing of the island of Corfu in Greece by Italian forces in 1923, the Japanese conquest of Manchuria in 1931, and the Italian conquest of Abyssinia in 1935; the league remained ineffective throughout all of these events, even though it imposed economic sanctions against Italy for an Ethiopian invasion. The chief defect of the League of Nations lay in its procedural arrangements. Under the covenant, the decisions of both the league assembly and the council were to be unanimous, except in certain specific spheres; second, the league could not prevent the withdrawal of its members; third, there was no provision for the compulsory reference of a dispute to the Permanent Court of International Justice; fourth, the supremacy of big powers prevented the league from forcing its members to solve their disputes by pacific methods; and finally, most members of the league lacked faith in its peacekeeping role.

League of Nations Assembly   The general conference of the League of Nations, which consisted of delegations from each of its member states. The league assembly was composed of three representatives from each member state but only one vote was permitted per state. Annual meetings were held in Geneva each September in the league's headquarters. The assembly elected its own president, who was traditionally chosen from smaller member nations. The assembly accomplished its principal agenda through committees. The rules of procedures for international organizations were determined by the assembly, which was the central organ of the entire system. The powers and functions of the assembly involved the election of nonpermanent members of the league council, election of its own officers, establishment of rules and procedures to control finances; consideration of disputes referred to it by the council, and reconsideration of league treaties as they became inapplicable. *See also* LEAGUE OF NATIONS; LEAGUE OF NATIONS COUNCIL.

Significance   The league assembly was the most original concept of the many innovations of the League of Nations. It was unique in that it was a world conference, meeting to discuss issues dealing with significant international matters. The league assembly was a public forum, not a legislative body; it recognized equal rights and offered podium opportunities to all members, whether they spoke for big or small nations. In discussion and debate, deliberative procedures were followed rather than diplomatic formalities. The assembly was the plenary organ of the League of Nations and its voting procedures required unanimity, except on matters of procedure or the appointment of committees to investigate particular situations—these required only a simple majority of members present. At its peak, the assembly totaled 59 members. The league instituted a useful practice—the general debate—which has been adopted by many international governmental and nongovernmental bodies.

League of Nations Council   The executive organ of the League of Nations. The league council was originally intended to consist of five great powers—the United States, Great Britain, France, Italy, and Japan—as permanent members, together with four others elected by the League of Nations Assembly for limited periods. But when the United States did not join the league, the permanent members were reduced to four, but increased to five again with the admission of Germany in 1926. Russia was given a permanent seat on the council upon becoming a member in 1934, but Japan and Germany withdrew from the league in 1935, thus leaving four permanent members. In 1922 the nonpermanent members were increased to six, and in 1926 this number was increased to nine. The Covenant of the League of Nations states that the council shall meet at least once a year, but it held ten sessions in the first year, and thereafter an average of five per year, each lasting about a week. In 1923 the council decided to hold regular meetings (four a year, later reduced to three) at fixed dates. The league council held its first meeting in Paris on January 19, 1920. *See also* COVENANT OF THE LEAGUE OF NATIONS; LEAGUE OF NATIONS; LEAGUE OF NATIONS ASSEMBLY.

Significance   The framers of the Covenant of the League of Nations expected the council to be the pivotal organ of the organization; it was to administer the league's policy. In addition, it was to serve as the principal mechanism for the peaceful settlement of disputes and collective security of the league. The other main purpose of the council was to demonstrate to the league the evil effects of the manufacture by private enterprise of munitions and implements of war. This included advice on how this type of manufacture could be prevented, due regard being given to the necessities of those members of the league who were not themselves able to manufacture the weapons of war necessary for their security. The council, like the league assembly, was intended to deal with any matter falling within the prescribed agenda of the league or any emerging issue affecting the peace of the world. Unanimity prevailed in voting, although exceptions were also to be noted.

League of Nations Secretariat   The administrative office of the League of Nations. The league secretariat was headed by a secretary-general and was composed of such secretaries and staff as were required. The staff of the secretariat totaled 600 persons, selected from more than 50 countries. Under the direction of the first secretary-general, Sir James Eric Drummond, the league organized an international civil service where all officials were to act independently of their own national authorities. A large number of experts were connected with the secretariat, and it was their task to prepare the groundwork for the league assembly, council, and various commissions. The work of the secretariat was organized along functional lines into 15 sections. The staff members of the secretariat enjoyed diplomatic immunity as international officials, provided for in Article 7 of the league covenant. The rules governing the conduct of members of the secretariat were laid down in the staff regulations, which were enforced by an administrative tribunal composed of three judges and three deputy judges. *See also* UNITED NATIONS SECRETARIAT.

Significance   The league secretariat grew with unexpected rapidity and represented a complete break with previously accepted ideas. The secretariat was the liaison office between different organs of the league, and the secretary-general was in constant touch with the member states. He made arrangements for investigations and considerations of disputes between members. The secretariat proved that an international civil service could function with an efficiency equal to that of any national organization. If the ideal of international civil service was not always realized, it is still true that—as a general principle—impartiality and independence governed the attitudes of the secretariat personnel. Its full growth was soon checked, however, by unrelenting budget cuts. The wealthiest members of the league reduced their contributions, and the work of the organization was hampered throughout by poverty-level support. The combined average annual budget of the League of Nations, the International Labor Organization (ILO), and the Permanent Court of International Justice (PCIJ) was $5,500,000.

League of Nations Secretary-General   The head of the secretariat of the League of Nations. The secretary-general of the League of Nations was assisted by a deputy secretary-general and three under secretaries-general. The first secretary-general of the League of Nations was Sir James Eric Drummond, who was named in an addendum to the league's covenant. Later, the secretary-general was appointed by the league council, with the approval of a majority of the league assembly. He was the ex-officio secretary-general of the assembly and of the council. The secretary-general appointed the members of the secretariat, with the approval of the council. He headed a staff of 600 persons and was in charge of carrying out tasks that would help the League of Nations to be successful. The members of the secretariat were responsible to the secretary-general alone, and they enjoyed diplomatic privileges and immunities in the discharge of their duties. *See also* UNITED NATIONS SECRETARY-GENERAL.

Significance   The first secretary-general of the League of Nations attempted to create an international civil service whose appointees could make decisions independently of their national governments in order to run the first world body objectively and efficiently. They were also in charge of promoting cooperation in international trade, finance, transportation, communications, health, and science. All activities of the League of Nations were basically coordinated by the secretary-general and his staff. The secretariat also represented a break with previously accepted ideas. It quickly proved that an international service could function with an efficiency equal to that of any national body. The bulk of the duties of the secretariat were similar to those carried out by officials of a national government. Its full growth, however, was soon checked—not by any direct opposition, but by an unrelenting campaign imposed by budget problems of the League of Nations.

Lebanese Civil War   A conflict between a mosaic of religious communities and their forces over the control of Lebanon. The Lebanese Civil War has had a long history. In the context of the Lebanese political formula, power is granted to the executive branch according to its 1926 constitution. As a result of national and international pressure, France granted Lebanon's independence on November 26, 1941. Following independence, Lebanon, through an unwritten national covenant of 1943, established a unitary and parliamentary government led by a chamber of deputies. Until 1952, the number of Christian deputies (of various denominations) in the parliament was 44; Muslim deputies numbered 20. In 1960 the number of Christian members of parliament rose to 54, and Muslims were more than doubled to 45. The division of seats in the parliament is accompanied by an equal division of government and army posts. The president is traditionally a Maronite, the prime minister a Sunni, the speaker of the house a Shiite, the deputy speaker an Orthodox Christian, and so on. The outbreak of the civil war in 1975–1976 divided Lebanon along sectarian lines. In September 1988, Lebanon slipped farther into crisis when the parliament failed to elect a successor to President Gemayel as a result of differences among the Christians, Muslims, and Syrians. Gemayel's final act, on September 22, was to appoint Aoun, the Maronite commander of the Lebanese armed forces, as prime minister; but the legitimacy of this government was disputed by the acting prime minister of the previous administration, Salim Hoss. This led to the establishment of two rival governments in Lebanon, and to virtual partition along sectarian lines. The violent eviction of Aoun from the presidential palace on October 13, 1990, removed the biggest single obstacle to the reunification of Lebanon. After having lived through more than two years of Aoun's occupation of the palace, President Elias Hrawi and his ministers are faced with an enormous task. On December 19, 1990, Prime Minister Hoss resigned to make way for a government of national unity and was succeeded by Omar Karami. The new cabinet, apparently formed with Syrian backing, included leaders of seven militias. *See also* ARAB-ISRAELI WARS.

Significance   The Lebanese Civil War is attributable to the heterodox character of the country's four million people, who embrace seven major religions and at least 10 minor sects, each of which demands social and cultural distinction. The disputes surround the allocation of seats in the parliament and in other representative bodies. In the beginning the allocation of government and parliamentary seats clearly favored the Christians because of the existence of their slight majority. Now the Shiites are more numerous than the Maronites. The civil war exemplifies the turmoil and conflict that exists in Lebanon. The conflict is intensified by the interference of Israeli and Syrian forces trying to promote their own national interests in Lebanon. Lebanese Christian forces are backed by Israel, while a Muslim coalition (Druze/Amal) is supported by Syria. Although many problems remain, Lebanon has made considerable progress in recent months toward national reconciliation peace.

M

Majoritarianism   The basic rule of the decision-making processes
regulating international organizations. The concept of majoritarianism has been variously applied within international bodies. There is a
clear historical trend away from the rule of unanimity to majority rule
in decision making within international organizations. The League of
Nations generally preserved the unanimity rule; within the United
Nations, the majority rule has become the norm in most bodies except
for the Security Council. There are differences in the voting systems,
depending on whether procedural or substantive issues are involved.
In the substantive cases, majority requirements are often by a two-
thirds vote rather than a simple majority. Article 18 of the Charter of
the United Nations provides that decisions on "important questions"
be made by a two-thirds majority. Majority rule prevails in the specialized agencies of the United Nations save in the financial bodies, where
a system of weighted voting (votes are determined by financial contributions) is followed. *See also* UNITED NATIONS GENERAL ASSEMBLY.

Significance   The majoritarian approach to decision making (by the
UN General Assembly, for example) is an improvement over that of
the League of Nations Assembly, which required unanimity. But a
remnant of unanimity lies in the veto power held by the five permanent members of the Security Council (the United States, the Soviet
Union, the United Kingdom, France, and China). The theory of majoritarianism springs from the concept of sovereign equality of nations
and the democratic idea that the will of the majority should prevail.
The one-country–one-vote formula in the General Assembly has a
philosophical appeal, but it does not reflect reality. Should Costa Rica,
without any military force, cast a vote equal to the powerful United
States or the Soviet Union? The most contemporary system in international organizations has two main components: (1) each member casts

131

one vote, and (2) this is done either by simple majority—50 percent plus one vote—or a majority of two-thirds.

Mandates System of the League of Nations   An alternative arrangement made by the League of Nations to facilitate annexation of territories by the victors of World War I. The mandates system placed the colonies of Germany and Turkey under the guardianship and tutelage of the Allied Powers. The mandates section of the League of Nations Secretariat assisted the Permanent Mandates Commission, which consisted of ten private experts, the league assembly, and the council, in reference to those questions concerning mandates. Mandated territories were classified into three groups according to their relative stages of development. Class A mandates (Arab territories formerly under the Ottoman rule) were regarded as ready for independence and self-government after a minimum mandate period. Class B mandates (East and West African colonies of Germany) were given no promises of early independence. Class C mandates (German South-West Africa and the Pacific Islands) were to be governed as "internal portions of the territory" with no promise of ultimate self-rule or independence. *See also* UNITED NATIONS TRUSTEESHIP COUNCIL.

Significance   The mandates system of the League of Nations was the first experiment by an international organization to improve the well-being of subject peoples. It was the beginning of international intrusion into the national system of colonialism. The main defect of such delegation of sovereignty was that it provided no machinery to ensure the due execution of the trust. The United States, not being a member of the League, was not party to the mandates arrangement; the United States negotiated separate treaties with most of the mandatories, securing its rights. Georg Schwarzenberger views the mandates system as an international disguise for the surreptitious continuation of colonialism.[33] It was a compromise between traditional imperialism and the future trusteeship system to be developed under the United Nations. However, the mandates system, adopted by the Treaty of Versailles, established a precedent that the world community has a responsibility for the well-being of colonial peoples. All mandated territories have now achieved independence; South-West Africa was the last one to be freed in 1990 under the new name of Namibia.

Mediation   The dispute-settlement practice under which the services of a third party are utilized as a means of reducing differences or of bringing about solutions. Mediation is a process of peaceful settlement of disputes by external assistance. Article 3 of The Hague Convention of 1899 provided that "Powers strangers to the dispute have the right to offer good offices or mediation even during the course of hostilities." The point of the offer is to permit contact to be resumed between the disputants, with the third state acting as go-between. If both or all accept the offer, negotiations may proceed through a third party. While The Hague Conventions of 1899 and 1907 provided certain procedures for mediation, it was not until the League of Nations was created that states assumed an obligation to submit disputes to the procedures of peaceful settlement. Under the UN system, members have undertaken even more precise obligations to settle disputes by peaceful means. *See also* GOOD OFFICES.

Significance Mediation is a technique frequently adopted when two or more disputants have deadlocked in their diplomatic negotiations. In such a case, the United Nations may approve the formation of a commission of inquiry and mediation, or the appointment of a UN representative, to visit the scene of the dispute to ascertain facts and seek an on-the-spot resolution. If the parties still are unable to settle the dispute, they may bring the matter before the Security Council or the General Assembly. After reviewing the situation as presented, the United Nations may then decide whether or not a threat to world peace and order exists. If so, the Security Council must decide whether to take specific action or to recommend to the conflicting parties those terms of settlement that it deems advisable. With the current proliferation of international organizations, such clear lines as formerly existed between mediation, good offices, arbitration, and judicial settlement have tended to become blurred.

N

Negotiation   A form of diplomacy in which bargaining occurs through formal, direct discussion between parties. Negotiation is a diplomatic technique for the peaceful settlement of disputes and differences. The choice of techniques to employ in diplomatic negotiation generally depends upon the degree of incompatibility between two or more nations' interests, their insistence upon their individual commitment to those interests, and the degree to which they are eager to reach agreement. Diplomatic negotiations—bilateral or multilateral—are the oldest and most commonly used method of peaceful settlement of disputes. In Article 33(1) the United Nations Charter prescribes that "The parties to any dispute . . . shall, first of all seek a solution by negotiation. . . ." However, obligation to negotiate does not entail an obligation to reach agreement. Nevertheless, the bulk of international disputes are settled by negotiation; thousands of treaties testify to this effect. *See also* DIPLOMACY.

Significance   In popular usage "negotiation" and "diplomacy" are often considered synonymous terms. Negotiation involves a balance between "giving what is asked and getting what is wanted."[34] Negotiation is a combination of art and technical skill that attempts to find a common ground among divergent positions. Diplomacy consists of the formal practices and methods whereby states conduct their foreign relations and seek to communicate, to influence each other, and to resolve conflicts through bargaining. There are distinct differences in negotiating techniques. For example, American negotiators tend to be legalistic and pragmatic. Unlike Americans, Soviet negotiators are apt to make generalized proposals, and desire to reach an agreement in principle. The Japanese are formalistic, and the Chinese are more solicitous. To be successful, negotiations should be carried out privately and discreetly by skilled diplomats and should promote the goals of each country's foreign policy.

New International Economic Order (NIEO)   A proposed set of trade, investment, and aid relationships demanded by Third World nations and intended to create a more even distribution of resources among rich and poor countries. The New International Economic Order was expounded at the Sixth Special United Nations General Assembly Session in 1974, convened at the end of the Arab oil embargo. Later in the year the Arab nations, along with other Third World countries, extended the scope of this proclamation by gaining United Nations approval of the Charter of Economic Rights and Duties of States. This document spelled out in detail the principle and practices needed to implement the NIEO. Since then, the nations of the world have coalesced into three major groupings—the North, the East, and the South (North is used to refer to the developed countries in the Northern Hemisphere; the East includes the socialist nations of Eastern Europe; and the South comprises the less-developed countries of the Southern Hemisphere). The South, in its demand for economic justice, has displayed a high degree of unity, working politically through the Group of Seventy-Seven (G-77). *See also* GROUP OF SEVENTY-SEVEN; THIRD WORLD.

Significance   The New International Economic Order calls for drastic changes, to the benefit of poor countries, in standards and procedures used in current international finance, trade, aid, and investments. This campaign by the countries of the South (mostly Third and Fourth World nations) against the North (mostly industrialized countries of the First and Second Worlds) is waged mainly within the United Nations and the United Nations Conference on Trade and Development (UNCTAD). More than any other document, the NIEO declaration outlines and symbolizes Third World views and calls for reform of the existing economic order in a world dominated by the highly industrialized nations. The future development of the South remains uncertain. A pivotal part of the success of the NIEO is the cooperation of the North, which thus far has been limited. The South has been notorious for playing the North and the East against each other; this can hardly continue since the North and the East are coming closer together with the increasing disappearance of totalitarianism in the East. Now that the socialist countries are asking for help from the North and introducing capitalist economic reforms, the South is likely to be in more jeopardy, economically and politically.

Nonaligned Movement (NAM)   A policy of asserting neutrality and independence from competing blocs of nations, especially those engaged in the East-West conflict. The nonaligned movement is one of only two associations used by the Third World to present a unified front on international issues (the other is the Group of Seventy-Seven, or G-77). In practical terms, the NAM sides with the United States on some issues and with the Soviet Union on other concerns, but refuses to become locked into either camp. It claims to find an identity and strength in numbers, thus permitting it to take a middle ground; two-thirds of the United Nations members belong to it. This movement is traceable to the 1955 Bandung Conference where 25 Afro-Asian nations met to proclaim themselves a third force in world politics. Initially, the NAM attracted great personal leadership like Gamal Abdul Nasser, Jawaharlal Nehru, Kwame Nkrumah, Ahmed Sukarno, and Marshal Tito. Under their leadership the NAM was institutionalized in 1961. *See also* GROUP OF SEVENTY-SEVEN (G-77); THIRD WORLD.

Significance   Nonalignment is a term that, through overuse and mis-use, has lost specific meaning. For some, it is inseparable from the more amorphous idea of Third World or the Group of Seventy-Seven. The nonaligned movement is organized separately from the G-77 and takes positions on a broader range of issues than does the latter group. The NAM today largely controls the machinery of the United Nations. Now that the stalwarts of the movement are dead, and with the growing attention of nations to their internal problems, some predict that the force of the NAM is waning. Thus the future of the nonaligned move-ment as a concept is uncertain. Indeed the nonaligned movement has been difficult for the West to understand. As Richard L. Jackson notes, "In a period of diminished U.S. idealism about the United Nations, critics regard the non-aligned as merely part of an uninterrupted, often unintelligible, flow of rhetoric in the world body."[35]

Nordic Council   A regional organization to promote economic, social, and cultural cooperation among the five Scandinavian coun-tries. The Nordic Council is composed of 78 elected and 45 appointed delegates from Denmark, Finland, Norway, Sweden, and Iceland. Meeting in session once a year, the council has as its purpose the responsibility of providing consultation on mutual problems among the governments and legislatures of member countries. A presidium is elected at the first meeting of each annual council session to head the work of the council until the following session. Some of the other structures are (1) the Council of Ministers, which has decision-making authority on all Nordic affairs; (2) five subject-matter standing com-mittees of the Nordic Council; and (3) two secretariats. *See also* EU-ROPEAN COUNCIL.

Significance   The Nordic Council has served its members as an interparliamentary body for deliberative purposes. Given the divergence of foreign policy attitudes of member nations of the Nordic countries, it is not surprising that one of the most often debated issues in past council meetings has been the problem of cooperation. The council has failed to achieve political integration. As far as its political outlook is concerned, the Nordic Council has one overriding goal, and that is to preserve peace. In the economic area it has been influential in facilitating a substantial number of agreements in commercial and trade matters, in creating a common labor market, and in establishing the Nordic Investment Bank. The Nordic Council also has encouraged closer cooperation on transportation, communications, and environmental problems.

North Atlantic Treaty Organization (NATO)   A regional military organization for the collective defense of Western Europe and North America. The North Atlantic Treaty Organization, created in 1949 in Washington, is a regional military alliance of democratic, capitalistic countries of the West. The 16 members of NATO are Belgium, Canada, Denmark, France, Germany, Greece, Iceland, Italy, Luxembourg, the Netherlands, Norway, Portugal, Spain, Turkey, the United Kingdom, and the United States. The principal organ is the Council of Ministers, represented by foreign, defense, or finance ministers of the members, or all three, depending upon the agenda of the meeting. The Council of Ministers meets several times a year and sets general lines of policy for the organization. NATO maintains that an attack on any member will be considered an attack against all members. Under the treaty, the member countries have adopted a policy of security based on the inherent right to individual and collective self-defense accorded by Article 51 of the United Nations Charter, while affirming cooperation among them in other spheres. *See also* CENTRAL TREATY ORGANIZATION (CENTO); SOUTHEAST ASIA TREATY ORGANIZATION (SEATO); WARSAW TREATY ORGANIZATION (WTO).

Significance   The North Atlantic Treaty Organization has been the most successful defensive alliance in history. NATO's main adversary—the Soviet Union—has accepted a unified Germany in the organization. In the words of the *New York Times*, NATO "alliance leaders proved in London [NATO summit meeting, July 5–6, 1990] that they are prepared to go beyond NATO. . . . This larger vision inspires the realistic hope that this time, Europe could become whole and at peace."[36] NATO has been the foundation of transatlantic freedom, and it has transformed the relationship with its old adversary, the Soviet Union. It now has pledged itself to use nuclear weapons as a last resort, while previously such weapons could be used at any time during a conflict. And NATO has, in essence, done more than that: It has deterred war without ever having to fight a war. It halted the spread of communism, which now is crumbling not only in Europe but also in other parts of the world. NATO kept the hope of freedom alive in the hearts of millions beyond the Iron Curtain. And finally, it convinced the Soviet leaders that the cold war, which was the main reason for the creation of NATO, wrought more damage upon their own country and cause—economically, politically, and morally—than it ever did to the democratic nations.

North-South Axis   A political, economic, and social relationship among wealthy industrialized nations and the less-developed countries (LDCs) of the world. The North-South Axis derives its name from the fact that most highly developed nations are in the Northern Hemisphere, and the poverty-stricken countries lie in the Southern Hemisphere. The North consists of West Europe, most of North America, Australia, New Zealand, and Japan, whereas the South includes Africa, Asia, and Latin America in general. The South occupies more than half of the world's surface and embraces 75 percent of its population. Over time, this group of some 130 nations has given various organizational expressions to their shared perspectives and aims. The nonaligned movement (NAM) and the Group of Seventy-Seven (G-77), to mention only two, have been instrumental in forging a loose-knit South, based on their mutual interests. The North, on the other hand, coordinates its joint policies through the twenty-four-member Organization for Economic Cooperation and Development (OECD). (The socialist bloc of nations is in a different category—neither rich nor poor.) The North-South issues have become a major preoccupation of the United Nations and other international organizations. *See also* NEW INTERNATIONAL ECONOMIC ORDER (NIEO); THIRD WORLD.

Significance   The disparity between the North and the South is nothing new. What has changed the situation is the rising expectations and heightened awareness of the poor Southern nations of their relative economic plight. The South presses the North to share its wealth and resources more equitably; the North has done relatively little to ameliorate the situation. Slowly, the gap between aspirations for development and lack of cooperation among nations is widening and becoming a source of serious international conflict. Many Southern countries face the serious problem of defaulting on loans or of having them canceled. Such a development might deprive them of future loans from the affluent countries. However, a sense of community has developed among many of the Southern nations—a community based upon a shared history and common economic and political problems. As a result, the South has achieved certain successes in garnering support for favorable decisions in many international organizations, but the North has refused to honor them.

Nuclear Proliferation   The spread of nuclear weapons and technology to non-nuclear states. Nuclear proliferation can be of two kinds: horizontal and vertical. Horizontal proliferation refers to the acquisition and development of nuclear weapons by nonnuclear nations. Vertical proliferation means an increase in number and capacity of weapons within the existing nuclear states. Only the United States possessed nuclear weapons in 1945, but their proliferation began in 1949 when the Soviet Union developed its first nuclear bomb. Next, Britain produced its nuclear weapon in 1952, France in 1960, China in 1964, and India in 1974. Officially these six nations are members of the so-called nuclear club and among them there are more than 50,000 nuclear weapons. The International Atomic Energy Agency (IAEA) and the nuclear nations have adopted strict guidelines to prevent the further spread of nuclear materials and technology for military purposes. *See also* INTERNATIONAL ATOMIC ENERGY AGENCY (IAEA); NUCLEAR WAR.

Significance   Nuclear proliferation is causing great concern to leaders of both the West and the East. Under the 1987 Intermediate-range Nuclear Forces (INF) Treaty, the two superpowers eliminated all intermediate-range nuclear missiles, short-range missiles, associated launchers, equipment, support facilities, and operating bases worldwide. The IAEA has been trying to stem the tide of nuclear proliferation by rigorous inspections and monitoring of nuclear plants in those nations without nuclear weapons that are signatories to the Nonproliferation Treaty (NPT) of 1968. Despite these attempts by the superpowers and many of the signatories to the NPT, a number of states, including Israel, Pakistan, South Africa, Argentina, and Brazil, are on the threshold of nuclear capability, and some may already have nuclear weapons.

Nuclear War   A confrontation involving the use of nuclear weapons. Nuclear war may be caused by human fallibility or electronic or mechanical disruption. In terms of destruction, nuclear war would result in far more deadly carnage than the world has ever witnessed, with suffering far exceeding that experienced in both World Wars I and II. The six nuclear powers possess over 50,000 nuclear weapons, equal in destructive power to one million Hiroshima bombs. The sheer size and complexity of modern nuclear weapons raises the risk of accidental nuclear war. Accidental nuclear war, or one by design, remains the most critical concern for all people. The Prevention of Nuclear War Agreement (1973) between the superpowers requires consultation between them if there is a danger of nuclear war. The Washington-Moscow hot line (a teletype communication link set up in 1963 and updated 1988) has helped the superpowers to ward off nuclear conflict. Similar hot lines exist between Paris and Moscow and between London and Moscow. *See also* NUCLEAR PROLIFERATION.

Significance   A general nuclear war might destroy the entire world. Such a war may so affect the earth's environment that it could no longer support living entities—human beings, plants, animals, fish, and so on. The United Nations has estimated that in a nuclear war the Northern Hemisphere would be attacked with a destructive force roughly equal to a thousand Hiroshima bombs. These attacks would quickly penetrate other areas of the world, making the survival of civilization itself doubtful. Why then are nations acquiring nuclear weapons? There are at least three reasons: (1) perceived national security, (2) prestige, and (3) domestic and international status and political and diplomatic advantage. However, it is also said that the primary value of nuclear weapons lies not so much in their utility as an instrument of war, but in their ability to prevent war.

O

Office of the United Nations Disaster Relief Coordinator (UNDRO)
The Office of the United Nations Disaster Relief Coordinator mobilizes relief on an emergency basis, coordinates efforts, reduces waste and duplication of effort, and improves supply of essential items. UNDRO, with headquarters in Geneva, began operations in 1972. An earthquake in Peru and a tidal wave in Bangladesh the preceding year prompted the UN General Assembly to authorize creation of the Office of the UN Disaster Relief Coordinator. The two principal functions of UNDRO are (1) relief coordination—mobilizing, guiding, and coordinating aid to stricken nations, and (2) prevention and preparedness in disaster-prone areas. UNDRO acts as the coordinating agency in emergencies for the United Nations Children's Fund (UNICEF), appropriate UN specialized agencies, other private and governmental donors, and such agencies as the Red Cross. UNDRO also promotes the study, prevention, control, and prediction of natural disasters. It provides planning assistance to prevent and minimize damage in countries subject to recurring natural disasters and calamities. *See also* UNITED NATIONS: REFUGEE PROGRAMS.

Significance   The Office of the UN Disaster Relief Coordinator acts as a focal point and clearinghouse for information on relief needs and on what donors are doing to meet those needs. In the years since World War II, major steps have been taken toward developing institutions and procedures for meeting the needs of refugees and for being responsive to the needs of those whose lives have been affected adversely by disasters. One of the major weaknesses of the UN disaster relief operations is the necessity to rely on self-reporting by governments. For example, the governments of various countries that are dependent on tourism trade are sometimes reluctant to notify the

141

World Health Organization (WHO) about outbreaks of cholera and other communicable diseases. At the same time, the inadequate infrastructure in those countries has interfered with the effective delivery of assistance to refugees. Some governments are also unwilling to admit the existence of food crises. Food crises, such as in Ethiopia and the Sahel, were not reported by their governments for political reasons; eventually, however, the United Nations and other international relief efforts succeeded in reaching the needy people. Because UNDRO is a small organization depending on voluntary contributions, it is unable to administer large-scale relief operations. Thus, when famine reached crisis proportion in Ethiopia during the 1980s, the United Nations established a special Office of Emergency Operations in Africa (OEOA).

Organization for Economic Cooperation and Development (OECD)
A regional economic association of 24 advanced industrialized states. Established in 1961, the Organization for Economic Cooperation and Development includes 17 Western European nations, Turkey, Iceland, Australia, Japan, New Zealand, Canada, and the United States. The OECD replaced the Organization for European Economic Cooperation (OEEC), established in 1948 to elicit common action among Marshall Plan recipient countries to aid their recovery from the ravages of World War II. According to the OECD Convention, member states are expected to promote the expansion of world trade on a nondiscriminatory, multilateral basis and to facilitate the processes of economic advancement in the less-developed countries (LDCs). Within the OECD a group called the Developed Assistance Committee (DAC) provides a channel through which the major donor nations attempt to coordinate their policies for economic assistance. *See also* COLOMBO PLAN; COMMONWEALTH OF NATIONS.

Significance   The Organization for Economic Cooperation and Development represents an improvement over other intergovernmental procedures in the working of its Development Assistance Committee. Each member must present to other members a statement of the sum of money that the contracting parties are committing to development assistance. Donald Blaisdell considers this to be a "setting similar to that of a witness before a committee of the United States Congress (where) each representative on the Committee is also quizzed by the other Committee members."[37] The OECD has established general policies and principles to guide member nations in defining their policies and programs and submitting them to inquiry. This is accomplished through the publication of statistics and research findings, while the deliberative process becomes a forum for analyzing and debating those policies.

Organization of African Unity (OAU)   A general-purpose regional body to promote African interests, composed of 52 African states. The Organization of African Unity's broad objective is to develop political solidarity, foster economic development, and provide security for member states. All independent African nations are members except South Africa. The OAU was formed in 1963 in Addis Ababa, Ethiopia, by what were then 30 independent African states. It evolved out of the Pan-African Congresses, which had begun in the early twentieth century. The OAU adopted the principles and goals put forth at the Afro-Asian People's Solidarity Conference (or Bandung Conference) in 1955 and later at the All-African People's Conference and the Conference of Independent African States, which were held in the late 1950s and early 1960s. The principles of the OAU charter call for sovereign equality of all states, noninterference in the internal affairs of states, respect for the sovereignty and territorial integrity of each state, peaceful settlement of disputes, condemnation of political assassination and subversive activities in other nations, and nonalignment with any blocs. *See also* AFRO-ASIAN PEOPLE'S SOLIDARITY CONFERENCE; ORGANIZATION OF AMERICAN STATES (OAS).

Significance   The Organization of African Unity is the most prestigious and encompassing organization on the African continent. The broad objectives are commonly accepted by members, but it has remained a loose association of independent states with lofty declarations but little in the way of common goals or concerted action. Its Pan-African outlook has been dimmed by internal political rivalries, ideological differences, conflicting ties with outside powers, and an overriding concern with preservation of personal power and state sovereignty. Security provisions in the OAU charter have seldom, if ever, been implemented. Cooperative cultural and economic programs have suffered from linguistic and regional barriers and lack of funds. The idea of achieving political unity among 52 independent member states is now recognized as unrealistic; political harmony and cooperation remain the desired objectives. Among the OAU's achievements is the establishment of an African Development Bank. In the United Nations, the OAU functions as an effective caucusing group when issues of common interest come before that world body. Its members also participate in the Afro-Asian groups' deliberations and with Third and Fourth World nations in the Group of Seventy-Seven (G-77).

Organization of American States (OAS)   A regional organization mandated to determine common political, economic, defense, and social policies and provide for coordination of various inter-American agencies. The Organization of American States was established by the Ninth International Conference of American States at Bogotá, Colombia, in 1948. Thirty-two Caribbean, Central, and South American states, as well as Canada and the United States, are members of the organization. OAS headquarters are in Washington. Cuba was expelled from membership in 1962. The OAS charter reaffirms the principle that "an act of aggression against one American state is an act of aggression against all the other American states," and solemnly proclaims the fundamental rights of individuals regardless of race, nationality, creed, or sex. The structure of the OAS includes the following principal organs: the General Assembly, the Meeting of the Consultation of Ministers of Foreign Affairs, three councils, the Inter-American Juridical Committee, the Inter-American Commission on Human Rights, the General Secretariat, specialized conferences, and specialized organizations. *See also* ORGANIZATION OF AFRICAN UNITY (OAU); PAN-AMERICAN UNION.

Significance   The Organization of American States is one of the oldest regional organizations. Its origin can be traced back to 1826, when Simón Bolívar sought the establishment of a Latin American League of Nations. Since its founding, the organization has changed remarkably as a result of a number of critical issues emanating from within the inter-American system. The main questions of peace and security have been linked increasingly to economic and social development, evolution of democratic institutions in many member countries, and respect for human rights. Despite the expulsion of Cuba from the OAS, the organization has been unable to adopt a common policy toward the Castro regime. As a superpower, the United States plays a dominant role in the OAS, especially in security matters. Many OAS members are hard hit by debt crises, and if the United States cannot work out a viable solution to their financial difficulties, the situation may worsen and multiply conflicts among the debtor members of the OAS and their creditors in the United States and Western Europe.

Organization of Arab Petroleum Exporting Countries (OAPEC)
An exclusive Arab oil cartel. The Organization of Arab Petroleum Exporting Countries, not to be confused with the Organization of Petroleum Exporting Countries (OPEC), was formed in 1968 to safeguard the interests of member countries and to determine ways and means to implement mutual cooperation in the Arab oil industry. The

members of the organization are Saudi Arabia, Kuwait, Algeria, Libya, Iraq, the United Arab Emirates, Bahrain, Egypt, Syria, and Qatar. Besides the establishment of close cooperative links (which have been shattered by the Iraqi occupation of Kuwait) and the protection of legitimate interests—individual and collective—of member countries, OAPEC is entrusted with the task of securing the supply of oil to consumer countries at equitable and reasonable prices and creating favorable conditions for capital and technological investments in the oil industry. The structure of the organization includes the Council of Ministers, the Executive Bureau, and the Secretariat. *See also* ORGANIZATION OF PETROLEUM EXPORTING COUNTRIES (OPEC).

Significance   The Organization of Arab Petroleum Exporting Countries has been instrumental in the success of the Organization of Petroleum Exporting Countries (OPEC) because of the former's embargo in 1973–1974, which created sufficient scarcity of oil to support oil price hikes. However, OAPEC action was fortuitous, rather than intended, in regard to oil pricing. OAPEC is dependent on OPEC because it needs the larger organization to arrive at consensus on oil production and oil prices; the two sister oil organizations are, in a sense, interdependent. OAPEC has played a key role in its efforts to improve inter-Arab cooperation on vital oil issues. But because of the Iraqi occupation of neighboring Kuwait, a war broke out between Iraq and eight Arab countries (six gulf nations, Egypt, and Syria) in association with an international coalition led by the United States. Unless the Arab nations reconcile their differences by peaceful means, Arab economic and political solidarity is doomed for a long time and the Arab cold war will continue.

Organization of Central American States (ODECA)   A regional organization devoted to fostering political, economic, and social cooperation in Central America. As signatories to the Charter of San Salvador, members of the Organization of Central American States include Costa Rica, El Salvador, Guatemala, Honduras, and Nicaragua. A revised charter was adopted at Panama City in 1962 and Panama was invited to join. The Charter of ODECA declares that the contracting parties constitute an economic-political community, aspiring to the integration of Central America; such an ultimate goal is to be pursued through the joint promotion of economic and social progress. The main action arms of ODECA are the meetings of heads of state, the conferences of ministers of foreign affairs, the Executive Council, the Legislative Council, the Central American Court of Justice, the Central American Economic Council, the Cultural and

Educational Council, and the Central American Defense Council. Decisions on substantive matters require unanimity; this is also required when determining whether a matter is substantive or procedural. See also CENTRAL AMERICAN COMMON MARKET (CACM); INTER-AMERICAN TREATY OF RECIPROCAL ASSISTANCE.

Significance   The Organization of Central American States has proven itself unable to attain its ambitious political goals, and activities concerning economic cooperation and integration have been entrusted to the Central American Common Market (CACM). Despite the inclusion of pacific settlement of disputes among its avowed purposes, ODECA has left this matter (as well as security affairs generally) to the Organization of American States (OAS). The long-standing dispute between Honduras and El Salvador represents one of the disturbing factors affecting unity of the region. However, ODECA continues to express—in organizational terms—the common cultural heritage, the common language, and the common memory of political unity in the early nineteenth century. Whether closer political unity is possible in the future will depend on the performance of the Central American Common Market and how serious the members are for political ties.

Organization of the Islamic Conference (OIC)   A group of Muslim nations to promote solidarity and strengthen cooperation. The Organization of the Islamic Conference was established in 1969; its main objectives are to support the tenets of Islam. Headquartered in Jeddah, Saudi Arabia, the main aims of the organization are to consolidate cooperation among 44 Muslim nations in economic, social, cultural, scientific, and other vital fields of activity; to facilitate consultations among member states in international organizations; to work toward elimination of racial segregation and discrimination; to take those measures necessary to support international peace and security; to coordinate efforts for safeguarding holy places; and to support the struggle of the people of Palestine. The question of Palestine has been an ever-present topic on the agendas of all Islamic summit conferences as well as Islamic conferences of foreign ministers. See also HOLY ALLIANCE.

Significance   The Organization of the Islamic Conference lends an aura of worldwide solidarity based on a particular religion—Islam. But the effective pursuit of the organization's goal has been adversely affected by recurring tensions and disputes between the Muslim nations. In the Iran-Iraq War the OIC attempted to mediate the dispute and to obtain a cease-fire, but its efforts proved to be in vain. The 1990 Iraqi occupation of Kuwait—with both countries being Muslim and Arab nations and members of the OIC—does not augur well for the working of the OIC. So far, the Arab-Israeli conflict remains the only item on the OIC agenda that has united the participants. But this formation is likely to change. The Palestine Liberation Organization (PLO) in 1990 lent support to Iraq, an act against the interests of the majority of Arab nations, which condemned the Iraqi action against Kuwait, and in 1991 eight Arab nations (all Muslim) went to a war against Iraq (an Arab and Muslim nation also).

Organization of Petroleum Exporting Countries (OPEC)   A group of Third World oil producing-exporting countries joined together to coordinate the oil policies of member countries and protect their individual and collective interests. The Organization of Petroleum Exporting Countries includes 13 members—six Arab nations (Algeria, Libya, Kuwait, Saudi Arabia, Qatar, Iraq, the United Arab Emirates), Iran, two African countries (Nigeria and Gabon), one Asian nation (Indonesia), and two Latin American countries (Venezuela and Ecuador). Membership in the Organization is open to any country that is a substantial net exporter of oil and has fundamentally similar interests to those of the member countries. Admission requires acceptance by three-fourths of the full members, as well as the concurrence of the five founders—Saudi Arabia, Kuwait, Iraq, Iran, and Venezuela. One of the major aims of the organization is to ensure the stability of oil production and prices in international markets. *See also* ORGANIZATION OF ARAB PETROLEUM EXPORTING COUNTRIES (OAPEC); THIRD WORLD.

Significance   The formation of the Organization of Petroleum Exporting Countries was not a new phenomenon in modern capitalism; neither were price fixing and trade embargoes. However, OPEC represented the first collective forum by Third World oil-producing countries to initiate structural changes in the market. The OPEC aspiration was unique and alarming, however, because it demonstrated that through collective action, the oil producing-exporting nations could generate the means or capacity to influence the oil market to their own advantage. This meant that a shift in structural power to protect national interests is possible despite control of the oil industry by multinational oil companies (MNOCs). The profound success of

OPEC raises the question of a redistribution of leverage in the international political economy. It may also provide an inspiration, a model, and possibly a financial base for similar initiatives by Third World raw materials-producing nations seeking market power.

P

Pacific Settlement of Disputes   Resolution of international conflicts without recourse to violence or force. Pacific settlement of disputes is arranged in such a manner that international peace and security are not endangered. There are many techniques for the peaceful settlement of disputes, such as arbitration, conciliation, good offices, inquiry, adjudication, mediation, and negotiation. These techniques are primarily concerned with international disputes to which sovereign states are party; they also may be applied to disputes between states and international organizations, and to those between international organizations. Private citizens do not have recourse to international settlement of disputes as they are not directly subjects of international law; these procedures, like any other aspects of international law, apply to nations and international organizations. *See also* HAGUE PEACE CONFERENCES.

Significance   The pacific settlement of disputes as a viable means of resolving conflicts has long been an ideal for both nations and individuals. The Hague Peace Conferences of 1899 and 1907 sought to capture that ideal through developed and codified mandatory multilateral procedures aimed at establishing peaceful settlement. These conferences carried the recommendation that states postpone hostilities while mediation was taking place. The League of Nations hoped to impose upon the parties a delay of some months before any war occurred. The United Nations unequivocally demands that disputants initially resort to peaceful settlement of disputes. The use of regional arrangements to develop and achieve pacific settlements of local or regional disputes is encouraged by the United Nations. The ultimate alternative to the pacific settlement of disputes is active hostility and war, with the possible unleashing of nuclear weapons.

Pan-American Union   The organization that emerged from various conferences between representatives of most of the independent nations of the Western Hemisphere that were held between 1826 and 1899. The Pan-American Union now functions as the secretariat for the Organization of American States (OAS), coordinates inter-American social, economic, juridical, and cultural activities, and promotes the welfare of members. The International Union of American Republics, formed in 1980, was assisted by the Commercial Bureau, which later came to be called the Pan-American Union. The Pan-American Union was formerly the central and permanent bureaucratic organ of the OAS. This function is carried out by the General Secretariat with a budget of more than $75 million. It is headquartered in Washington, D.C., and is headed by a secretary-general, elected by a council. That office may participate in any activity of OAS organs, but does not have the right to vote. The General Secretariat consists of over 1,200 international staff; many are highly skilled professionals in various fields. *See also* ORGANIZATION OF AMERICAN STATES (OAS).

Significance   The Pan-American Union has broad membership and a broad mandate, but its powers are limited. Until World War II, the organization concerned itself with nonpolitical issues. A spirit of collaboration engendered by the war, and the vital need for effective security arrangements, made for an inevitable strengthening and improvement of the Pan-American system. As a result, the Inter-American Treaty of Reciprocal Assistance of 1947 developed a system of collective security whereby an act of aggression committed within the Western Hemisphere would be acted upon jointly by the signatory nations. The Pan-American Union has been the unifying factor in developing models for an effective regional system.

Peace   The absence of war. Peace can usher in amity between those who have been at war or in a state of enmity. Since the Middle Ages, persons and private groups were associated with the quest for peace. In modern times, governments also have played an increasing role in seeking to establish or diminish warfare. The Congress of Vienna in 1815 sought to stabilize Europe through wide-ranging arrangements. In The Hague Conference of 1899, delegates from 26 governments discussed disarmament, rules of warfare, and the arbitration process. In 1907, representatives from 44 states assembled in The Hague to examine similar issues. The main purpose for the establishment of the League of Nations and the United Nations was to maintain peace and security in the world. In the post–World War II period, world peace is based mainly on nuclear deterrence. *See also* UNITED NATIONS: PEACE-KEEPING; WAR; WORLD GOVERNMENT.

Significance   Peace is the highest political goal of nation-states, and they seek it through their constitutional declarations; no nation proclaims war as its constitutional principle. Peace is the objective of every nation, since it is a blessing and its opposite—war—is a scourge. Relations between nations are dominated by misunderstandings, misinterpretations, and the inability to view other nations in a nonegocentric manner. To establish peace in the world, nations must abandon their ignorance of one another by mutual exchange and organization of information regarding their histories and culture. As in domestic affairs, where internal peace is maintained by a government having superior authority over local bodies, a world government concept seems to many to offer a logical solution to the problems of international conflict and the attainment of security. But how to establish an acceptable world government remains elusive. So far, the United Nations is the only step in that direction.

Peacekeeping Forces: United Nations Command in Korea (UNCK)
The United Nations peacekeeping force in Korea. The United Nations Command in Korea was established in 1950 to repel an armed attack by troops from North Korea and restore peace in South Korea. The UN Security Council declared the armed attack against South Korea to be a breach of the peace and called for a cease-fire and withdrawal of North Korean forces to the 38th parallel. The Security Council declared North Korea an aggressor and recommended that members of the United Nations furnish the necessary assistance to South Korea to repel the attack and restore international peace and security in the region. The United States announced that it had ordered its air and sea forces to give cover and support to the troops of the South Korean government. Later it authorized the use of ground forces. The United Nations Command constituted troops from 16 nations, and five others supplied medical units. The Soviet Union considered the Security Council's decision illegal. China sent a volunteer force to fight on the side of North Korea. *See also* PEACEKEEPING FORCES: UNITED NATIONS TRUCE SUPERVISION ORGANIZATION (UNTSO).

Significance   The organization of the United Nations Command in Korea had initial success because of the voluntary absence of the Soviet Union from the Security Council. The preponderance of troops supplied by the United States in response to the UN decision to send an international force to Korea makes it difficult to assess the effectiveness of the UN action. Many of the major decisions were taken outside of the UN framework, much of the political debate and argument is only hinted at in the records of the General Assembly and the Security Council, and the formal reports of the commander are clearly inadequate as a historical record of the changing military situation. Further, the United States' domination of the military command in Korea became most evident in the controversy involving General Douglas MacArthur that led to his removal by President Harry Truman. Most of the Allies and many Americans viewed MacArthur's plan to bomb military bases in Manchuria as serious provocation to the Chinese. He was removed from the command because of his challenge to the authority of the U.S. president. Finally, though the North Korean aggression was halted and an armistice reached, Korea remained tense and politically divided, and large numbers of American troops remain in the South 40 years later.

Peacekeeping Forces: United Nations Emergency Force I (UNEF I)
An international emergency security force created by the General Assembly in 1956 to prevent four-nation hostilities. The United Nations Emergency Force I was established to help resolve a severe crisis in the Middle East and stem the Anglo-French and Israeli invasion of Egypt. It was designed as a temporary police force, operating with the consent of Egypt and the cooperation of contributory states. UNEF I primarily was assigned the task of supervising withdrawal of foreign troops from Egyptian territory and ensuring compliance with the UN resolutions. This critical situation in the Middle East was precipitated by a 1956 British, French, and Israeli invasion of Egypt when that nation nationalized the Suez Canal. When the Security Council was prevented from action by Anglo-French vetoes, the General Assembly, acting under the Uniting for Peace Resolution of 1950, which provided that the General Assembly could assume jurisdiction over peace and security matters when the Security Council was stymied by a veto, authorized the creation of an emergency force. The principles elaborated by the secretary-general centered mainly upon an effort to establish and secure recognition of the international character of UNEF I. The commanding officer of UNEF I was so defined as to make him fully independent of control by any one nation. The United Nations authorized an emergency force of 6,000 men to supervise a cease-fire and troop disengagement on the Egyptian front and control a buffer zone between the combatants. UNEF I was withdrawn in 1967 at the request of Egypt. *See also* PEACEKEEPING FORCES: UNITED NATIONS

EMERGENCY FORCE II (UNEF II); PEACEKEEPING FORCES: UNITED NATIONS
TRUCE SUPERVISION ORGANIZATION (UNTSO).

Significance   The establishment of the first United Nations Peacekeeping Force was a formidable task for the General Assembly in its
first emergency special session; the concept of a peacekeeping force
had no real precedent. Concerned with a great number of far-reaching duties and responsibilities, the force has been recognized as an
important model for any international organization's technique of
peacekeeping. UNEF I became the prototype of a small police force
that the international community might find useful at other times of
crises. Indeed, it was the continuing success of UNEF I that encouraged the formation of UNEF II in 1973 as a "weapon for peace." With
the help of UNEF I, a regional war in the Middle East was brought to
an end, a menacing situation was stilled, and a reasonable stability
became possible in one of the world's most volatile regions. The creation of UNEF I as a tool of peaceful settlement was a positive step in
United Nations preventive diplomacy. If political and financial conditions permit, recourse to emergency forces can make valuable contributions to peace and stability in the world, with the General Assembly
serving as a backup to the Security Council in handling such matters.

Peacekeeping Forces: United Nations Emergency Force II (UNEF II)
The second United Nations peacekeeping operation in the Middle
East. The United Nations Emergency Force II was created in 1973,
after the fourth Arab-Israeli war broke out. The purpose of the Egyptian attack against Israel was not to destroy the Jewish state, but to
regain the occupied territories. Egyptian forces swept over the Israeli
Bar-Lev Line of defensive fortifications and pressed inland. Israel was
also attacked by Syria from the Golan Heights. With rapid mobilization of Israeli reserves, a sizable force was assembled and took to the
field within days of the initial fighting. The United States rushed
military supplies to Israel, but the Soviet Union mustered a similar
effort in support of Egypt and Syria. Within a week, the tide of battle
had turned in favor of Israel. Both Egypt and Syria were defeated,
and the Egyptian Third Army was cut off on the Sinai side of the Suez
Canal. President Anwar Sadat of Egypt appealed for joint Soviet-
American forces to be sent to the Middle East to restore peace. The
Soviet Union agreed, while the United States suggested an enlarged
military observation group. While this disagreement continued, the
UN Security Council decided to set up immediately a United Nations
Emergency Force, to be composed of personnel drawn from member

states—except from the permanent members of the Security Council (China, France, the United Kingdom, the Soviet Union, and the United States). *See also* PEACEKEEPING FORCES: UNITED NATIONS EMERGENCY FORCE I (UNEF I).

Significance   The United Nations Emergency Force II performed its assignments successfully and kept hostile forces at a distance from each other. It then faced the Security Council's demand for the return of former combatants to the positions they had occupied on October 22, 1973. While discussion for this demand dragged on, the United States and the Soviet Union jointly called for negotiations on a just and durable peace in the Middle East. As a result, under the auspices of the United Nations, the Peace Conference on the Middle East was convened in Geneva in December 1973. This conference discussed the disengagement of forces in the Egyptian sector as well as a comprehensive settlement of the Middle East problem, but the result was indecisive. On the Syrian front, military action persisted until May 1974, when a disengagement agreement was signed at Geneva by Syria and Israel, with provision for a UN peacekeeping force. Such a force—the United Nations Disengagement Observer Force (UNDOF)—was established to supervise disengagement and patrol the border area; UNDOF performed its mission well in so far as it kept the warring nations separate from each other. At the same time, the warming of relations between Egypt and the United Nations, and the new heights of popularity of President Sadat, culminated in the 1979 Camp David Accords and peace treaty between Egypt and Israel. There also came into being the first political and territorial settlement between Israel and an Arab country, and the first opening of diplomatic relations between them.

Peacekeeping Forces: United Nations Force in Cyprus (UNFICYP) The United Nations peacekeeping involvement in Cyprus. The United Nations Peacekeeping Force in Cyprus was established in 1964 to invoke law and order between warring Greek and Turkish factions. Since then, the Cyprus conflict has been constantly on the UN agenda. Cyprus became independent from Britain in 1960, with a constitution that was intended to balance the interests of the island's Greek and Turkish populations. A relative peace prevailed in Cyprus until 1963, when the situation gradually deteriorated because of political differences between the two communities; as a result, fighting broke out. Following this outbreak of hostilities, the UN Security Council met to consider a complaint by Cyprus charging Turkey with intervention in its internal affairs and aggression. Turkey maintained that the

Greek Cypriot leaders had tried for more than two years to nullify the rights of the Turkish Cypriot community and denied all charges of aggression. The Security Council unanimously recommended the creation of, with the consent of the government of Cyprus, a United Nations peacekeeping force in Cyprus. To promote a peaceful solution to the Cyprus problem, it also asked the secretary-general to designate, upon agreement with the four governments concerned (Cyprus, Greece, Turkey, and the United Kingdom), a UN mediator. *See also* PEACEKEEPING FORCES: UNITED NATIONS TRUCE SUPERVISION ORGANIZATION (UNTSO).

Significance　　The United Nations Force in Cyprus has effectively performed its mandate to curb violence and has succeeded in maintaining law and order in Cyprus. Ever since its involvement in Cyprus, the United Nations has been trying to win approval from both sides (Turkish and Greek) of a reunification of Cyprus under one government. Both the General Assembly and the Security Council have affirmed numerous times their recognition of the Greek Cypriot government and their opposition to permanent division of the island. A new crisis developed in 1974 when a military coup in Cyprus prompted Turkey to invade the island. UNFICYP was involved in the fighting and suffered some casualties before a cease-fire was agreed upon. The result was a division of the territory that strongly favored the Turkish position. UN Secretary-General Pérez de Cuéllar opened talks with the belligerents in 1989, but they ended in failure. Currently there is no visible peace effort, but the UN peacekeepers remain vigilant in Cyprus.

Peacekeeping Forces: United Nations Good Offices Mission in Afghanistan and Pakistan (UNGOMAP)　　An international peacekeeping force to monitor the full withdrawal of Soviet troops from Afghanistan in February 1989. The United Nations Good Offices Mission in Afghanistan and Pakistan continues to fulfill its tasks with regard to the Geneva Accords, which are to promote a comprehensive political solution in Afghanistan. During Christmas week in 1979, when Soviet troops entered Afghanistan to install a pro-Soviet leader after months of domestic conflict, nearly every member of the United Nations condemned the invasion. The General Assembly adopted scores of resolutions calling for a Soviet withdrawal and a halt to attacks on civilians. Years of UN diplomacy finally produced four agreements, one dealing with Soviet troop withdrawal: the Geneva Accords of April 4, 1988. On the political front, little progress has been made since the signing of the Geneva Accords. Afghan President

Najibullah has urged a settlement with the mujahiddin (insurgents or holy warriors) and offered to give rebel leaders posts in the army and government. But the mujahiddin have declined such offers. In the meantime, UNGOMAP—a force of fifty observers—keeps monitoring the pledges of the United States, Pakistan, and the Soviet Union not to meddle in Afghan affairs. See also UNITED NATIONS OBSERVATION GROUP IN LEBANON (UNOGIL).

Significance   The small United Nations Good Offices Mission in Afghanistan and Pakistan successfully monitored the full withdrawal of over 100,000 Soviet troops from Afghanistan. Throughout the continuing conflict and fluid political situation within Afghanistan, the United Nations has repeatedly called upon the parties involved in the Afghan problem to ensure that they carry out the obligations they assumed under UN auspices—that is, to promote a political solution in Afghanistan with dispatch. The failure of the Security Council to reach a consensus on renewing UNGOMAP's mandate on March 15, 1990, led to the establishment of the Office of the Secretary-General in Afghanistan and Pakistan (OSGAP). The UN secretary-general's personal representative maintains contacts with all parties in an attempt to achieve an intra-Afghan dialogue. He also maintains close contact with various segments of the Afghan population, both inside and outside the country. Clearly this kind of activity for the purpose of achieving a broad-based government falls within the framework of domestic affairs of nations. Although the Security Council was unable to extend the mandate of UNGOMAP, the General Assembly allowed the secretary-general to appoint a personal representative with apparent authority to interfere in the internal affairs of Afghanistan, thus giving the appearance of acting contrary to provisions of the UN Charter that rule out UN intervention in the domestic affairs of member nations.

Peacekeeping Forces: United Nations India/Pakistan Observation Mission (UNIPOM)   An international peacekeeping operation in India and Pakistan. The United Nations India/Pakistan Observation Mission was an administrative adjunct of the United Nations Military Observer Group in India and Pakistan (UNMOGIP), set up as a temporary measure for the sole purpose of supervising the cease-fire along the India-Pakistan border outside of Kashmir. The background of the formation of UNIPOM lies in the breakdown in 1965 of the cease-fire agreement of 1949 between India and Pakistan, when they had fought another war. The first war broke out between the two countries over the Rann of Kutch. A United Nations tribunal settled this dispute, but hostilities again broke out in Kashmir in 1965. The Security Council called for a cease-fire and the fighting came to an end with the assistance of UNMOGIP. Since the conflict extended beyond the Kashmir cease-fire line, the secretary-general decided to establish UNIPOM for the sole purpose of supervising the cease-fire along the India-Pakistan border. The function of UNIPOM was primarily to observe and report on breaches of the cease-fire. In case of breaches, the observers were also to do all they could to persuade the local commanders to restore the cease-fire but had no authority to order a cessation of firing. *See also* PEACEKEEPING FORCES: UNITED NATIONS MILITARY OBSERVER GROUP IN INDIA AND PAKISTAN (UNMOGIP).

Significance   The United Nations India/Pakistan Observation Mission was quite effective in terminating hostilities between the two countries. It had successfully—though not without difficulties—helped achieve a cease-fire, and it played an indispensable role at the military level in bringing about the withdrawal of armed personnel within their own borders. UNIPOM, like UNMOGIP, was not charged with finding a long-term solution to the problem of Kashmir—which still persists. Although the two organizations were separate, the functions of cease-fire observation and assistance in troop withdrawals were acknowledged by the secretary-general as being closely interwoven. He argued that UNMOGIP had duties specifically in relation to the 1949 Kashmir cease-fire line, and that the 1965 fighting had occurred along international frontiers as well as across the Kashmir cease-fire line. However, this dispute over the functions of the two peacekeeping operations ended shortly thereafter when UNIPOM was closed in 1966.

Peacekeeping Forces: United Nations Interim Force in Lebanon (UNIFIL)   An international peacekeeping mission in Lebanon. The United Nations Interim Force in Lebanon was established in 1978 after Israeli forces invaded southern Lebanon in response to a Palestinian commando raid into Israel. Sectarian strife and public disorder had kept Lebanon in a state of anarchy since the outbreak of civil war in 1975. The situation deteriorated further after another Israeli invasion of southern Lebanon in 1982. The mandate of UNIFIL, which was sent to restore Lebanese sovereignty in southern Lebanon, was extended, and the strength of the force was increased from 6,000 to about 7,000. The situation in Lebanon was further complicated by the presence of Syrian troops, Palestinian guerrilla groups, and multinational forces composed of American, British, French, and Italian troops. Lacking a credible central authority, any would-be leader could assert authority if he was capable of doing so. One such person was General Michel Aoun, who asserted the hegemony of Christian forces under his command over local militias and rallied the country against Syrian occupation. But in 1990 Aoun gave up his fight and took asylum in the French embassy in Beirut, thus ending a protracted civil war, and, temporarily at least, the country returned to a semblance of normalcy. *See also* PEACEKEEPING FORCES: UNITED NATIONS OBSERVATION GROUP IN LEBANON (UNOGIL).

Significance   The efficacy of the peacekeeping operations of the United Nations Interim Force in Lebanon has been problematic from the beginning. The job of UNIFIL was particularly difficult because the numerous internal factions and various foreign elements in Lebanon were in conflict and continued fighting. UNIFIL has been unable to prevent clashes not only between Israeli forces and Palestinian guerrillas, but also between Lebanese Christians and Muslims. Like other UN peacekeeping forces, UNIFIL has no combat authority and no enforcement power and requires the cooperation of the parties concerned to fulfil its tasks. A further problem arises from the lack of a clear definition of UNIFIL's area of operation (the Security Council resolution establishing UNIFIL was the result of a compromise and was vague on this point). Meanwhile, UNIFIL continues to cooperate with the Lebanese authorities and various UN agencies in extending humanitarian assistance—distributing food and medicine—to the local population.

Peacekeeping Forces: United Nations Iran-Iraq Military Observer Group (UNIIMOG)   An international cease-fire observation force along borders between Iran and Iraq. The United Nations Iran-Iraq Military Observer Group was established in 1988 to supervise a cease-fire while the secretary-general began negotiations with the parties for settlement of the dispute between Iran and Iraq that began with Iraq's invasion of Iran in 1980. At that time Iraq had asserted its determination to achieve full control over the Shatt al-Arab waterway and reverse the Algiers Accord of 1975, in which both countries had agreed to joint sovereignty over the Shatt River. Between 1980 and 1988 the Security Council adopted many resolutions and issued numerous statements calling for a withdrawal of forces to internationally recognized boundaries, respect for the right of free navigation and commerce in international waters, restraint from actions that would endanger peace and security, and an exchange of prisoners of war. Finally, on July 17, 1988, Iran informed the secretary-general of its acceptance of Resolution 598 (1987), which called for an immediate cease-fire "on land, at sea, and in the air," deplored the initiation of the war, and advocated an inquiry into "responsibility for the conflict." Following intensive discussion in New York with the foreign ministers of the two countries, the secretary-general announced on August 8, 1988, that a cease-fire would go into effect that day. *See also* PEACE-KEEPING FORCES: UNITED NATIONS EMERGENCY FORCE I (UNEF I); UNITED NATIONS EMERGENCY FORCE II (UNEF II).

Significance   The 350-person United Nations Iran-Iraq Military Observer Group, together with the necessary military and civilian staff, supervised the cease-fire. At the same time the secretary-general engaged in negotiations with envoys from Iran and Iraq for the full implementation of Resolution 598 and a comprehensive solution to the conflict. Since September 1988, however, numerous rounds of face-to-face negotiations in New York and Geneva have made little progress toward a comprehensive settlement. Both parties stubbornly pursued political goals at the negotiating table that had eluded them on the battlefield; meanwhile, the Security Council renewed UNIIMOG's mandate. However, in the wake of an Iraqi invasion of Kuwait on August 2, 1990, Iraq decided to unilaterally withdraw its troops from the Iranian border, return Iranian territory occupied during the eight-year war (1980–1988), and exchange prisoners of war with Iran. Thus, finally, without direct involvement from the United Nations or UNIIMOG, Iraq and Iran resolved their problems and re-established diplomatic relations. Iraq's actions, however, were less a matter of complying with UN resolutions than adjusting to the new set of affairs in the region that pitted Iraq against a UN-authorized force composed of military units from 28 countries. The UN force, largely American, sought to make Iraq withdraw from Kuwait, which it had invaded and tried to integrate as its nineteenth province in the latter half of 1990 and early 1991.

Peacekeeping Forces: United Nations Iraq-Kuwait Observer Mission (UNIKOM)   An international peacekeeping force to monitor the peace in Iraq and Kuwait. The United Nations Iraq-Kuwait Observer Mission is charged with monitoring the 15-kilometer-wide and 200-kilometer-long demilitarized zone between Iraq and Kuwait. Established by UN Security Council Resolution 687 of April 9, 1991, UNIKOM mandated a formal cease-fire between Iraq and Kuwait and those nations cooperating with Kuwait. The same resolution also called for a Special Commission to oversee the destruction of Iraq's biological, chemical, and nuclear weapons capabilities as well as its ballistic missiles. UNIKOM has deployed 300 military observers and

680 soldiers along the demilitarized zone. Eventually 1,400 troops from 36 countries—among them Bangladesh, China, Fiji, Ghana, Hungary, Pakistan, the United States, and the Soviet Union (but no Middle Eastern states) will be patrolling the area by land and air. These forces are intended to serve as a deterrent to cross-border violations and as observers of any hostile actions that might be launched by one state against another. UNIKOM may use force in self-defense but is not authorized to use force to prevent entry of military personnel or equipment into the demilitarized zone. The cost of the UNIKOM operation is estimated at $83 million for the first six months and $40 million for the following six; these sums are to be raised from assessed and voluntary contributions. *See also* PEACEKEEPING FORCES: UNITED NATIONS IRAN-IRAQ MILITARY OBSERVER GROUP (UNIIMOG).

Significance   Iraq reluctantly accepted all phases of the humiliating UNIKOM resolution but had little or no intention of complying fully or cooperating with the UN inspectors looking for nuclear weapons—making material in Iraq. In June, 1991, Iraq twice denied a UN inspection team access to a reported uranium-enrichment device. Upon learning of these incidents, U.S. President George Bush himself accused Iraqi President Saddam Hussein of violating the Gulf war cease-fire agreement, reiterating his pledge that the United States would not permit Iraq to continue to violate solemn international agreements. While diplomatic options are sought by the United States and other nations, the possibility of a renewed Gulf war cannot be ruled out if Iraq continues to flout the UNIKOM resolution.

Peacekeeping Forces: United Nations Military Observer Group in India and Pakistan (UNMOGIP)   An international military observer group designated to supervise a cease-fire in Kashmir between India and Pakistan. Established in 1949, the United Nations Military Observer Group in India and Pakistan has largely been involved in observation, reporting, and a joint investigatory system, agreed upon by both parties, used for controlling violations. In 1948 India had complained to the UN Security Council of a situation whose continuation was likely to endanger international peace and security: India claimed that Pakistan was giving aid to invaders who were mounting incursions into Kashmir (one of the more than 500 states ruled by princes in preindependent India, which had been given the choice of joining either India or Pakistan). Kashmir's Hindu maharaja had joined India without ascertaining the wishes of the Muslim majority population. Pakistan rapidly submitted countercharges, and the Security Council invited both countries to participate in its debates. The Security Council established the three-member Commission on India and Pakistan (UNCIP) to go to Kashmir to investigate the facts and exercise a mediatory influence. Upon the advice of UNCIP, the Security Council finally set up a 20-member military observer group to supervise a cease-fire in Kashmir. Since then Kashmir has remained divided by a cease-fire line. *See also* INDIA-PAKISTAN WARS; PEACE-KEEPING FORCES: UNITED NATIONS INDIA/PAKISTAN OBSERVATION MISSION (UNIPOM).

Significance   The United Nations Military Observer Group in India and Pakistan did not solve the Kashmir dispute—alternatively referred to as the India-Pakistan question—but it helped to bring about an atmosphere that is more conducive to diplomatic negotiations and peaceful settlement of issues. UNMOGIP's duties included observation of the cease-fire line, and it was also vested with "the competence to decide whether or not there is a violation of the Cease-Fire Agreement by either side." This adjudicative function has been carried out discreetly and with a minimum of publicity. In this way an attempt has been made to keep military facts distinct from political propaganda. UNMOGIP's functions also entail recording the identity and deposition of units of the two armies, as well as any general troop information that might be useful to the charge of its mandate. Like all UN forces and observer groups, UNMOGIP has developed a detailed practice over the years for fulfilling its broad mission as stipulated by the United Nations. The Indian-Pakistani conflict over Kashmir still remains one of the most prolonged and unsettled disputes before the United Nations.

Peacekeeping Forces: United Nations Observation Group in Lebanon (UNOGIL)   The largest of the three United Nations observer missions (the other two are the United Nations Yemen Observation Mission and the United Nations India/Pakistan Observation Mission). The United Nations Observation Group in Lebanon, consisting of 600 men, was established in 1958 at a Lebanese request to police the Lebanon-Syria border. A rebellion, which had started in the predominantly Muslim city of Tripoli, soon spread to Beirut and the northern and northeastern areas near the Syrian border. It soon assumed the proportion of a civil war. The Lebanese government requested a meeting of the UN Security Council to consider its complaint "in respect of a situation arising from the intervention of the United Arab Republic [a union of Egypt and Syria from 1958 to 1961] in the internal affairs of Lebanon, the continuance of which is likely to endanger the maintenance of international peace and security." The Security Council authorized a UN observation group to proceed to Lebanon to ensure that there was no illegal infiltration across her borders. UNOGIL was established on June 11, 1958, more than one month before the landing of the U.S. Marines in Lebanon. The United States subsequently informed the Security Council that U.S. forces were not in Lebanon to engage in hostilities but to help the Lebanese government in its efforts to stabilize the situation until the United Nations could take steps to protect the integrity and independence of Lebanon. *See also* PEACEKEEPING FORCES: UNITED NATIONS INDIA/PAKISTAN OBSERVATION MISSION (UNIPOM); PEACEKEEPING FORCES: UNITED NATIONS YEMEN OBSERVATION MISSION (UNYOM).

Significance   The United Nations Observation Group in Lebanon assumed a strictly limited role, seeking to observe whether illegal infiltration was occurring. Its intended main role, however, was based on the strategy that its very presence on Lebanon's borders would contribute to the cessation of any such traffic. The assignment of UNOGIL created no major problems for the United Nations. The relationship between UNOGIL and the Lebanese government remained basically cordial, though Lebanon resented the considered opinion of UNOGIL that there was no substantial infiltration from the neighboring countries. However, months after the establishment of UNOGIL in November 1958, the Lebanese government informed the United Nations that relationships between Lebanon and the United Arab Republic had improved considerably and asked the world body to remove its complaint from the Security Council agenda. Thus UNOGIL's brief operation in Lebanon was closed on December 9, 1958.

Peacekeeping Forces: United Nations Observer Mission for the Verification of the Elections in Nicaragua (ONUVEN) A peace process established to monitor elections in Nicaragua in 1990. The United Nations Observer Mission for the Verification of the Elections in Nicaragua was established to verify free and fair elections. While many proposals to end the fighting between the Nicaraguan Sandinista forces and the U.S.-backed Contra rebels failed, continued efforts by the five Central American countries (Costa Rica, El Salvador, Guatemala, Honduras, and Nicaragua) produced positive results. An accord was reached to disband the Contras in return for the advancement of presidential, legislative, and municipal elections in Nicaragua. In July 1989, Nicaragua agreed to the terms for the creation of ONUVEN. In September, the United Nations and the Organization of American States (OAS) established the International Support and

Verification Commission (CIVA), a combined task force. Another agreement, designating the UN Observer Group in Central America (ONUCA) as a mechanism for verifying the security aspects of the operation, was signed in October 1989. Two UN missions traveled to Central America in the fall of 1989 to lay the groundwork for the conciliatory outcomes. One was a joint UN/OAS mission to Honduras and Nicaragua, and the other was a UN technical planning mission for ONUCA. To help coordinate the increasingly complex UN involvement in the Central American region, the UN secretary-general appointed a personal representative for the peace process. *See also* PEACEKEEPING FORCES: UNITED NATIONS GOOD OFFICES MISSION IN AFGHANISTAN AND PAKISTAN (UNGOMAP).

Significance The United Nations Observer Mission for the Verification of the Elections in Nicaragua was the first UN operation to monitor an electoral process within a member state at its request. The United Nations, which has had long experience in observing elections in former colonies as they gained independence and decided territorial issues, now, for the first time, monitored elections in a sovereign country. The complete electoral process—not only during the voting day—was monitored, from voter registration, to the political campaign, to the final vote count. The Sandinistas were beaten in the elections; they accepted their defeat and permitted a change in government. ONUVEN succeeded in verifying that political parties in Nicaragua enjoyed freedom of organization and mobilization, without hindrance or intimidation, and that they had equal access to the media. The observer group in Central America was the first UN military mission in the Western Hemisphere that monitored the commitment of the Central American governments to deny aid to Contra forces based in Honduras. The breakthrough was a direct consequence of the historic agreements reached by the five Central American presidents. Monitoring the Nicaraguan election was a turning point in UN history and an exemplary success story among its accomplishments.

Peacekeeping Forces: United Nations Operations in the Congo (ONUC) The United Nations peacekeeping operations in the newly independent Congo between 1960 and 1964. The United Nations Operations in the Congo was organized following disorder in what is now Zaire. With the abrupt termination of the Belgian administration when independence was suddenly granted to the Belgian Congo in 1960, violence broke out due to mutiny in the Congolese army. Belgium immediately rushed troops back to the region in order to protect its nationals and its interests. Soon the provinces of Katanga and Kasai seceded. As the situation deteriorated, the possibility of East-West involvement became certain. Belgian troops were sent as belligerents without permission of the Congolese government, which then requested the United Nations to intervene and to dispatch a military force to end external aggression as well as internal secession and strife. The Security Council established the United Nations Operations in the Congo on July 14, 1960. *See also* PEACEKEEPING FORCES: UNITED NATIONS OBSERVATION GROUP IN LEBANON (UNOGIL).

Significance   The United Nations Operations in the Congo was the largest peacekeeping operation ever undertaken by the United Nations. At one point it reached a strength of 20,000 troops from 29 countries and cost more than $400 million. The long struggle by ONUC to reestablish the control of the central Congolese government and free the country from foreign troops and mercenaries lasted until 1964. The activities of ONUC became the subject of a major East-West controversy during the heyday of the cold war. Operations were threatened when the Soviet Union was given 24 hours to get its personnel out of the Congo. The Soviet Union then withdrew its support of pro-Soviet leader, Patrice Lumumba, alleging that ONUC was backing pro-Western factions in the Congo. The UN force faced an almost insoluble dilemma of trying to restore order while avoiding the charge of intervention in a civil war. While the civil war among the Congolese was going on, ONUC could do little more than protect civilians and try to keep the fighting within bounds. The UN force prepared the grounds for political stability in the Congo, and by the time it had disbanded in 1964, the force had accomplished its primary mission: preventing the Congo crisis from triggering a general war.

Peacekeeping Forces: United Nations Security Force in West New Guinea (West Irian)   An international peacekeeping operation in West New Guinea. The United Nations Force in West New Guinea was created in 1962 because of a prolonged dispute between Indonesia and the Netherlands. This dispute began over the Dutch territory of West New Guinea about the same time the Netherlands formally recognized the independence of Indonesia. Sovereignty over West New Guinea remained in dispute between the two countries, and repeated appeals were made by both parties for UN intervention. The situation became very serious in 1961 when Indonesian President Ahmed Sukarno ordered total mobilization of armed forces, announced his decision to seize the territory by force, and began dropping paratroopers in the disputed territory. The Netherlands charged that the landings were an act of aggression by Indonesia. After negotiations held at the U.N. Headquarters, an agreement was signed in New York on August 15, 1962, that provided for the administration of West New Guinea to be transferred to a UN Temporary Executive Authority (UNTEA). It also provided for\a United Nations security force to assist UNTEA. The agreement required the inhabitants to decide to "remain with Indonesia" or "to sever their ties with Indonesia" in a plebiscite to be held no later than 1969. Consultative assemblies in the territory were held between July 14 and August 2, 1969, and pronounced themselves without dissent as favoring the territory's remaining with Indonesia. *See also* PEACEKEEPING FORCES: UNITED NATIONS OPERATIONS IN THE CONGO (ONUC).

Significance   The United Nations Security Force in Indonesia had at that time the distinction of being the only peacekeeping force to leave the scene of action with its mission fully accomplished. For the first time the United Nations assumed direct responsibility for the administration of a territory. In addition, all costs for the UN operation were shared by the two disputants—Indonesia and the Netherlands. The objective of the United Nations in West New Guinea was to avoid conflict, and this was achieved. The United Nations pursued a policy of preventive diplomacy, acting as a buffer between nations on the verge of armed conflict. The settlement of this dispute by providing for decision by plebiscite in the disputed West Irian territory set a precedent for settling other disputes by—in the best tradition of democracy—a direct vote of the inhabitants of the area in dispute. Since cold war issues were not involved in the dispute, the great powers were not committed to opposing sides and were willing to accept the final outcome.

Peacekeeping Forces: United Nations Special Committee on the Balkans (UNSCOB)   An international organization established in 1947 to monitor border violations by the Soviet bloc states in support of leftist Greek rebels. The United Nations Special Committee on the Balkans was set up solely to report on the question of the establishment of good neighborly relations on the frontiers of the four nations involved in the dispute—Albania, Bulgaria, Greece, and Yugoslavia. In 1946, a serious situation had arisen and was brought to the attention of the UN Security Council when Greece charged that Albania, Bulgaria, and Yugoslavia were aiding communist guerrillas in northern Greece. A United Nations commission of investigation supported the Greek accusations. When the Security Council was unable to agree on a resolution to deal with the problem, the General Assembly adopted a resolution requesting the parties concerned to negotiate their differences; it also established a special committee to facilitate peaceful settlement of the dispute. The Soviet Union refused to cooperate in these efforts. UNSCOB fielded a border watch team of 20 observers in the Balkans. *See also* PEACEKEEPING FORCES: UNITED NATIONS TRUCE SUPERVISION ORGANIZATION (UNTSO).

Significance   The designated efforts of the United Nations Special Committee on the Balkans were only one small part of a very complex story. It may be argued that to understand the importance of UNSCOB in perspective is to realize that its function was mainly that of an observer and this role was too narrow and weak to withstand the pressure of surrounding events. But the operation of UNSCOB is nonetheless of genuine historical and diplomatic interest. It marked the United Nations' first tentative steps toward peacekeeping through the establishment of subsidiary organs in the field; it showed an early realization of the limits of enforcement action and the need for consent of host countries. UNSCOB further illustrated, at this early stage, the inevitable need for an active General Assembly role in such operations as a backup to the Security Council in case the latter's role is nullified by a veto. Indeed, the Uniting for Peace Resolution adopted by the General Assembly in 1950 is a testimony to such a development; that resolution was adopted by the General Assembly when the Security Council became unable to deal with the Korean crisis because of Soviet veto in the council.

Peacekeeping Forces: United Nations Transition Assistance Group (UNTAG)   An international group that supervised elections in Namibia and oversaw its transition to independence. Established in 1989, the United Nations Transition Assistance Group assisted the United Nations in oversight of free and fair elections of a constituent assembly in Namibia. In 1976, the Security Council demanded that South Africa accept elections for its territory of South-West Africa, named Namibia by the nationalists, under the supervision and control of the United Nations, so that people might freely determine their national future. It also declared that adequate time was required to enable the United Nations to establish the necessary machinery for the elections in Namibia and to permit the Namibian people to organize politically. In 1980, the South African government accepted the election plan proposed by five powers—Canada, France, Germany, the United Kingdom, and the United States. According to the proposal, elections for a constituent assembly would be held under UN auspices, and every stage of the electoral process would have to be conducted to the satisfaction of a special representative for Namibia appointed by the secretary-general. A United Nations Transition Assistance Group would be at the disposal of the special representative to help him supervise the political process and to ensure that all parties observed the provision of the agreed solution. *See also* PEACEKEEPING FORCES: UNITED NATIONS OBSERVER MISSION FOR THE VERIFICATION OF THE ELECTIONS IN NICARAGUA (ONUVEN).

Significance The United Nations Transition Assistance Group's operation of a military-civilian force of 7,500 gave Namibia its start on the road to independence. It was a unique operation, undertaken (for the first time) by a United Nations presence that combined military and civilian components. A 1988 tripartite agreement among Angola, Cuba, and South Africa, mediated by the United States, was signed at the U.N. Headquarters in New York. This agreement committed the signatory states to undertake a series of measures necessary to achieve peace in the region and opened the way to independence for Namibia in accordance with the UN plan. A bilateral agreement between Angola and Cuba was signed at the same time. In accordance with a stipulation set forth in this agreement, the United Nations dispatched an observer mission—the United Nations Angola Verification Mission (UNAVEM)—to Angola to verify the redeployment northward and the phased withdrawal of Cuban troops. In a very difficult existing situation, UNTAG acted with impartiality and performed its duties of monitoring the cease-fire; monitoring the withdrawal, restriction to base, and demobilization of forces; and assisting the civilian component in the supervision and control of free elections in Namibia. Under the watchful eyes of UNTAG, Namibia—the last African colony—achieved its independence on April 1, 1990, and became a member of the United Nations.

Peacekeeping Forces: United Nations Truce Supervision Organization (UNTSO) The first peacekeeping operation in the Middle East to supervise armistice. The United Nations Truce Supervision Organization is still carrying on its work of supervising the armistice agreements between Israel and its neighbors. UNTSO was created during the Arab-Israeli War of 1948 to supervise the truce called for by the UN Security Council. This need developed as a result of the formation in 1947, by the United Nations, of the State of Israel. On May 14, 1948, Israel proclaimed its independence, and the next day the Arab armies, under the banner of the Arab League, invaded the new Jewish state. Armies from Egypt, Jordan, Iraq, Syria, and Lebanon, as well as contingents from Saudi Arabia, attempted to terminate Israel. The Arab armies moved to within ten miles of Tel Aviv,

Jordanian troops overran the West Bank and stormed East Jerusalem, and the Iraqi army moved within five miles of the Mediterranean Sea. The Syrian troops moved through the Galilee. The Israelis responded by either beating back the Arab advance or holding firm. In 1949, armistice agreements were signed by Israel with Egypt, Jordan, Lebanon, and Syria; Iraq has refused to sign any agreement with Israel. Only one Arab country—Egypt—has signed and ratified a peace treaty with Israel, as a result of American pressure and foreign aid promises.

Significance   The need for the United Nations Truce Supervision Organization is found in the protracted history of the Palestinian dispute. Failure to find a solution to this problem led to fighting of such intensity that it could only be halted by the Security Council using its full authority under Chapter VII of the Charter of the United Nations to demand a truce; the basic function of the Truce Commission—UNTSO's forerunner—was to supervise the maintenance of the truce. With the signing of the armistice agreements between Israel and its neighbors, the Truce Commission was named the Truce Supervision Organization and is still carrying out its tasks. In the Middle Eastern wars of 1956, 1967, and 1973, the functions of UNTSO varied according to changing circumstances, but it remained in the region, acting as go-between for the hostile parties and preventing escalation of conflicts into a major catastrophe. UNTSO's services are also available to form a nucleus for other UN peacekeeping operations. The chief of staff of UNTSO is directly responsible to the UN secretary-general, who in turn reports to the Security Council. While a wide range of discretion is granted to the chief of staff, it is the secretary-general who formulates the overall policy guidelines.

Peacekeeping Forces: United Nations Yemen Observation Mission (UNYOM)   An international peacekeeping initiative in Yemen. The United Nations Observation Mission in Yemen was established in 1963 to observe a military disengagement agreement between the parties to the Yemeni Civil War. The Yemeni Civil War of 1962 was provoked by the overthrow of the imamate (monarchy) of Imam Mohammad al-Badr by a group of Yemeni army officers loyal to Egyptian President Gamal Abdul Nasser. Nasser accepted responsibility for the coup and dispatched a large number of Egyptian forces to reinforce the Yemeni revolutionary command. The Imam had the support of the Saudi Arabians, who perceived the coup as an indirect attack on their traditional rule. Thus Egypt found itself in conflict with Saudi Arabia as well as the royalist (Imam's) forces. The new republican government was recognized by Egypt and the Soviet Union, but other major powers, including the United States and the United Kingdom, withheld recognition. The UN Security Council undertook a peace initiative that led to the creation of the United Nations Yemen Observation Mission. Its terms of reference were restricted to observation and reporting, and responsibility for implementation lay with the two parties to the agreement—Saudi Arabia and Egypt. *See also* PEACEKEEPING FORCES: UNITED NATIONS OBSERVATION GROUP IN LEBANON (UNOGIL).

Significance The United Nations Yemen Observation Mission was a small team of less than 200 observers, and it is considered to be the least successful of all UN peacekeeping operations—it exerted very modest restraining influence on hostilities. The planned operational organization did not suit the needs of the mission, nor was it of sufficient size to cover effectively the vast and difficult terrain over which it was required to operate. The presence of UNYOM made little difference to the situation in Yemen; the deep-seated nature of the Egyptian and Saudi Arabian military and political engagement was such that the planned disengagement was extremely difficult to achieve. The repeated violations of the disengagement agreements by the parties concerned led to the withdrawal of UNYOM in 1964. In 1990, North and South Yemen overcame their differences and united into the new nation of Yemen, and their two UN memberships became one.

Permanent Court of Arbitration A panel of international jurists established in 1900 under the 1899 Hague Convention (modified in 1907), readily available to serve as arbitrators in international disputes. The Permanent Court of Arbitration is neither permanent nor a court; it is essentially a group of potential arbitrators skilled in international law. Each party to the convention can appoint four individuals of recognized competence in international law; the four arbitrators then select an umpire. A special section procedure deals with cases where there is no agreement on the appointment of the umpire. Members of the Permanent Court of Arbitration only serve for six years and have no regular session. The court has not been called upon since 1940 and prior to that date was utilized only 23 times. The parties identify the points at issue, define the authority of the panel, and agree that a decision made within those limitations will be accepted as legally binding. *See also* UNITED NATIONS INTERNATIONAL COURT OF JUSTICE (ICJ); PERMANENT COURT OF INTERNATIONAL JUSTICE (PCIJ).

Significance The Permanent Court of Arbitration is a misnomer, since in fact it consists of a standing list of persons who might be selected as arbitrators whenever signatories avail themselves of these services. It is "permanent" in the sense that it is equipped with a standing professional staff and board of control. The Permanent Court of Arbitration remains technically in existence. After the establishment of the Permanent Court of International Justice as an adjunct of the League of Nations, the Permanent Court of Arbitration was continued "primarily for those states (like the United States) not connected with the League of Nations, and has had no cases since the United States joined the United Nations."[38] The International Court of Justice (ICJ), established under the Charter of the United Nations, has linkage with the Permanent Court of Arbitration since the members of the former are elected from a list of persons nominated by the national groups in the Permanent Court of Arbitration.

Permanent Court of International Justice (PCIJ)   The first global tribunal created by the League of Nations to settle conflicts between states and render advisory opinions upon any dispute or question referred to it by the league. The Permanent Court of International Justice came into being pursuant to Article 14 of the league's covenant under a treaty known as the Statute of the Permanent Court of International Justice. The court first met in 1922, and annual sessions were held until 1936, when the statute was amended to provide continuous sessions. The court did not meet during World War II, and its final session was held in 1945, after which its functions were subsumed by the International Court of Justice (ICJ), established by the United Nations. Neither the United States nor the Soviet Union were parties to the Permanent Court of International Justice. The judges of the court (originally 11, later changed to 15) were elected by absolute majorities of the league council and assembly from a list of persons nominated by the national groups of the Permanent Court of Arbitration. The Peace Palace at The Hague was the seat of the Permanent Court of International Justice. *See also* UNITED NATIONS INTERNATIONAL COURT OF JUSTICE (ICJ); PERMANENT COURT OF ARBITRATION.

Significance   During its lifetime, the Permanent Court of International Justice discharged considerable business. It took under consideration 65 new cases and handed down 32 judgments and 27 advisory opinions. At no time did a state refuse to accept the PCIJ's judgment or opinion; this attests to the court's thoroughness in its deliberations, as well as to its impartiality. A total of 550 international treaties were concluded during the lifetime of the PCIJ, thus authenticating the jurisdiction of the court. These treaties represented a large portion of the accepted international law of the time. The PCIJ developed judicial techniques that provided a blueprint for its successor, the International Court of Justice. It also resolved some serious international disputes, many of which were related to interpretation of the 1919 Treaty of Versailles, which ended World War I. More than any other international organization, the PCIJ broadened the reign of law among nations.

Power   The ability of nations, leaders, institutions, or organizations to exercise influence over others. Power is also an accepted quality marking the relationship between nations or international actors. According to Hans Morgenthau, power "may comprise anything that establishes and maintains control of man over man [and it] covers all social relationships which serve that end, from physical violence to the most subtle psychological ties by which one mind controls another."[39] Studies of power recognize that it is a mixture of capabilities derived from both domestic and international activities. The concept of power has been undergoing changes, as is evidenced by the ability of the Organization of Arab Petroleum Exporting Countries (OAPEC) to impose an oil embargo on the powerful Western nations and Japan in 1973, and the Organization of Petroleum Exporting Countries' (OPEC's) repeated and successful attempts to increase the price of oil. *See also* ORGANIZATION OF ARAB PETROLEUM EXPORTING COUNTRIES (OAPEC); ORGANIZATION OF PETROLEUM EXPORTING COUNTRIES (OPEC).

Significance   Power is a concept that denotes anything that establishes and maintains the control of one actor over another. For example, nation A has power over nation B, which means A has the ability to force, influence, or persuade B. The exercise of power may take many forms, including control, coercion, and warfare. Thus power is relative. It is also situational, depending on the realities of various situations. Many observers speak of the two superpowers at the top, trailed at great distance by all the rest. Significant world power centers are the United States, the Soviet Union, the European Community, Japan, and China. It is one thing to define power; it is another thing to measure it. However, almost invariably, the list of tangible elements contributing to positions of power includes geography, population, economic capability, and military strength. Elements of intangible power are those that cannot be measured easily. Leadership, personality, morale, type of government, societal cohesiveness, and characteristics of nations may serve as some of the examples of intangible power.

Public International Unions   International agencies of the nineteenth century concerned with problems in various essentially nonpolitical fields. Public international unions represented almost every field of human endeavor at one time or another. They covered such diverse fields as science and art, communications and transit, economics and finance, and health and morals. In the nineteenth century various international river commissions emerged in Europe—the Central Rhine Commission dates back to 1804. The International Telegraphic Union was formed in 1865 and the Universal Postal Union came into being in 1874; both have become specialized agencies of the United Nations. In other fields, the Metric Union (1875), the International Sugar Union (1902), and the International Institute of Agriculture (1905) serve to illustrate the breadth and type of activity undertaken. Twentieth-century public organizations are called international governmental organizations (IGOs). Among the global IGOs are the League of Nations and the United Nations. Some regional ones are the North Atlantic Treaty Organization (NATO), the Organization of American States (OAS), and the Organization of African Unity (OAU). *See also* INTERNATIONAL GOVERNMENTAL ORGANIZATIONS (IGOS).

Significance   Public international unions represented the initiation, not the consummation, of a trend toward international control of those specific affairs of the world with which they were concerned. They serve as a central focal point for collecting vital information and discussing international problems and their solutions. Sovereign states of the nineteenth century recognized that there were certain areas within their national jurisdiction that required international cooperation; international organizations based on the sovereign equality of nations were needed to handle such issues of mutual concern. The nineteenth-century nonpolitical or functional organizations produced organizational inventions that were of fundamental benefit to their twentieth-century descendants. For example, the nineteenth-century Bureau of the International Telegraphic Union became the prototype of contemporary secretariat of international organizations. The chief problem of the various public international unions was a lack of coordination of their activities—a deficiency that has been partially overcome through voluntary cooperation but still exists among modern international organizations.

R

Red Cross   A worldwide humanitarian agency with national affiliates in almost every country. The Red Cross aims to uphold the fundamental principles of a neutral institution in order that the military and civilian victims of wars or internal troubles receive protection and assistance. It serves on a humanitarian level and acts as an intermediary between parties. The International Red Cross consists of three components: (1) the International Committee of the Red Cross, (2) the League of the Red Cross, and (3) the national Red Cross societies. An international conference held every four to six years includes representatives not only of these three groups, but also of those governments adhering to the Geneva conventions. Founded in Geneva in 1863, the Assembly of the Red Cross consists of 25 Swiss citizens and has headquarters in Geneva. Some Muslim nations call the Red Cross by the name Red Crescent, and in Iran the Red Lion and Sun are used.

Significance   To many people, the words "Red Cross" suggest "nurse." In the beginning nursing care of the wounded during wartime was one of the chief motives for the existence of most national Red Cross societies. But the scope of the Red Cross has been widened to include all kinds of emergencies. The wartime activities of the Red Cross have included such diverse services as providing ambulances, hospitals, and medical and nursing personnel, operating canteens for troops in transit, distributing food in occupied territories, and locating families and friends displaced by hostilities. The scope of the peacetime activities of the Red Cross has increased enormously since the end of World War II and now covers many aspects of health and welfare. Members and former members of the armed forces and their families are given financial aid, counseling, referral, and other services. Procurement of blood and the maintenance of a blood supply are among the most critical activities of Red Cross societies.

Regional Cooperation for Development (RCD)   A policy organization formed by Iran, Pakistan, and Turkey in Istanbul, Turkey, in 1964 to provide for economic cooperation and cultural exchange. Regional Cooperation for Development was envisioned as a means of establishing an Asian common market that would promote trade, assist in joint enterprises, and enhance the well-being of the people of the three countries. It was potentially a model program that demonstrated the advantages of working together to achieve development goals. The heads of states of the three member countries agreed (1) to a free movement of goods by all practical means, such as the conclusion of trade agreements; (2) to establish closer collaboration among existing chambers of commerce, and eventually found a joint chamber of commerce; (3) to formulate and implement joint-purpose projects; (4) to reduce the postal rates to the level of internal rates; (5) to improve the air transport service within the region and eventually establish a competitive airline among the three countries; (6) to investigate the possibilities of securing close cooperation in the field of shipping, including the establishment of a joint maritime line; (7) to undertake necessary studies for construction and improvement of rail and road links between the three nations; (8) to sign an agreement to promote tourism; (9) to abolish the use of travel visas among the three countries; and (10) to provide technical assistance to one another in the form of exchange of experts and establishment of training facilities. *See also* ASSOCIATION OF SOUTHEAST ASIAN NATIONS (ASEAN); CENTRAL TREATY ORGANIZATION (CENTO).

Significance   The Regional Cooperation for Development never measured up to the intentions of its creators. Iran was less than inspired; Turkey's economic interests were oriented toward the West; and Pakistan's enthusiasm waned after the death of President Mohammad Ayub Khan, who had proposed the formation of the organization. Other states were invited to join the RCD but none did, as the three member states were in those days identified with the Central Treaty Organization (CENTO). The binding element that the three countries shared was their mutual disenchantment with the West. There is no evidence to suggest that the RCD was supported in any way by the United States and Britain, or the Soviet Union and China. Yet some observers maintain that the United States prompted Pakistan to form the RCD. Although the organization no longer exists, it did briefly demonstrate that regional cooperation in development can be useful, but political factors can also quickly destroy its utility.

Regional Economic Groups   Regional organizations or associations aimed at coordinating the economic development of member nations. Regional economic groups are established to encourage economic, social, and sometimes cultural cooperation among members in a defined region of the world. There are many such groups; some of the principal ones are the Amazon Pact (1978), Andean Common Market (1969), Asian and Pacific Council (1966), Association of Southeast Asian Nations (1967), Caribbean Community and Common Market (1973), Central American Common Market (1960), Council of Mutual Economic Assistance (1949), European Free Trade Association (1959), European Economic Community (1958), Latin American Integration Union (1960), Organization for Economic Cooperation and Development (1961), South Asian Association of Regional Cooperation (1985), and Southern African Development Coordination Council (1980). *See also* COLOMBO PLAN; COMMONWEALTH OF NATIONS.

Significance   Taken together, these regional economic groups extend almost worldwide in their efforts to eradicate poverty, hunger, and malnutrition, remove trade and custom barriers, improve social and cultural life, and seek regional cooperative arrangements to enhance the quality of human life. They also attempt to harmonize economic policies of member nations for a fuller realization of economic benefit and (in some cases) integration. But, as within most regional groups, members with stronger economies push for freer trade, but the weaker nations are reluctant to give up protection for their indigenous industry and commerce. Typically, the stronger members initiate most proposals; thus the more-developed nations play key roles in policy development. The regional economic organizations try to establish credentials as nonpolitical bodies, concerned with improving the well-being of all members.

Regional Financial Institutions   Banks and other economic organizations created to foster regional development. Regional financial institutions have been established in Asia, Africa, the Middle East, the Caribbean, and Latin America. Some of the main regional financial institutions are the African Development Bank (ADB), Asian Development Bank (ADB), Arab Bank for Economic Development in Africa (BADEA), Arab Monetary Fund (AMF), Caribbean Development ment Bank (CDB), and Central American Bank for Economic Integration (CABEI). The African Development Bank was established in 1964 to promote economic development in Africa. The Asian Development Bank was instituted in 1966 to foster economic growth and cooperation in the Asian Pacific region. The Arab Bank for Economic Development in Africa, formed in 1973, contributes to the economic development in Africa by providing aid to African countries faced with devastating economic situations. The Arab Monetary Fund, set up in 1976, assists Arab countries in coping with balance-of-payments difficulties and, in general, promotes Arab monetary cooperation. The Caribbean Development Bank, organized in 1969, is a financial body aimed at assisting in the economic growth and development of its member countries. See also REGIONAL ECONOMIC GROUPS.

Significance   There is no general agreement whether regional financial institutions have been of great financial help to the particular regions with which they are identified. Nevertheless, they have played a role in the conduct of research on economic and social problems, making recommendations to member governments and advising on matters within their respective competencies. They have obviously promoted economic development as a means of attacking both poverty and slow economic development in the regions. None of these activities, however, is carried out without the approval of the countries concerned. The regional financial institutions have been mainly concerned with improving the quality of life of the member nations and hastening the economic development of the regions they serve.

Regional Military Groups   Regional organizations established to provide mutual security for their members in a defined area. Regional military groups came into existence at the end of World War II, in 1949, when the North Atlantic Treaty Organization (NATO) was created to block the threat of Soviet military aggression in Europe. Since then at least five other regional military organizations have been set up: the Australia, New Zealand, and United States Pact (ANZUS, 1951; now defunct); the Central Treaty Organization (CENTO, 1955; now defunct); the Southeast Asia Treaty Organization (SEATO, 1954; now defunct); the Warsaw Treaty Organization (WTO, 1955; now disbanded); and the Western European Union (WEU, 1955). ANZUS, which remained in force until 1986, was aimed at providing safeguard and security of the Pacific area against communist threat. SEATO, dissolved in 1977, was a security pact among Australia, Great Britain, France, New Zealand, Pakistan, the Philippines, Thailand, and the United States to meet the common danger of communism in the designated area. CENTO, disbanded in 1979, was a regional alliance among Iran, Pakistan, Turkey, and Great Britain (the United States was an informal member) to provide security in the Middle East against communist aggression. The WTO is a military association of East European states formed to counter NATO. The WEU is to defend Western Europe from attack, to control German rearmament, and to cooperate with NATO in defense of the Atlantic

community. *See also* NORTH ATLANTIC TREATY ORGANIZATION (NATO);
WARSAW TREATY ORGANIZATION (WTO); WESTERN EUROPEAN UNION (WEU).

Significance Of the six regional military organizations, the Asian,
Middle Eastern, and Pacific defense groups (SEATO, CENTO, and
ANZUS) and the Warsaw Treaty Organization are no longer functional. As for the remaining two, NATO is operational in Western
Europe and North America and the WEU in Western Europe. These
defense organizations were formed to protect anticommunist nations
against communist threat. Now that communism has collapsed and
Germany has reunited as one nation, bringing the former East Germany within the fold of NATO, and the WTO has been completely
disbanded, the vision of a united and democratic Europe is rising. As
the WTO has been abandoned, is there any need for NATO or the
WEU? The answer may depend upon how successfully the anticommunist elements in Eastern Europe move toward democratization and
the creation of market economy. If the 1990–1991 trend continues, it
is quite possible that NATO and the WEU will become history in the
not-too-distant future.

Regional Political Groups Regional bodies aimed at promoting a
multitude of objectives, principally political. Regional political groups
are prevalent in all parts of the world, except in Eastern Europe.
Among the principal regional political groups is the Commonwealth
of Nations, which grew out of the British Commonwealth of Nations
of the nineteenth and twentieth centuries—an association of 50 independent nations that were formerly British colonies, plus the United
Kingdom. The League of Arab States (Arab League), established in
1945 to coordinate member nations' activities, safeguards independence and encourages cooperation of all Arab nations in social, economic, and cultural matters. The Council of Europe, formed in 1949,
is a quasi-parliamentary body that encourages political, economic, and
social cooperation among its members—Belgium, Denmark, France,
Britain, Ireland, Italy, Luxembourg, the Netherlands, Norway, Sweden, Austria, Cyprus, Germany, Greece, Iceland, Malta, Switzerland,
Turkey, and Hungary (the first East European nation to join the
Council of Europe, on November 6, 1990). The European Community, founded in 1952, is a common body organized to make decisions
for the European Economic Community (EEC), the European Coal
and Steel Community (ECSC), and the European Atomic Energy
Community (EURATOM). The members are Belgium, France, Denmark, Ireland, Germany, Italy, Luxembourg, the Netherlands,
Greece, Spain, Portugal, and the United Kingdom. The Nordic Council

is a Scandinavian regional body, set up in 1952, that recommends common policies and programs to its members. Membership includes Finland, Norway, Sweden, and Iceland. The Organization of African Unity (OAU) is an African organization that includes all African nations except South Africa. The OAU was established in 1963 to develop unity, end colonialism, foster economic development, and provide security for the members. The Organization of American States (OAS) is an inter-American system that includes all North American countries and Latin American states except Cuba. The OAS was formed in 1948 to determine political, economic, defense, and social policies for the Americas and the Caribbean. *See also* REGIONAL ECONOMIC GROUPS; REGIONAL MILITARY GROUPS.

Significance   The broad objectives of all regional political groups include the following: coordinating political activities, assisting members in developing a sense of unity of purpose, fostering economic development, and safeguarding security interests. The prolific growth of regional political organizations since the end of World War II has stemmed from an emphasis on regional development as a means for achieving national goals. The effectiveness of these regional organizations will continue so long as a common interest in maintaining unity persists. The Third World political organizations, such as the OAU and the Arab League, have been sapped by internal rivalries, ideological differences, personality clashes, conflictual ties with outside powers, and an overriding zeal for preservation of personal power.

Rhine River Commission   Serves to ensure that the Rhine River will remain open to all nations for commercial purposes. The Rhine River Commission formulates regulations for navigation, hears complaints for alleged violations of rules, and maintains the technical facilities necessary for full navigation at all times. In 1804, France and Germany created the Central Rhine Commission to direct and supervise the establishment and collection of navigation tolls and to hear appeals on problems relating to the administration of the Rhine. The Rhine River Commission was formed in 1815 at the Congress of Vienna and promotes unrestricted navigation on the Rhine River for ships of all nations. Nations represented on the commission are Belgium, Germany, France, the Netherlands, Switzerland, and the United Kingdom. The Rhine is an international waterway, flowing from east-central Switzerland to the North Sea. *See also* CONGRESS OF VIENNA; DANUBE RIVER COMMISSION.

Significance   The Rhine River Commission is the first modern international governmental organization (IGO). It was given considerable authority to amend its own rules and to act as a court of appeals for the decisions of local courts regarding problems and issues. Following the examples of the Rhine River Commission, similar commissions were later established for the Danube, Elbe, Duoro, and Po rivers. The principle of free navigation on the Rhine was extended in 1918 to ships of all countries, and not merely to the riverine states. Plans exist for extending navigation through the Alpine Rhine into Switzerland by canalizing the Aar system, and a Swiss-German Convention of 1929 envisaged canalization of the High Rhine between Rheinfelden and the Lake of Constance.

Rotary Club   A private civic organization of business and professional persons, united worldwide, who provide humanitarian service, encourage high ethical standards in all vocations, and help build goodwill and peace in the world. The Rotary Club (Rotary International is the association of Rotary Clubs throughout the world) was founded in Chicago in 1905 by Paul Harris, a lawyer. It received its name "Rotary" because the members met in rotation at their places of business. There are approximately one million members, in more than 23,000 Rotary Clubs, established in over 165 countries. The Rotary Club maintains the Rotary Foundation, which offers scholarships to outstanding students. The foundation has also a Health, Hunger, and Humanity program that marshals Rotary manpower and resources to accomplish large-scale humanitarian projects in the area of immunization, health care, polio, rehabilitation, and nutrition.

Significance   The Rotary Clubs center their activities on community improvement, the fostering of good citizenship, promotion of high standards, the improvement of rural and urban understanding, the advancement of international goodwill, and many other civic-oriented goals. The members are required to take a four-way test of the things they say or do: (1) Is it the truth? (2) Is it fair to all concerned? (3) Will it build goodwill and better friendship? and (4) Will it be beneficial to all concerned? The Rotarians are supposed to use these four-way tests in their dealings with business, government, and schools as an effective measuring stick for conduct. They maintain that these tests comprise a guide to right thinking. By coming together in weekly meetings, Rotarians enjoy a common fellowship and undergird the club's service goals by continual discussion.

S

Self-Determination   The right of a people to choose the political entity under which they would like to live. Self-determination denotes the process by which national entities establish themselves as independent states. The phrase "self-determination of peoples" is used in the United Nations Charter (Articles 1 and 55) without further explanation. The concept that lies behind this term reaches back to the "consent of the governed" in the American Declaration of Independence in 1776, and to the "divine right of the people" in the French Revolution of 1789. The history and growth of the idea of self-determination link it closely to the development of various forms of nationalism in nineteenth-century Europe. The right of national independence, which came to be called self-determination, is, in general terms, the belief that each society or national group has a right to become an independent, sovereign state and determine its own government and laws. *See also* INDEPENDENCE; UNITED NATIONS: DEPENDENT TERRITORY.

Significance   Self-determination of peoples in the United Nations Charter does not indicate which groups have self-determining powers. Usually, large, compact groups and peoples separated from a colonial power by distance have been listed as having such powers. It is also used to support claims for independence or autonomy by minority groups or colonial areas within established states. Following World War I, President Woodrow Wilson, in his famous Fourteen Points, spoke for adjustment of colonial claims based upon strict observance of the principle that, in determining all such questions of sovereignty, the interests of the populations concerned must have equal weight with the claims of a government whose title is to be determined. Self-determination is a theory about the relationship that should prevail between the nation and the state, the latter being understood as any independently governed political community. Most

180

non-self-governing or colonial territories of the world have imple-mented the principle of self-determination since the end of World War II, with almost one hundred new states in Asia, Africa, Latin America, the Caribbean, and Europe. In the 1990s, the major chal-lenge to the application of the principle will come from those republics and regions of the Soviet Union, Yugoslavia, and any other countries that seek independence.

Sino-Indian War   A military confrontation between China and In-dia in 1962. Also known as the Indo-Chinese War, the Sino-Indian War was caused by a boundary dispute between the two largest Asian nations. The border conflict had its origin in the nineteenth century, when the colonial powers of Europe, as well as Japan, were busy carving up weak and helpless China. China wanted to have all the borders that had been imposed by British imperial power renegoti-ated. The Indian government argued that its frontiers with China were firmly established by the McMahon Line—drawn in 1910 by Sir Henry McMahon, the head of the British delegation at the Simla Conference, which negotiated the frontier between Tibet and India. Disputing the Indian claim, the Chinese army launched an offensive at the western end of the McMahon Line, followed by a similar offensive at the eastern end. Within a month of these offensives, China advanced more than 100 miles south of the McMahon Line at the western end, and 25 to 30 miles south at the eastern end. China, however, returned to the McMahon Line unilaterally, thus ending the brief war. *See also* INDIA-PAKISTAN WARS.

Significance   The Sino-Indian War was one of the most dramatic events of international relations in the late twentieth century. It sharply reduced the role of India in world affairs. Friendship with China had been the keystone of India's foreign policy of nonalign-ment—its refusal to join either the Communist or anti-Communist bloc. The border dispute, and the war that was its climax, confirmed the general view prevailing in the world in the 1960s, of China as a bellicose and expansionist power. China's show of force, however, failed to bring India to the negotiating table. India refused to compro-mise its vital strategic interests in the region. The Indian position was supported by both superpowers. The Soviet Union terminated its aid to China, and it agreed to deliver Soviet Mig fighters for the Indian Air Force. In the final analysis, the Sino-Indian War can be character-ized as nothing but China's attempt to humiliate India in the eyes of the world and to demonstrate to the world that China was a power to be reckoned with. Pakistan, India's archenemy, benefited from the

Sino-Indian War by the demarcation of its common border with China within the area of Kashmir, which came under Pakistani control.

South Asian Association for Regional Cooperation (SAARC)   An organization of the seven South Asian countries to promote regional cooperation on a footing of sovereign equality, territorial integrity, political independence, noninterference in the internal affairs of other states, and mutual benefit. The South Asian Association for Regional Cooperation was formed in Dhaka, Bangladesh, in 1985 by Bangladesh, Bhutan, India, the Maldives, Nepal, Pakistan, and Sri Lanka. The principal aim was to provide an arrangement which would be of some tangible benefit to the peoples of South Asia—improving their quality of life, strengthening their collective self-reliance, strengthening cooperation among them in the international forum on matters of common interest, and interacting with those international and regional organizations with similar aims and purposes. *See also* ASSOCIATION OF SOUTHEAST ASIAN NATIONS (ASEAN).

Significance   The South Asian Association for Regional Cooperation is not a practical response to the problems that bedevil interstate relations in the South Asian region. An analysis of historical, social, political, and economic realities in the region provides SAARC with an imperative to seek peace, stability, and fruitful development for the people of South Asia. At the same time, it is only realistic to bear in mind that the intrinsic asymmetry obtaining among South Asian countries cannot be ignored or dismissed in the regional, as well as in the global, contex. But such asymmetries, if not corroded by narrow and selfish interests, can coexist with a fair degree of harmonious cooperation. Although SAARC, to be successful by any real measure, has a long way to go, its participating members have demonstrated their belief that progress has been made. They perceive these achievements as a triumph of reason and good sense, and of the common effort to promote peace and harmony in the region and the world.

South Pacific Commission (SPC)   An agency to promote the economic and social welfare and the general well-being of the peoples of the South Pacific region. The South Pacific Commission was established in 1947 by the six governments with colonies in the area: Australia, New Zealand, the United States, France, the United Kingdom, and the Netherlands. Each member nation is represented by two commissioners in the secretariat, which is located in Noumea, New Caledonia. There is also a research council and a South Pacific conference.

The South Pacific Commission's purpose is to encourage and strengthen international cooperation by promoting the advancement of the peoples of the non-self-governing territories in the region. Health education, including nutrition, is a high priority. The SPC maintains close cooperation with many specialized agencies of the United Nations.

Significance   The South Pacific Commission is essentially an advisory agency concentrating upon the nonpolitical problems of that region. The commission has dealt with soil and land use, subsistence economies, the coconut and rice industries, fisheries, and plant collection and introduction. It serves as one instrument for all six major administering powers for interterritorial cooperation in the region. In some areas of the South Pacific, such as the hinterlands of Papua New Guinea, native peoples still live under the fiction of political independence. In other areas, such as Western Samoa, articulate spokesmen for the indigenous population are seeking and receiving self-government. Nations responsible for the administration of the South Pacific territories have recognized the realities and signs of dependence.

Southeast Asia Treaty Organization (SEATO)   A now-defunct mutual defense alliance that called upon the signatories to consult and to meet the common danger of communism. The Southeast Asia Treaty Organization was created by the Southeast Asia Collective Defense Treaty, signed in Manila, the Philippines, in 1954. The representatives of Australia, France, New Zealand, Pakistan, the Philippines, Thailand, the United Kingdom, and the United States formed the alliance. SEATO came into force in 1955. It was precipitated by several major historical developments, among them the communist takeover of China (1949), the invasion of South Korea by North Korea (1950–1953), and the defeat of the French in Indo-China (1953). SEATO functioned through a council and a secretariat located in Bangkok, Thailand. The treaty area covered the general region of Southeast Asia, including the specific territories of its Asian members and the general area of the Southwest Pacific. Following American withdrawal from Vietnam in 1973, SEATO collapsed, and was dissolved in 1977. *See also* AUSTRALIA, NEW ZEALAND, AND UNITED STATES PACT (ANZUS); CENTRAL TREATY ORGANIZATION (CENTO).

Significance   The Southeast Asia Treaty Organization was a loose and flexible organization, and its area of operation was not well defined. It was intended to be the Asian counterpart of the North

Atlantic Treaty Organization (NATO), but some of the major regional powers, such as India, refused to join the alliance, arguing that communism posed no serious threat to that region. Pakistan joined the organization in the hope of obtaining arms to use against its enemy—India—but the treaty did not permit such use against a noncommunist nation. SEATO failed to develop an effective command structure, an allied military strategy, or a major commitment of troops by member states. The Asian member countries received considerable economic aid, mainly on a bilateral basis, from the developed members of the organization—the United States, the United Kingdom, Australia, and New Zealand.

Southern African Development Coordination Council (SADCC)
A collaborative effort to develop the region of southern Africa and to reduce its dependence upon South Africa. The Southern African Development Coordination Council seeks to forge regional integration to mobilize resources for promotion and implementation of national, interstate, and regional policies and to encourage concerted action on behalf of international cooperation. The nine members of SADCC are Angola, Botswana, Lesotho, Malawi, Mozambique, Swaziland, Tanzania, Zambia, and Zimbabwe. The supreme authority of SADCC is a summit meeting, which is convened annually; it provides overall policy direction. *See also* ORGANIZATION OF AFRICAN UNITY (OAU).

Significance In contrast to regional financial organizations in other areas of the world, the responsibility for coordinating the activities of SADCC ultimately rests with individual members, who enjoy substantial freedom in carrying out their assignments. In other words, SADCC has arrived at a peculiarly African administrative structure, which is highly decentralized and nonbureaucratic and functions on the basis of consensus. This loose structure respects state sovereignty and ensures that the larger states will not dominate or dictate overall SADCC programs. Although this loose construct seems to have worked well, it does present problems in the overall development of the area, and sometimes national policies do not fit—or may even duplicate—the overarching policies of the region. However, SADCC has developed a relatively successful program to decrease dependence on South Africa and also has been effective in attracting foreign aid.

Sovereignty The supreme power; the highest authority to decide and enforce obedience. Sovereignty refers to national independence and the ability of states to act freely with little or no outside interference. According to Jean Bodin, a French scholar, sovereignty is the state's supreme authority over citizens and subjects. Originally derived from the Latin word *superanus*—giving rise to the French term *souverainete*—the English derivation means to possess the equivalent of supreme power. Prior to the French Revolution (1789), the territory of a state was considered to be property of the ruler. This was the patrimonial theory, and was displaced in the French Revolution. Independence is the central element of sovereignty. The basic idea is that a sovereign nation is free to order itself internally and to make and enforce domestic law without foreign interference. National sovereignty is becoming obsolete, and advanced nations are moving toward regional and global integration and common markets, which invites the abolition of customs, tariffs, and other impediments to the free flow of trade across national boundaries. *See also* INDEPENDENCE.

Significance   Sovereignty implies that governments have the supreme decision-making and law-making authority within their own territorial boundaries. However, sovereignty in a practical sense does not mean that states enjoy absolute freedom of action—some states are obviously more powerful militarily and economically than others. But the United Nations recognizes the sovereignty and therefore the legal equality of all nations, which is really possible only in theory. In reality, smaller nations are not equal to larger ones, especially the superpowers. In the UN Security Council, this fact of political life is recognized by according the veto power exclusively to the five permanent (great power) member nations. Yet, despite the ambiguities, states are proud to call themselves sovereign. It gives the peoples and governments of nation-states a powerful belief in their own legitimacy, and a claim that they are "in charge" of their affairs free from external influence.

Specialized Agencies of the United Nations   The single-purpose, multi-purpose, or functional international organizations of the United Nations with broad responsibilities in various fields. Specialized agencies of the United Nations are autonomous bodies but maintain close relationships with it. Article 57 of the Charter of the United Nations established these agencies "having wide international responsibilities, as defined in their basic instruments, in economic, social, cultural, educational, health, and related fields." There are 16 specialized agencies and they report annually to the Economic and Social Council (ECOSOC) of the United Nations. These specialized agencies are the (1) International Labor Organisation (ILO); (2) Food and

Agriculture Organization (FAO); (3) United Nations Educational, Scientific and Cultural Organization (UNESCO); (4) World Health Organization (WHO); (5) International Bank for Reconstruction and Development, or World Bank (IBRD); (6) International Development Association (IDA); (7) International Finance Corporation (IFC); (8) International Monetary Fund (IMF); (9) International Civil Aviation Organization (ICAO); (10) Universal Postal Union (UPU); (11) International Telecommunication Union (ITU); (12) World Meteorological Organization (WMO); (13) International Maritime Organization (IMO); (14) World Intellectual Property Organization (WIPO); (15) International Fund for Agricultural Development (IFAD); and (16) United Nations Industrial Development Organization (UNIDO). The common organizational structures of the specialized agencies include (1) a general assembly or conference of all members, functioning as the principal policy-making organ, (2) a board or executive council that implements policies, and (3) a secretariat that performs administrative duties for the agencies. *See also* UNITED NATIONS ECONOMIC AND SOCIAL COUNCIL (ECOSOC).

Significance   The specialized agencies of the United Nations are intergovernmental organizations related to the world body by special arrangements. Yet they are separate and autonomous organizations that work with the United Nations and one another through the coordinating machinery of the Economic and Social Council. But, as Inis Claude notes, the specialized agencies are "looking to the United Nations proper for coordination and guidance but enjoying essential freedom of action in their respective fields."[40] This decentralized pattern of operations permits each agency of the UN system to enjoy a certain independence within its field of operation. Thus, each specialized agency is designed to deal with specific, generally nonpolitical, economic and social problems. The UN system functions through specialization and division of labor.

State   A defined territory organized under a common political institution. A state, when independent, fulfills the basic requirements for entrance into the community of nations. There are more than 165 independent states in the world today, and most of them are members of the United Nations. The terms *state, nation-state, country*—or even *government*—are used interchangeably to mean a territorially defined geographical entity having its own independent government exercising sovereign control over its domestic and foreign policy. The universally cherished political characteristic of a state is sovereignty. The requirements of a state system are territory, population, government, and independence. States emerged out of the collapse of feudal order in Europe, and today the peoples of the former subject states stand in sovereign equality to one another. *See also* INDEPENDENCE; SOVEREIGNTY.

Significance   A state is a tangible entity and is the most powerful actor as an independent body on the world political stage. All states have equal standing in international law, despite demographic inequalities. China has over one billion people, yet it is considered juridically equal—under international law—to some of the smallest nations of the world, such as Grenada. In terms of international law, regional organizations constitute a mixed challenge to the traditional relationship between the state and the international system. The United Nations was to replace the state as the paramount basis of institutional value by establishing a constitutional concert of powers. However, the United Nations has succeeded only in underscoring the existing tension between the drive to maintain the state and the goal of maintaining the system. States are expected to abide by the legal norms established by the international community and are subject to restraints embodied in treaties and other principles of law, especially if they have accepted the law by ratifying treaties that contain it.

Summit Diplomacy   Diplomatic discussion or negotiation between two or more heads of state or government; often discussions take place between monarchs, presidents, and prime ministers. Summit diplomacy encompasses at least five principal elements: (1) policy formulation, (2) communication, (3) participation, (4) state visits, and (5) negotiation. It emerged during the era of absolute monarchy and has continued since that time. World War II and its aftermath evoked an unusual number of summit conferences. President Franklin Roosevelt attended many critical conferences with Allied heads of state and government at Casablanca, Quebec, Tehran, Cairo, and Yalta. In recent years President Ronald Reagan attended three summit meetings with Soviet President Mikhail Gorbachev, and, as of August 1991, President George Bush had participated in six such conferences with the Soviet leader. Summit conferences may focus on several problem areas, but all have a political bent to them. Most are ad hoc, but some have become regularized. An economic summit, for example, is held annually by the major industrialized countries and is aimed at developing common approaches to current problems. Initiated in 1975 by the Group of Five (Britain, France, Japan, Germany, and the United States), it became the Economic Summit of the Group of Seven in the 1980s when Italy and Canada were invited to participate.

Significance   Summit diplomacy represents the highest level of contact and diplomatic activity. It is a most dramatic manifestation of the role of heads of state or government in conducting world affairs and their response to immediate problems and to the need for understanding among various national leaders. The technique of summitry is also employed to improve the climate of relations between nations. The drama of negotiation involving crucial matters between the top level of government is a most newsworthy occurrence, but it also may make failure at the summit more spectacular, frustrating, and dangerous. Summit diplomacy is a risky undertaking, since when the heads of state fail to resolve an issue or a dispute, there is no higher governmental authority to which it can be referred. Whether successful or not, top governmental leaders relish summit meetings because they offer grandeur, pageantry, and entertainment, as well as enhance their political status in their own countries.

Supranational Organizations   International bodies with some of the attributes of governments, but falling short of achieving a sovereign independence. However, decisions made by majority consensus within supranational organizations usually are enforced by member governments even though they may dissent from the policy. Member states of supranational organizations with policy-making and policy-implementing powers, such as the European Community and the Nordic Council, use the argument that their sovereignty remains unaffected because they have delegated certain authority to a body of international civil servants. There are several forms of supranationalism. Hegemonic supranationalism exists when a superior power takes over decision making for a weaker nation. In the case of a protectorate, the subordinate state voluntarily relinquishes part of its sovereignty. The United Nations has exercised supranational authority on many occasions in performing its peacekeeping functions. *See also* EUROPEAN COMMUNITY (EC); NORDIC COUNCIL; WORLD GOVERNMENT.

Significance   Supranational organizations have the authority to initiate actions that have direct application to individuals and some legal entities, such as corporations. They are more independent from national governments than the agencies of international organizations, and their sphere of jurisdiction is more penetrating and concrete. The supranational executive has authority over private individuals, including the power of taxation, while the supranational court enjoys compulsory jurisdiction over nations and citizens. Advocates of the functional approach to supranationalism argue that it is possible to design supranational organizations to share sovereignty in a relatively noncontroversial and less political arena. They maintain that peace will emerge gradually as more technical institutions are organized. Whether this type of organization will become more numerous, and whether supranational organizations will evolve further, still provoke considerable speculation in scholarly circles. Yet we can cite several examples of successful supranational organizations. For example, the European Community in a few years will function in economic areas as a supranational organization, and the UN Security Council's decision to embargo trade with Iraq in 1990 is binding on all members of the world organization.

T

Third World   A largely noncohesive group of economically under-developed countries located in Asia, Africa, and Latin America. The Third World, however, is somewhat united by a common historical and political experience, and by a common contemporary outlook on development, human rights, and anticolonialism. Most of the 125 countries in this category are struggling with problems of survival. At one extreme of the Third World group are the new-rich oil-exporting countries, such as Saudi Arabia and Kuwait. At the other extreme are impoverished nations, such as Bangladesh and Ethiopia. The latter are so indigent that the United Nations has put them in a separate category—the less-developed countries (LDCs) or "Fourth World," the poorest of the poor. The Third and Fourth Worlds stand in contrast to the highly industrialized and comparatively rich countries of the West and Japan, which constitute the First World, and to the communist and former communist countries of Eastern Europe, often referred to as the Second World. In between the newly rich and the low-income countries are such newly industrialized nations as Brazil and South Korea. The Third World nations are members of the United Nations, and over one hundred have joined the nonaligned movement (NAM) and the Group of Seventy-Seven (G-77). Despite the desires of many nations forming the Third World to think of themselves as a bloc, they are nevertheless beset by differences among them. The phrase "Third World" devolved from the French *tiers monde;* it came into common use in the world in the 1960s. *See also* GROUP OF SEVENTY-SEVEN (G-77); NONALIGNED MOVEMENT (NAM).

Significance   The Third World presents diverse and complex problems that defy sweeping generalizations. What the Third World countries make of their freedom will depend primarily on how they conduct themselves in the realm of philosophy and thought, since it is ideas that generate action. Colonialism bequeaths them a formidable

190

legacy: massive problems that they must face and resolve. This requires that they channel their emotional impulses into powerful, constructive endeavors. The problems of poverty, hunger, disease, and illiteracy cannot be solved by a magic wand of freedom alone. Slowly, the gap between aspirations for technological development and the ties to traditional ways of life is widening, and is thus becoming a source of internal conflict. Many countries face serious problems of defaulting on loans or of having them canceled. This Third World foreign debt crisis is having a serious negative impact on their development and modernization because of the increasing difficulty in securing loans from the affluent countries of the First World, loans desperately needed to sustain Third World growth.

Treaty A written agreement between two or more states, which becomes international law and may, if applicable, become part of the national law of the consenting nations. A treaty may cover a wide range of subjects, from purchase or lease of territory, to the formalization of established rules, the creation of new rules of international trade, arms control, peace, and so on. Thus a treaty may perform the same function as a contract between individuals or a statute enacted by a national legislature. Many treaties are bilateral, creating what is called "particular" international law (which binds only two signatories). Multilateral treaties are called "general" international law, binding upon the signatories and also the nonsignatories. Sovereign states have full treaty-making capacity; international organizations may enter into agreements among themselves or with states. Treaties are variously called agreements, conventions, arrangements, pacts, covenants, declarations, charters, accords, acts, general acts, protocols, and concordats. More than 30,000 treaties have been registered with the United Nations since its creation in 1945. *See also* TREATY OF VERSAILLES.

Significance Treaties have been in evidence throughout recorded history, and they have promoted development of international relations, international organizations, and international law. Treaties and agreements are the main source of international law in the contemporary world. The number and diversity of treaties has expanded greatly in recent years, as nations have been involved with a wide variety of new problems. Treaty-making as a process involves negotiations, signatures, ratification, exchange of ratifications, publication, proclamation, and execution. A treaty usually consists of a preamble, the dispositive articles, and the so-called final clauses. The preamble will contain a statement of the broad objectives of the treaty and the names of the contracting parties and their representatives. The preamble is an integral part of the treaty and may furnish basic indications of its ensuing interpretations. However, specific statements of rights and obligations in the dispositive articles will, in case of conflict, prevail over general pronouncements in the preamble. The heart of a treaty is in the dispositive clauses, which may be supplemented by maps, appendices, or additional notes and protocols.

Treaty of Versailles   The agreement that ended World War I and established the League of Nations. The Treaty of Versailles also declared that universal peace must be based on social justice, and thus called for a progressive improvement in conditions of the world labor force by creating the International Labor Organisation (ILO) to function in support of the league. The provisions of the Treaty of Versailles were primarily drawn up by President Woodrow Wilson, with some contribution from British Prime Minister Lloyd George, French Premier Georges Clemenceau, and Italian Prime Minister V. Orlando. Germany—the vanquished nation—was not consulted. German colonies became mandates of the League of Nations, and Alsace-Lorraine was returned to France. Germany was also forced to accept responsibility for the war, agreeing to huge reparations payments and the surrender of equipment. Its army was limited to 100,000 troops, it relinquished vast holdings to Poland (including the Polish Corridor), and it was forced to demilitarize the Rhineland. *See also* WORLD WAR I.

Significance   The defeat of the Treaty of Versailles in the U.S. Senate prevented President Wilson from bringing about American participation in the League of Nations, which he had helped to establish. He was also unable to prevent the incorporation of certain provisions in the peace treaties that were damaging to its success. Many critics maintain that the League of Nations was handicapped from the start by the tie between the league covenant and the Treaty of Versailles. Critics also point out that the League of Nations became an instrument for upholding a dictated and unjust peace. However, with the conclusion of the Treaty of Versailles, the Americans, the British, and the French felt that their main task had been completed: Germany had, beyond any shadow of doubt, been the chief enemy, and the Treaty of Versailles was the price that Germany had to pay following her defeat in World War I. Primarily, Germany suffered from loss of territory, and the map of Europe was redrawn. This treaty was an instrument of retribution imposed by the conquerors upon a crushed and humiliated foe, and in the 1930s it was used by Adolf Hitler to win power and rebuild a militarily powerful German state.

U

Union of Banana Exporting Countries   An association to determine a coordinated policy for its member countries with regard to the technical and economic development of the banana industry, and to further international cooperation in connection with world banana trade. Other principal aims of the Union of Banana Exporting Countries are to secure fair remunerative prices for bananas; promote common policies with a view to rationalizing output, exports, transportation, and marketing; and to explore new markets. The union was established in 1974 in Panama. Its present members include Colombia, Costa Rica, the Dominican Republic, Guatemala, Honduras, Nicaragua, Panama, and Venezuela. The structure of the union includes a conference of ministers, composed of the ministers of economy or agriculture of the member countries. It is headquartered in Panama City, Panama. *See also* INTERNATIONAL TIN COUNCIL (ITC); INTERNATIONAL WHEAT COUNCIL (IWC).

Significance   The Union of Banana Exporting Countries periodically reviews the world supply and demand for bananas to consider possible solutions to current problems. Formed at the end of the Arab oil embargo in 1974, the union was concerned with price levels, because bananas were one of only a few perishable primary commodities whose prices had not substantially increased. In the face of this price behavior, and because of the protectionist tendency among the consuming industrialized nations, the union has been urging the conclusion of an international agreement between exporting and importing nations. It has close relationships with the United Nations Development Program (UNDP), the Food and Agricultural Organization (FAO), and the United Nations Conference on Trade and Development (UNCTAD). The union also has a cooperative relationship with the Organization of American States (OAS). The Union of Banana Exporting Countries has also concluded a number of scientific and

193

technical agreements with national and international research institutes with a view to exchanging information and collecting statistical data.

Union of International Associations (UIA)   An international body to facilitate the evolution of the activities of the worldwide network of nonprofit organizations, especially nongovernmental and voluntary associations. The Union of International Associations promotes understanding of international organizations representing valid interests in every field of human activity or belief, whether scientific, religious, artistic, educational, political, economic, commercial, or labor-related. Since its establishment in 1910 at Brussels, the UIA has set up a number of criteria for defining international nongovernmental organizations (INGOs) covering aims, membership, governance, and financing. The UIA's purpose is to establish a permanent relationship between international organizations and thus assist their activities; to study all questions relative to the organizations—coordination, unification of common methods; and to promote cooperation between them in research and documentation. It collects, analyzes, and publishes data on over two thousand governmental and nongovernmental international organizations. *See also* INTERNATIONAL GOVERNMENTAL ORGANIZATIONS (IGOS); INTERNATIONAL NONGOVERNMENTAL ORGANIZATIONS (INGOS).

Significance   However admirable the purpose of the Union of International Associations, its ultimate aim of coordinating the activities of so many organizations with such diverse interests seems to lack practicality. What can be useful is the grouping of international organizations that have specific common interests, combined with a close and cooperative relationship with intergovernmental organizations working in the same fields. Happily, such cooperation is being developed and continues to become more important. The Union of International Associations was established because of the growth of private unions. It laid down as a condition of membership that the association should establish a permanent office; that its objective should be of interest to all or a number of nations; and that it should be nonprofit and genuinely international. Despite the distinction between private and public associations, a number of organizations have mixed membership, with representatives of government bodies joining together with individual members.

United Nations (UN)   An organization of sovereign nations arising from a desire on the part of many of them to foster world peace and security and international cooperation. The United Nations is a voluntary association of 166 nations to seek to achieve freedom from war and aggression and to further international cooperation by solving global economic, social, political, and military problems. The United Nations officially came into existence on October 24, 1945 (since known as United Nations Day), when its charter was ratified by China, France, the Soviet Union, the United Kingdom, and the United States and by a majority of other signatories. The charter was drawn by the representatives of 50 countries at the United Nations Conference on International Organization, which met in San Francisco from April 25 to June 26, 1945. The six principal organs of the United Nations are the General Assembly, the Security Council, the International Court of Justice (ICJ), the Secretariat, the Economic and Social Council (ECOSOC), and the Trusteeship Council. All members of the United Nations are members of the General Assembly; each has one vote. The Security Council has five permanent members—China, France, the United Kingdom, the Soviet Union, and the United States—and ten nonpermanent members, elected by the General Assembly for two-year terms and not eligible for immediate reelection. The United Nations also has 16 specialized agencies. The official languages are Arabic, Chinese, English, French, Russian, and Spanish. The work of the Secretariat is carried on in English and French. *See also* LEAGUE OF NATIONS.

Significance   The United Nations is not a world government and it does not have authority to interfere in the internal affairs of any country. The name "United Nations" was devised by President Franklin Roosevelt and was first used in the "Declaration by the United Nations" of January 1, 1942, when representatives of 26 countries joined in an alliance and pledged their governments to continue fighting against the Axis powers. The United Nations is based on the sovereign equality of all its members, who undertake to fulfill in good faith their charter obligation—to settle international disputes by peaceful means and without resorting to war. Although the United Nations boasts of a proud record of accomplishment, it has been beset by myriad problems and difficulties. However, after years of being dismissed as a failure and a forum for Third World demagoguery, the United Nations suddenly has been transformed into an active mechanism through which the world community hopes to unite against aggressors. Since August 2, 1990, when Iraq invaded Kuwait, in the most sustained show of unanimity in the United Nations' 46-year history, the UN Security Council passed a succession of resolutions charging Iraq with aggression, demanding Iraqi withdrawal from Kuwait, imposing comprehensive and far-reaching economic and military sanctions against the aggressor, and authorizing the use of force by member nations against Iraq if it failed to withdraw from Kuwait on or before January 15, 1991.

United Nations: Amendment Process   Procedures established to govern any alterations to the Charter of the United Nations. Amendments to the charter are voted for adoption by two-thirds of the members of the General Assembly, with ratification by two-thirds of the member states, including the five permanent members of the Security Council. The basic constitutional documents of all international governmental organizations (IGOs) make provision for amendments, and the most frequent use of these provisions has been to change structural features. By 1991, four charter articles had been amended, one of them twice. In 1965, the membership of the Security Council was increased from 11 to 15 (Article 23), and the number of affirmative votes needed on procedural matters was increased from 7 to 9; on all other matters it was also increased to 9, including the concurring votes of the five permanent members (Article 27). Also in 1965, the membership of the Economic and Social Council (ECOSOC) was increased from 18 to 27, and in 1973 was further increased to 54 (Article 61). In 1968, the number of votes required in the Security Council to convene a general conference to review the charter was increased from 7 to 9 (Article 109). Amendments adopted are binding on all member states, whether ratified by them or not, so long as they remain UN members. *See also* CHARTER OF THE UNITED NATIONS.

Significance   In the wake of the decolonization of the world in the early 1960s and the sudden and substantial increase in the number of IGOs, most of them adopted amendments increasing the size of their smaller units. Because each permanent member of the Security Council possesses a veto over possible amendments, the charter has been altered more by interpretation, international custom, and usage than by the formal amendment process. Since the tenth annual session of the United Nations, a conference to review the charter can be called by a majority vote of the General Assembly and a procedural vote of the Security Council (no veto). If a conference is held, proposed amendments will be effective when ratified by two-thirds of the members, including all of the permanent members of the Security Council. In the past, when the Security Council was stymied because of the inability of the permanent members to achieve unanimity, the General Assembly increasingly took action on matters that under the charter were the exclusive preserve of the Security Council.

United Nations: Assessment Problems   Difficulties involved in finding an equitable but adequate financial formula by which to operate the United Nations budget. Obviously related to the assessment problem is the matter of ensuring adequate financing for the activities of the United Nations. The UN General Assembly in Article 17 of the charter is given the power to "consider and approve the budget of the Organization as well as to apportion the expenses among the members of the United Nations." In the formative years of the United Nations, the United States contributed about 40 percent of the total budget of the organization; the other members added 60 percent. The United Nations faced no problems with its financial assessment and the contributions of member nations until the creation of the United Nations Emergency Force (UNEF) in 1956 during the Suez Canal crisis. In some years the total contributions of the United States to the United Nations system and various related programs and agencies had approached 50 percent, but recently it has declined to about 25 percent. Many members, including the United States, have refused to pay their share of the UN budget and for its specialized agencies for political reasons and to underscore their opposition to particular programs and situations. In the early 1990s, the United Nations again faced a financial crisis because of the failure of a number of member nations to pay their assessed contributions, with the United States the leading "deadbeat," owing over $500 million. However, heartened by the UN system's response to events in the Persian Gulf, Congress late in 1990 approved full payment of 1990 dues to the UN budget. *See also* UNITED NATIONS: FINANCING.

Significance   Assessments for the payment of contributions to the United Nations' budget are determined according to a scale adopted by the General Assembly upon recommendation of its Committee on Contributions. The scale is calculated primarily on the basis of each country's total national income relative to that of other states. For poor nations, the national income is adjusted downward by a special allowance formula. The maximum that any country can be assessed is 25 percent of the UN budget; the minimum assessment is .01 percent. One answer to the assessment and other financial problems is to find new sources of income for the United Nations. Riggs and Plano, among other scholars, suggest eleven potential funding sources for the United Nations. In brief, they are (1) private contributions; (2) charges levied by UN agencies for services performed; (3) tolls for various transportation and communications; (4) fees for international travel; (5) profits from exploitation of mineral and other wealth in international waters and seabeds; (6) royalties from exploitation of resources of seabeds and Antarctica; (7) fees from fishing, whaling, and sealing rights in international waters; (8) revenue charged for the use of outer space, the moon, and other planets; (9) taxes levied on member states; (10) taxes levied on individuals; and (11) international trading currency.[41] The sovereign right of nations and political accommodation create barriers for implementation of most of these noble ideas.

United Nations: Caucusing Groups   Various member nations acting as interest groups by forming caucuses that meet regularly to determine common approaches to issues before the world body. Caucusing groups are active mainly in the General Assembly, which is the "parliament" of the United Nations. These groups are mostly organized on regional and geographical bases, such as the African, the Asian, the Arab, the Latin American, the Eastern European, the Western European, the European Community, and the Nordic caucuses. The two large groups—the nonaligned movement (NAM) and the Group of Seventy-Seven (G-77) are not regional but rather encompass nations from the three continents of the Third World: Africa, Asia, and Latin America. G-77 is the caucusing group composed of almost all nations of Africa, Asia, and Latin America, totaling about 125 nations. Most of these nations share a common historical past of colonial rule by Western nations. *See also* BLOC POLITICS IN THE UNITED NATIONS.

Significance   Caucusing groups have formed at the United Nations for the obvious purpose of achieving common objectives through concerted action. They fight for an equitable share of the elective seats in many UN organs. They exist primarily for these elections, for passing or defeating resolutions that come before the assembly, and for exchange of information. Caucusing groups have helped somewhat to change the decision-making process in the General Assembly, from one that primarily reflects the Western influence to one that underlines the concerns of the poorer, Third World nations for the advancement of their socioeconomic and political systems. There is a difference of opinion as to whether or not the caucusing system has a salutary effect on the United Nations, or whether they have created a parochial and narrow view of the world organization. On the positive side, caucusing groups provide additional channels of communication and socialization and a forum for harmonization of views.

United Nations: Collective Security   A system embodied in the Charter of the United Nations that governs a collective resort to dispute settlement, to determination that aggression has occurred, and to the levying of sanctions against an aggressor. The objective of these actions is to maintain international peace and security under the authority of the United Nations. Collective security is based on deterrence; if it fails, then the Security Council may decide to authorize military actions against the aggressor. Following World War II, collective security acquired its substantial legal basis through the United Nations Charter. According to the charter, the Security Council is primarily charged with maintenance of world peace and may ask all members to invoke sanctions against aggressor states under Chapter VII. This provision of the UN Charter was invoked after Iraq invaded Kuwait on August 2, 1990, and a comprehensive trade sanction was imposed by the Security Council against the aggressor, along with a decision that authorized the possible use of military action against Iraq if economic sanctions failed to secure its withdrawal from Kuwait. *See also* UNITED NATIONS: SANCTIONS.

Significance   The term *collective security* has been applied indiscriminately in regard to almost any agreement among two or more countries involving the possibility of their joint military action. The basic principle of collective responsibility is that all states in the international community must have a role in making or implementing collective decisions. However, because of great differences in national resources of member states, something resembling "ability to pay" governs the financial support requirements. Collective security to be successful involves much more than enforcement of peace. The system is most effective when it functions in harmony with provisions for peaceful settlement of disputes and with the successful conclusion of disarmament agreements. The policy of collective security, when attempted, has typically overestimated the amount of collective power that can be effectively mobilized to confront a violator of peace. Some critics charge that it has also underestimated the possibility of noncoercive methods of preventing or ending war. There have been many differences of opinion between the five permanent members of the Security Council (China, France, the United Kingdom, the Soviet Union, and the United States) regarding the composition of the UN force, when and how it will be used, and what strategy and tactics should govern its use. In the face of such sharply divergent attitudes of the major powers, the practical side of organizing an effective UN program for collective security appears bleak.

United Nations: Committees   Subgroups assigned to facilitate the division of work of the General Assembly. The General Assembly can establish as many committees as it believes are necessary to carry on its responsibilities. Four types of committees have been established: (1) the main committees, to which matters of substance are referred; (2) procedural committees, which organize the assembly's work and conduct business; (3) the standing committees, which perform continuing functions related to their specialized jurisdiction; and (4) the ad hoc committees or commissions established from time to time for a special purpose. The main committees are the First Committee (disarmament and related international security matters); the Special Political Committee (known as the Ad Hoc Political Committee; in 1956 it was made permanent); the Second Committee (economic and financial); the Third Committee (social, humanitarian, and cultural matters); the Fourth Committee (decolonization matters); the Fifth Committee (administrative and budgetary matters); and the Sixth Committee (legal matters). Two procedural committees—the General Committee and the Credentials Committee—deal with the organization of the General Assembly and the conduct of business. Voting in committees and subcommittees is by simple majority. See also UNITED NATIONS GENERAL ASSEMBLY.

Significance   Because of the great number of questions the General Assembly is called upon to consider each year, it allocates most questions to its main committees. Without the committee system it would be impossible to proceed with discussion and debate in full General Assembly meetings with any degree of efficiency. Agenda items are referred to the committees, and their primary task is to draft or consider resolutions and present them for discussion and final decision in the plenary session. Some questions are considered only in plenary sessions, rather than by one of the main committees, and all questions are voted on in plenary meetings after the committees have completed their consideration and submitted draft resolutions to the plenary assembly. In plenary meetings, resolutions may be adopted by acclamation, without objection or without a vote, or the vote may be recorded or taken by roll call. In keeping with UN tradition, and being conscious of political implications, each committee elects its own chairman, vice-chairman, and rapporteur—usually on the basis of geographical distribution, experience, and competence factors.

United Nations: Constitutional Evolution   The constitutional development of the United Nations through its charter. Over the years, the Charter of the United Nations has evolved through interpretation by its members and by its major organs—the General Assembly, the Security Council, the Secretariat, and the International Court of Justice (ICJ). Ratified as a multilateral treaty, the UN Charter became the constitution of the world organization with its establishment on October 24, 1945. Inis Claude has summarized the composite of forces and interactions that resulted in the United Nations Charter. According to Claude, the charter "was the product of past experience in the building and creation of international institutions, wartime planning, great power and particularly American leadership, intensive negotiation amid an intricate pattern of national disagreements and conflicts of interest, and popular pressures for realization of the desperate demand and noble aspiration for a just and durable peace."[42] The constitutional evolution of the United Nations represents a reaction to the extreme decentralization of the traditional system of international relations and the constantly increasing complexity of the interdependence of states. See also CHARTER OF THE UNITED NATIONS.

Significance   The process of constitutional development is not so clearly delineated in the United Nations as in many national systems. The charter as the basic constitutional document of the world body is inherently dynamic, quite unlike a multilateral treaty. Article 103 establishes the preeminence of the charter over any other international obligation. It stipulates, "In the event of a conflict between the obligations of the Members of the United Nations under the present Charter and their obligations under any other international agreement, their obligations under the Charter shall prevail." Thus, although the charter is a treaty, it is a treaty of a special kind that, short of amendment to change this provision, has priority over future treaties in a way not unlike a constitution's priority over ordinary law. Yet the United Nations is not a superstate or anything resembling a world government. However, to the extent the United Nations organizes the unorganized world, it may be regarded as a manifestation of the organizing process and may be considered a further expression of developing constitutional and legal structures in world affairs.

United Nations: Dependent Territory   A territorial possession of an independent state. Dependent territories or colonies were established by conquest, occupation, settlement, and cession in centuries past. The European powers—Great Britain, France, Belgium, Spain, Portugal, Germany, Italy, and the Netherlands—have had colonial possessions in much of Africa, Asia, and Latin America. Several non-European powers, including the United States and Ottoman Turkey, also maintained colonies. The issue of dependent territories became critical after World War II, and since then more than 80 new nations emerging from colonies have joined the United Nations as sovereign states. The decolonization efforts of the United Nations derive from the charter principle of "equal rights and self-determination of peoples." Since 1960, the United Nations has also been guided by the General Assembly's Declaration on the Granting of Independence of Colonial Countries and Peoples (Resolution 1514 [XV]). There are currently 16 dependent micro-territories, mostly in the Atlantic and the Caribbean islands and the Pacific Ocean. *See also* INDEPENDENCE.

Significance   Despite the great progress made by dependent territories to achieve independence, over 3 million people still live under colonial rule. The United Nations continues its unrelenting efforts to help achieve self-determination for these people, mostly islanders. Possession of dependent territories provided markets for colonial powers and offered them power and prestige. Article 73 of the UN Charter charges all members responsible for administering dependent territories to govern in such a manner as to promote the well-being of the inhabitants. In the process of administering their colonies, metropolitan powers fulfilled many of the provisions of Article 73. However, this article was also interpreted as a call for independence and set the stage for colonies to seek national independence. The United Nations helped hasten the process of dismantling the colonial system.

United Nations: Development Decades   Ten-year periods during which the United Nations put forth exceptional efforts—both multilateral and bilateral—to expand the flow of resources to the Third World and improve their utilization. The Development Decades covered the 1960s, the 1970s, and the 1980s. The first was undertaken in 1961, when General Assembly Resolution 1710 (XVI) called attention to the need for long-range planning and "to mobilize and to sustain support for the measures required on the part of both developed and developing countries to accelerate progress toward self-sustaining growth of the economy of the individual nations and their social advancement." The resolution outlined broad policies that would help to increase economic growth in the developing nations by at least 5 percent by the end of the first decade (1960–1970). The second decade (1970–1980) set a goal of 6 percent as the minimum average annual rate of growth in the gross domestic product (GDP) of the developing countries as a whole. The third decade (1980–1990) called for attainment of an annual aggregate GDP growth of 7 percent for the developing countries. The fourth decade (1991–2000) has been launched. *See also* THIRD WORLD; UNITED NATIONS DEVELOPMENT PROGRAM (UNDP).

Significance   The three Development Decades failed to achieve their major development goals; the first decade lacked planning and the second and third decades were unable to implement the UN recommendations. At the end of the third development decade, a committee established by the General Assembly to evaluate the implementation of the development plans and programs found the gap between the two types of countries—developed and developing—had widened over the years and that the developed countries' aid to the developing countries in terms of development assistance had decreased. However, the Development Decades succeeded in dramatizing UN development efforts and highlighted the need to sustain economic growth and close the gap between the haves and have-nots. The eradication of major pockets of poverty through a fairer distribution of the world's wealth could mean a safer and more stable world.

United Nations: Disarmament   The reduction or eradication of armed forces and specific classes of armaments under the auspices of the United Nations. Disarmament can be unilateral, bilateral, or multilateral. Disarmament has been used to advance distinct ideas: (1) the destruction or reduction of the armament of a defeated nation, (2) bilateral or multilateral agreements applying to specific areas, and (3) universal limitation of armaments by international agreements. The United Nations established the Disarmament Commission in 1952, for the discussion and negotiation of disarmament issues. Under the UN Charter, the General Assembly is empowered to "consider principles governing disarmament and the regulation of armaments" and to "recommend action to be taken by Member States." The Security Council was given responsibility for formulating a system for reducing the quantity of armaments in the world. *See also* UNITED NATIONS DISARMAMENT COMMISSION (UNDC).

Significance   The United Nations has used a variety of methods, techniques, and approaches in the search for disarmament. The General Assembly's first resolution addressed the question of disarmament; it sought the elimination of all atomic weapons that could destroy the world. Disarmament in its absolute form—general and complete disarmament—requires the worldwide destruction of weaponry and the elimination of all armed forces. The advocates of disarmament argue that (1) arms races can be the causes of war and (2) disarmament releases funds needed for the socioeconomic betterment of the peoples of the world. Opponents counter these arguments by pointing out that weapons are not the causes but the consequences of conflictive relationships. Many observers believe that the ultimate survival of the human race depends on the ability of the United Nations to limit the spread of nuclear weapons. While the argument and counterargument go on, some steps toward disarmament have been taken. In 1987, the superpowers eliminated all intermediate-range nuclear missiles, short-range missiles, associated launchers, support facilities, and operating bases worldwide. On November 19, 1990, the 34 nations of the Western and Eastern blocs signed the most ambitious arms control treaty ever, pledging to destroy tens of thousands of tanks, artillery pieces, combat vehicles, and attack aircraft from the Atlantic to the Ural Mountains deep inside the Soviet Union.

United Nations: Domestic Jurisdiction   Authority of nations within their frontiers concomitant with national sovereignty. However, the United Nations is more and more inclined to define its competence so broadly that virtually nothing is left to domestic jurisdiction. But Article 2 (7) of the UN Charter provides: "Nothing contained in the present Charter shall authorize the United Nations to intervene in matters which are essentially within the domestic jurisdiction of any state or shall require the Members to submit such matters to settlement under the present Charter; but this principle shall not prejudice the application of enforcement measures under Chapter VII." The inclusion of this provision came primarily at the insistence of the great powers in order that they might be protected from undue interference in their domestic society and economy. The borderline between questions of national versus international concern has been narrowing in recent years. Tariff policies, immigration laws, and the treatment of minorities are some of the issues that are commonly treated as domestic. *See also* INDEPENDENCE; SOVEREIGNTY.

Significance   Domestic jurisdiction implies that international law is not universal, but is limited to those issues and topics that have been agreed upon by sovereign states. Collective action to maintain international peace and security is specifically excluded from the domestic jurisdiction clause of the United Nations, but beyond this no definition is provided as to what constitutes an international problem and a proper subject for consideration of the United Nations. In setting boundaries between national and international jurisdiction, problems of interpretation inescapably arise. The most difficult problem is to resolve the question of human rights and self-determination. Finally, the questions of domestic jurisdiction are decided by UN agencies by their voting procedure.

United Nations: Expulsion, Suspension, and Withdrawal   Procedures by which membership in an international organization can be terminated or suspended. Expulsion, suspension, and withdrawal are seldom, if ever, applied by the United Nations, its members, or other international governmental organizations (IGOs). Any member country that has persistently violated the principles of the UN Charter may be expelled by the General Assembly on the recommendation of the Security Council. There is no provision in the charter for reentry into the organization of an expelled member. The charter provides for the rights and privileges of membership to be suspended by the General Assembly upon the recommendation of the Security Council when preventive or enforcement action has been taken against the member (Article 5). Although the charter does not provide for withdrawal, it is generally assumed that each state has the exclusive right to make such a determination. Indonesia is the only nation to have exercised this right (1965); in 1966, it rejoined the world body. *See also* CHARTER OF THE UNITED NATIONS.

Significance   The United Nations Charter makes clear provisions for expulsion, suspension, but not withdrawal. However, the framers of the charter approved a declaration that admitted the right of withdrawal from the world organization. Indonesia, which used this right in the face of requests not to do so, including that of the secretary-general, soon returned to the world body. At the United Nations Conference on International Organization in San Francisco, it was made clear that it was not the purpose of the United Nations to compel a member "to continue its cooperation in the Organization," if that member felt constrained to withdraw due to "exceptional circumstances." The predecessor of the United Nations, the League of Nations, experienced several examples of withdrawal and expulsion: Germany, Italy, and Japan withdrew from the League of Nations after committing aggression, and the Soviet Union was expelled from the league for its attack on Finland in 1939. So far, the UN Charter provisions to suspend or expel members have not been invoked. A member of the United Nations can also disappear as a result of union with another member; for example, East and West Germany were both members of the United Nations, but as they united as one nation in 1990, Germany became a single member. Similar was the case of North and South Yemen; when they united as one nation in 1990, Yemen too became a single member of the world body. Also, what if the Soviet Union, Yugoslavia, or any other states, break up? There will be a new problem of admitting 10 or 15 (or more) new states that formerly were represented in the United Nations by the Soviet Union, Yugoslavia, or other states.

United Nations: Financing   The function of raising operating funds for overhead expenses of the United Nations. The financing operations of the United Nations are divided into four major budget categories: (1) the regular budget, (2) the specialized agencies, (3) voluntary programs related mainly to economic development, and (4) peacekeeping operations. Article 17 of the charter specifies that the expenses of the United Nations shall be apportioned among member states by the General Assembly. Almost all regular budget income comes from contributions assessed member states according to a formula that takes account of national incomes and per capita incomes. Each state must pay the major portion of its assessment in dollars, with the balance payable in local currencies. Financial assessments range from about 25 percent for the largest contributor, the United States, to the established minimum of .01 percent required of nearly one-half of the members. *See also* UNITED NATIONS: ASSESSMENT PROBLEMS.

Significance   Financing of the United Nations is a reflection of political realities existing in the member states and the world at large. At various times, over 25 member nations withheld portions of their financing of the United Nations' operations because of political reasons. Some have even refused to pay their share for peacekeeping operations because they opposed the use of UN peacekeeping forces in particular instances. During its more than 45 years of existence, the membership of the United Nations has more than trebled and the number and scope of its activities have also greatly increased, but financing has not grown proportionately. Under severe criticism by the United States for alleged inefficient management and top-heavy administration, the United Nations has now begun to restrain its budget growth and institute efficient and effective management techniques. Members of the United Nations have shown little interest in developing independent sources of income for the world organization that would weaken their control over decision making.

United Nations: Foreign Aid   Multilateral assistance on generally concessionary terms from the United Nations or an international governmental organization (IGO) to supplicant governments. Foreign aid issues involve economic, technical, and social assistance rendered by the United Nations or other IGOs; foreign aid is also proferred by certain wealthy nations to poorer countries. Under the UN system, many global and regional institutions render financial and technical assistance exclusively to Third World countries. Generally, foreign aid issues include technical assistance, capital grants, development loans, guarantees for investments, and trade credits. Major international technical and financial aids are carried by the United Nations Development Program (UNDP), International Bank for Reconstruction and Development (IBRD), International Monetary Fund (IMF), International Finance Corporation (IFC), International Development Association (IDA), and other specialized agencies of the United Nations. Each acts independently in its own funding practices and decision-making processes. Foreign aid can take many forms: grants of money or food or other resources that are donated as gifts, and loans that must be repaid but carry nominal or no interest charges and export credits. Financing for specific capital development projects by Western nations usually takes the form of loans supplied by the IBRD or World Bank groups. *See also* INTERNATIONAL BANK FOR RECONSTRUCTION AND DEVELOPMENT (IBRD); INTERNATIONAL MONETARY FUND (IMF); INTERNATIONAL DEVELOPMENT ASSOCIATION (IDA); INTERNATIONAL FINANCE CORPORATION (IFC); UNITED NATIONS DEVELOPMENT PROGRAM (UNDP).

Significance   The UN system covers an enormous range of development activities in economic, social, and technical sectors. The developing nations prefer to receive foreign assistance through the United Nations because this implies an international partnership and satisfies the recognition of their sovereignty as nation-states. The United Nations has been quite successful in channeling and administering foreign aid, even though political considerations sometimes limit its effectiveness. Too often, aid has been used to fund highly symbolic but economically unwise projects. Inefficiency and corruption have also diverted aid. Some international-assistance critics charge that certain recipient countries have used aid to allow national budgetary funding to be diverted to noneconomic and nondevelopmental projects. Yet, multilateral assistance, as evidenced by the donors' commitment to these programs, ensures a kind of collective solidarity among both the sponsors and the recipients.

United Nations: Functional Cooperation   International activities that relate directly to economic, social, technical, and humanitarian matters or problems that may be tentatively described as nonpolitical. Functional cooperation is a method that overlaps political divisions with a spreading network of international activities and agencies into which the special interests of nations will be gradually integrated. The UN system has provided widely accepted standards for national conduct in such technical and noncontroversial areas as, for example, communication and transportation. The functionalist format encourages the development of piecemeal nonpolitical cooperative organizations, which can be established most effectively in the economic, scientific, technical, and social sectors. The UN system was, in its original conception, a full-fledged experiment in the application of the functional-sectors approach to world problems. Since its founding in 1945, the United Nations has steadily enlarged and diversified its own operations and also its functional program. The main organization—and the various specialized agencies—have devoted particular attention to the promotion of functional cooperation. *See also* FUNCTIONALISM.

Significance   In the functionalist argument there is a dichotomy between technical and political, with a strong bias toward the former. In general, "technical" connotes economic and social, as opposed to security, matters. Functional activities are concerned with such immediate values as prosperity, welfare, and social justice, rather than the prevention of war and the guarding of national security. The functionalists maintain that the spread of functional cooperation is expected to trigger a spillover (demonstration) effect. Although the functionalist argument seems to explain adequately the development of many international organizations, it does not explain the creation of all. Nor does it offer a rationale for the establishment of successful organizations in some fields and not in others. What is certain is that international organizations have been largely confined to the work of helping governments to help themselves, as well as encouraging them to help each other.

United Nations: Human Rights   Fundamental and natural rights as defined by the United Nations. Human rights have been a major concern of both global and regional international organizations since the end of World War II. Of the seven references to human rights in the UN Charter, the two most important are found in Article 1 (3) and Article 55 (c). They advocate (1) "international cooperation in solving international problems of an economic, social, cultural, or humanitarian character, and in promoting and encouraging respect for human rights and fundamental freedoms for all without distinction as to race, sex, language, or religion" and (2) "universal respect for, and observance of, human rights and fundamental freedoms for all without distinction as to race, sex, language, or religion." Human rights were historically concerned mostly with civil and political rights, but have expanded in the contemporary period to include social, economic, and cultural rights. Since 1946 the General Assembly of the United Nations and the Economic and Social Council (ECOSOC) have carried on many activities to ensure the protection of human rights; the most notable principle adopted by the UN General Assembly, in 1948, was the Universal Declaration of Human Rights. *See also* UNIVERSAL DECLARATION OF HUMAN RIGHTS.

Significance   The involvement of the United Nations in human rights issues has been hesitant and cautious. There was at first a groping effort to identify aspects of human rights problems that were truly international, and then a gradual movement toward international action. Both the General Assembly and ECOSOC are given authority by the charter to promote the protection of human rights. The United Nations and other international organizations can encourage and exhort nations to adopt certain human rights practices, they can provide technical and material assistance, and they can condemn practices of which they do not approve. But it is exceedingly difficult for them to force recalcitrant states to take actions they do not like. Various early nongovernmental organizations (NGOs) emphasized separate action within national societies to achieve common goals relating to human rights. Only as the connections among societies increased did it become apparent that these seemingly national social and legal matters had international aspects and that international action was essential for solutions.

United Nations: Legal Framework   The body of laws and rules governing the UN system. The legal framework of the United Nations is based primarily upon its charter, statutes, and treaties, as well as upon the universal principle of the law of nations (international law). It also includes decisions by the International Court of Justice (ICJ). The basic principles of international conduct are set forth in Article 2 of the charter, which members accept by its ratification, and which include (1) the sovereign equality of all nations, (2) fulfillment of charter obligations in good faith, (3) peaceful settlement of international disputes, (4) nonuse of force or threat of force for aggressive purposes, (5) support for UN enforcement action, and (6) nonintervention by the United Nations in domestic affairs of nations. The Third World nations challenge the international legal system because (for the most part) they had no role in shaping the norms to which they are expected to conform. In their view, the present international legal system benefits Western nations and the big powers in the UN Security Council, who have veto powers. The five nations with veto powers are China, France, the United Kingdom, the Soviet Union, and the United States. Thus, some of the newly independent Third World nations selectively accept only certain principles of international law as may suit their purposes. *See also* CHARTER OF THE UNITED NATIONS; INTERNATIONAL LAW.

Significance   The distinction between the legal framework for the guidance of states in their political relations and rules of international law relating to international peace and security is not always clear. For example, the UN Charter declares that states "shall refrain in their international relations from the threat or use of force against the territorial integrity and political independence of a state," and in the further development of this principle, the General Assembly has proclaimed that "war of aggression constitutes a crime against peace." But nonrenunciation of war implies its legal recognition as an instrument for defending existing rights and for changing the present system of rights. This means then that war is justified for defending as well as for overthrowing the status quo. If war is considered legal in spite of the inherent contradiction in the above argument and in the logic of its defense, then the rival parties would try to vindicate their respective positions in war in opposite directions.

United Nations: Membership   States that are members of the United Nations. The membership of the United Nations has been a decisive factor in determining its role in international affairs and its effectiveness in achieving its declared purposes. The 51 original members of the United Nations were the states that took part in the Conference on International Organization (San Francisco Conference) in 1945 and signed and ratified the charter or had previously signed the Declaration by the United Nations. At its peak the United Nations had 160 members, but in 1990 the two Yemens merged into one country and the two Germanies are also reunited, thus reducing the UN membership to 159. However, with the admission of seven new members— North Korea, South Korea, Estonia, Latvia, Lithuania, the Marshall Islands, and Micronesia—in 1991, the membership climbed to 166. Any country wishing to become a member must submit an application to the Security Council, including a declaration that it accepts the obligations set forth under the charter. If the Security Council recommends admission of the new member, the application is then passed to the General Assembly, which must accept it by a two-thirds majority. Any member nation that has persistently violated the principles of the charter may be expelled from the United Nations. *See also* CHARTER OF THE UNITED NATIONS.

Significance   The United Nations limits its membership on a qualitative basis to those states that provide some evidence of capacity and worthy conduct and intention. However, to be effective, the program of the United Nations must be universal in scope, and can be served best by a universal membership. With this objective in mind, the UN General Assembly has admitted many ministates—Antigua and Barbuda, Dominica, the Seychelles, São Tomé and Principe, and Saint Kitts and Nevis—all with less than 100,000 population, suggesting that the United Nations is becoming truly universal in its membership. When the remaining 16 dependent territories in the world become independent (should this happen) and the two Koreas join, either as two members or one (in the event of their unification), the United Nations will then become fully universal.

United Nations: Monetary and Debt Crisis   The critical financial condition in the world as a result of Third World debt. Monetary and debt crises have forced nations to realize that they cannot sustain large fiscal deficits indefinitely through excessive borrowing. Latin America, beset with the interconnected problems of overpopulation, debt, drugs, crime, capital flight, and emigration, stands at a portentous crossroads. Africa, especially the sub-Saharan region, has suffered drought, famine, and disease to a degree unknown elsewhere. Only in the developing countries of Asia did economic growth top the average global gross national product (GNP) of 3.2 percent in 1989. Recently, the International Bank for Reconstruction and Development (IBRD) has assumed an increasingly greater role in stimulating sustainable economic growth in debtor countries through policy-based, fast-disbursing loans. The IBRD and the IMF (International Monetary Fund) are providing financing to Third World nations to encourage new commercial debt reduction agreements and to assist debtor nations in pursuing fundamental economic reforms. *See also* INTERNATIONAL BANK FOR RECONSTRUCTION AND DEVELOPMENT (IBRD); INTERNATIONAL MONETARY FUND (IMF).

Significance   The United Nations faces one of its greatest and most difficult challenges in its efforts to manage and resolve the international monetary and debt problem, which has reached the level of crisis. With communism in the retreat from economic pressures and the Third World tottering on the brink of bankruptcy, the United Nations is being compelled to make some rapid, and often painful, decisions concerning international economic assistance and financial management. What does the emergence of independent Eastern Europe mean to the poor nations of the Third World? Just as they were gearing up for greater debt relief in the 1990s, Third World nations now fear they will face a new competitor—the former Soviet satellite countries of Eastern Europe, whose turn toward democratic institutions and market economy has stirred global admiration. After two decades mired in the intractable problems of Afro-Asian development and Latin American debt, the IMF and its sister institution, the IBRD (World Bank), are turning attention—and resources—to the newly liberated nations of Eastern Europe. In 1991 alone, Eastern Europe is expected to receive a total of $17 billion from the IMF, the World Bank, and Western nations.

United Nations: Peacekeeping   Maintenance of peace and security in the world. The peacekeeping system is centralized in the UN Security Council, which is charged with a primary responsibility for the maintenance of international peace and security. Under the UN Charter, the General Assembly may consider general principles for peacekeeping cooperation and make recommendations on such principles. It may also discuss any question relating to the maintenance of international peace and security brought before it by a government or by the Security Council. The methods and machinery for preventing or terminating conflicts have taken many forms. In some cases, the United Nations has acted through peacekeeping forces, observer or fact-finding missions, plebiscite, supervision, good offices missions, third party negotiation, conciliation, panels, mediators, and special representatives. In other cases, it has provided a forum for debate and negotiation and a channel for quiet diplomacy. From 1948 to date (1991), nearly two dozen UN peacekeeping operations have been authorized by the United Nations; "peacekeeping" was first used to describe the work of the UN Emergency Force (UNEF) during the 1956 Suez Canal war. *See also* UNITING FOR PEACE RESOLUTION.

Significance   The United Nations peacekeeping forces have helped to supervise cease-fires in various volatile regions, mostly in the Third World. The United Nations was born from the despair resulting from the League of Nations' inability to prevent the outbreak of war, thus its main objective is to prevent the outbreak of war, and should it fail to do this, then to limit and contain the conflict until it can be resolved. In this effort, the United Nations has achieved some successes and arrived at some stalemates. The success or failure of various peacekeeping approaches to peace and security by the United Nations has depended not merely upon the nature of a particular conflict, but also upon the nature and degree of international cooperation among the members of the United Nations, especially the five permanent members of the Security Council (China, France, the United Kingdom, the Soviet Union, and the United States). Judging from the success achieved so far by various peacekeeping operations, we can conclude that they are the most promising line of action currently available to tamp down and control international crises. It is precisely for this reason that the United Nations' peacekeeping operations received the 1988 Nobel Peace Prize.

United Nations: Refugee Programs   Plans and programs to resettle displaced persons. Refugee programs are for people who have been forced to leave their homeland because of war, economic deprivation, or denial of basic human rights by the people or the government. Additionally, a refugee is a person who, because of fear of persecution for reasons of race, religion, nationality, ethnicity, or political opinion, leaves his own country and is unwilling to return. The international refugee problem was first recognized in 1921, with the appointment of a League of Nations High Commission for Refugees. In 1943 the United Nations Relief and Rehabilitation Administration was established; it was replaced in 1946 by the International Refugee Organization. The Office of the United Nations High Commission for Refugees (UNHCR) was then established in 1951 to replace the International Refugee Organization. The UNHCR relies on an operational partnership in the field to implement assistance programs it has helped to plan and finance. Many international nongovernmental organizations (INGOs), such as the Red Cross, play a crucial role in helping refugees all over the world. *See also* UNITED NATIONS HIGH COMMISSION FOR REFUGEES (UNHCR).

Significance   The refugee problem is truly worldwide, growing in size and complexity. Every war and civil war produces homeless persons, and the total number of such refugees is now in the millions. As strangers in foreign countries where they have sought sanctuary, refugees are often without any legal or political rights and frequently are in dire economic condition. With no status as citizens, many times they are almost reduced to nonentity status and seen as a threat to the well-being of those countries to which they applied for refuge. Assistance offered by the United Nations has helped to stabilize populations endangered by nature or man in many instances. Equipment, food, and foreign expertise are hallmarks of UN assistance, along with neutral international monitors to verify the necessary cooperation to stabilize war zones and, sometimes, to separate opponents.

United Nations: Regional Commissions   Five commissions established by the Economic and Social Council (ECOSOC) of the United Nations that seek to maintain and strengthen economic relations among countries, both within and outside the regions. The five regional commissions are the Economic and Social Commission for Asia and the Pacific (ESCAP), the Economic Commission for Africa (ECA), the Economic Commission for Europe (ECE), the Economic Commission for Latin America and the Caribbean (ECLAC), and the Economic and Social Commission for Western Asia (ESCWA). ECOSOC established the Economic Commission for Europe and the Economic Commission for Asia and the Far East (now ESCAP) in 1947 to assist the countries devastated by World War II. ECLAC was established in 1948; ECA in 1958; and ESCWA in 1974. In 1977, the General Assembly made the regional commissions the main regional economic and social development centers (within the UN system) for their respective regions. They work closely with various UN agencies and other international governmental and nongovernmental bodies. *See also* UNITED NATIONS: REGIONALISM.

Significance   The regional commissions are playing a vital and expanding role in a wide variety of activities. They are aimed at raising the standard of living in their areas of jurisdiction. Because the various member states belonging to these regional commissions have different priorities and economic conditions, the impact of the commissions varies from region to region. The ECE helped Europe to recover economically from the damages of World War II, and that continent is far ahead of other regions in which regional commissions are operating (Africa, Asia, Latin America and the Caribbean, and the western Asia). While Europe is moving toward one unit in 1992, the developing areas of the world are lagging far behind. However, the main objective of these commissions has been to provide research and planning, which can stimulate the spirit of self-help in meeting regional problems, and in this respect the various commissions have achieved some success.

United Nations: Regionalism   The growth of international organizations and other kinds of common ties among nations in a geographical area. Regionalism is built upon the narrower concerns of a particular region through membership in an organization aimed at meeting the political, economic, military, and cultural objectives of its limited constituency. The rapid increase of regional international governmental organizations (IGOs) followed the conclusion of World War II, when economic cooperation programs were seen as providing solutions for the ravages of the war. Today, more than two-thirds of all forms of IGOs are regional in scope. Some of the better-known regional organizations are the European Community (EC), Council of Mutual Economic Assistance (COMECON or CMEA), the North Atlantic Treaty Organization (NATO), the Warsaw Treaty Organization

(WTO), the Organization of African Unity (OAU), the Organization of American States (OAS), and the Arab League. Article 52 of the UN Charter provides some general rules by stating that "Nothing in the present Charter precludes the existence of regional arrangements or agencies for dealing with such matters relating to the maintenance of international peace and security as are appropriate for regional action, provided that such arrangements or agencies and their activities are consistent with the Purposes and Principles of the United Nations."

Significance   Regionalism is recognition of the viability of regional organization by the United Nations and implies acceptance that not all problems are global or national in nature. There are problems in defining regions, as Couloumbis and Wolfe note, in that "different criteria for identifying regions yield altogether different regional configurations." They cite four criteria: (1) geographical, (2) military-political, (3) economic, and (4) transactional.[44] Other scholars, while emphasizing the predominant role of universal organizations, recognize that regional and more limited organizations have a place within the global system. Recourse to regional arrangements may be ascribed to beliefs that the United Nations, under present circumstances, cannot wholly suffice to protect or further the interests of nation-states. Consequently, states have turned to regional groups as a supplement to unilateral national action; regionalism is considered more effective, and it tends to produce greater support from "neighbors."

United Nations: Sanctions   Enforcement measures—economic restrictions or collective military action—against violators of international law. Sanctions may be imposed through trade embargo or joint military action on behalf of the UN Security Council. The Security Council has two forms of sanctions available to it—those described in Article 41, not involving the use of armed force, and those described in Article 42, involving action by air, sea, or land forces. Before deciding upon either, the council must "determine the existence of any threat to the peace, breach of the peace, or act of aggression" under Article 39. The UN Charter specifies that the council may invoke voluntary or compulsory sanctions against the law-breaking state. If the Security Council fails to act on a threat to the peace, breach of peace, or act of aggression because of lack of agreement among its members, the General Assembly, under the Uniting for Peace Resolution, "shall consider the matters immediately with a view to making appropriate recommendations to Members for collective measures." Following the 1990 Iraqi invasion of Kuwait, the Security Council imposed comprehensive economic sanctions against Iraq, which were enforced by air, sea, and land blockade by multinational forces.

Significance   To levy sanctions the Security Council must determine the existence of any threat to the peace, breach of the peace, or act of aggression by a nonprocedural vote in which the veto can be used by any of the five permanent members of the Security Council (China, France, the United Kingdom, the Soviet Union, and the United States). To undertake such actions, therefore, the unanimity of the permanent members is essential. It is unlikely that any sanction can be imposed by the Security Council against any of the permanent members; the General Assembly, under the 1950 Uniting for Peace Resolution, can recommend enforcement action against any state, including the permanent members. Under the provision of the League of Nations Covenant, each member nation was left to determine for itself whether an act of aggression had been committed, and upon that decision rested the obligation of supporting a recommendation against the aggressor by the league council. In contrast, the UN Charter empowers the Security Council, and not the individual members, to determine the existence of any threat to the peace, breach of the peace, or act of aggression. The Security Council passed 12 resolutions after the Iraqi invasion of Kuwait in 1990, levying an economic embargo and outlining other potential enforcement actions. For the first time in the United Nations' 46-year history, the Security Council thus authorized member nations to take future military action against aggressor Iraq, if deemed necessary, without a UN flag or UN command. Nevertheless, national military action undertaken as a result of Security Council approval would be an implementation of UN-voted sanctions.

United Nations: Sessions   Meetings of the General Assembly. The General Assembly meets in regular sessions, in special sessions, and in emergency special sessions. Regular and special sessions are provided for by the UN Charter (Article 20). Regular sessions must be held at least annually. The General Assembly meets every year on the third Tuesday in September until a closing date set by the assembly upon the recommendation of the General Committee. These meetings normally take place at the U.N. headquarters in New York, although a majority of members can establish some other meeting place. Special sessions are convoked by the secretary-general, either at the request of the Security Council or of a majority of the UN members. The charter contains no provision for emergency special sessions. Emergency special sessions are authorized by the Uniting for Peace Resolution of 1950, according to which the General Assembly may meet on twenty-four-hours' notice if requested by the Security Council or by a majority of the members of the United Nations. *See also* CHARTER OF THE UNITED NATIONS; UNITING FOR PEACE RESOLUTION.

Significance   Although the regular session of the General Assembly lasts only three months each year, the assembly's work continues in special committees dealing with issues such as apartheid, science and technology, natural resources and outer space; in the activities of bodies it has established, such as the United Nations Development Program (UNDP), the World Food Council (WFC), the United Nations Environment Program (UNEP), the United Nations Conference on Trade and Development (UNCTAD), and the United Nations Children's Fund (UNICEF); in the work of the secretariat; and at international conferences on specific problems. Some questions are considered in plenary sessions—meetings of the whole—which may speak and act officially in the name of the General Assembly. Thus, recommendations and resolutions adopted in plenary sessions have the authority of the General Assembly behind them, while matters considered and adopted in the main committees and other bodies are work preparatory to consideration in the plenary sessions. Plenary meetings may be private, but are almost always public. Final decisions on agenda items are not usually made until a committee report has been received.

United Nations: Technical Cooperation for Development   Promotion of bilateral and multilateral technological skills among the developing and the developed regions of the world. Technical cooperation for development is offered by the developed nations to the developing countries. Technical assistance programs of the international organizations have sought to develop managerial, industrial, educational, public health, agricultural, mining, and administrative skills. Within the UN system, the United Nations Development Program (UNDP), the United Nations Fund for Population Activities (UNFPA), the International Bank for Reconstruction and Development (IBRD), and the International Development Association (IDA) are responsible for most international technical cooperation development loans. In support of technical cooperation activities, the General Assembly in 1978 set up the Department of Technical Cooperation for Development (DTCD) as an executing agency for the UNDP and the UNFPA. In general, the DTCD establishes a framework for growth by assisting (1) in the preparation of comprehensive plans to promote balanced economic and social development and the best use of available financial, physical, and human resources; (2) in the exploration, exploitation, and effective use of natural resources, such as water, minerals and energy supplies; and (3) in the improvement of national statistical and public administration systems. *See also* UNITED NATIONS: DEVELOPMENT DECADES; UNITED NATIONS DEVELOPMENT PROGRAM (UNDP).

Significance   Technical cooperation for development is understood to include the application of scientific and human skills to the solution of problems in the practical or industrial arts. In other words, technology applies the laws of the physical and biological sciences to engineering, agriculture, and industry. It is a scientific and social process to serve human needs. The level of technology depends mainly upon research and development—the acquiring of new basic knowledge and its application to innovation. The process of modernization in the contemporary world involves the transfer of skills from the technically advanced nations to the developing countries. Technology is thus culture-bound and difficult to transfer, because it shapes not only the way people live but also tends to shape the way people think. Even though the United Nations and other international organizations have been playing a catalytic role by helping to mobilize the capital investment required for worldwide technical cooperation and development, many of the international projects have failed to achieve the desired goals because of the complex nature of the problem and the ideological underpinnings of the decision-makers in both the developed and the developing worlds.

United Nations: Trust Territory   A dependent territory placed under the United Nations trusteeship system. The last trust territory (Micronesia)—composed of the former Japanese-mandated islands of the Marshalls, the Marianas (with the exception of Guam), and Palau—consists of more than 2,000 islands and atolls covering 7.8 million square kilometers of the western Pacific. It is a strategic trust territory administered by the United States under an agreement approved by the UN Security Council in 1974. In 1986 the Trusteeship Council recommended that the United States, as the administering authority, had discharged its obligations under the trusteeship agreement and that it was appropriate for that agreement to be terminated upon entry into force of the Compact of Free Association for the Marshall Islands, Palau, and Micronesia and the Commonwealth Covenant for the Northern Mariana Islands. The agreements have come into force everywhere except in Palau, where the draft compact, which would allow the United States to place weapons on the territory, failed to obtain the required 75 percent majority vote of the population required by Palau's constitution. The trust territory is overseen by the Trusteeship Council on behalf of the Security Council. Each year the Committee on Decolonization examines the question, although the United States maintains that under Article 83 of the UN Charter, only the Trusteeship Council and Security Council have jurisdiction. *See also* UNITED NATIONS: DEPENDENT TERRITORY; UNITED NATIONS TRUSTEESHIP COUNCIL.

Significance   By 1990 almost all trust territories had been granted independence or were united with a neighboring country on the basis of plebiscite held under UN supervision. Under the terms of the Compact of Free Association, the Federated States of Micronesia, the Marshall Islands, and Palau would be self-governing. They would have authority over internal and foreign affairs; defense and security matters would be the responsibility of the United States. The compact can be terminated unilaterally by any signatory at any time. The United States has not always functioned with the best interests of the inhabitants of the trust territory as a guide. However, after many years of demands for self-government by the people of the trust territory, the United States now plans to terminate the trusteeship arrangement while retaining responsibilities over defense and security matters for at least 15 more years.

United Nations Center for Human Settlements (Habitat)   A body serving as a focal point for human settlement action and coordinating related activities within the UN system. The center assists nations and regions in solving their habitation problems, promoting greater international cooperation in that sector, together with a comprehensive approach to human settlement problems. The first international meeting on the subject was convened by the United Nations in Vancouver, Canada, in 1976 under the title Habitat: UN Conference on Human Settlements. Acting upon recommendation of the conference, the General Assembly decided in 1977 to turn the Committee on Housing, Building and Planning into the Commission on Human Settlements, and in 1978 the General Assembly established the UN Center for Human Settlements, with headquarters in Nairobi, Kenya. (The Commission on Human Settlements is the governing body of the Center for Human Settlements.) The commission has 58 members, regionally chosen for four-year terms on the basis of 16 from Africa, 13 from Asia, 10 from Latin America, 6 from Eastern Europe, and 13 from Western Europe and other areas. The Habitat serves as the secretariat. Annually, the first Monday in October is designated World Habitat Day. *See also* UNITED NATIONS: REFUGEE PROGRAMS.

Significance   The chief concern of the United Nations Center for Human Settlements is the worldwide problem of homelessness; its global strategy for the solution is to provide adequate shelter for all. With this objective in mind, Habitat offers technical cooperation to government programs, organizes meetings of experts on housing and demographics, gives workshops, and publishes and disseminates information throughout the world. Habitat maintains cooperation with various UN bodies, specialized agencies, and other intergovernmental as well as nongovernmental organizations. Technical cooperation projects cover national settlement policies and programs, urban and regional planning, rural and urban housing, slum upgrading, low-cost building technology, and the establishment of institutions responsible for human settlements. Habitat has over 220 projects underway in nearly 100 countries.

United Nations Children's Fund (UNICEF)   An organization established by the UN General Assembly in 1946 to provide emergency supplies of food, clothing, and medicine to destitute children in war-ravaged countries. Originally it was called the United Nations International Children's Emergency Fund (UNICEF), but when the General Assembly extended its mandate permanently, the words "International" and "Emergency" were dropped from the name, although its famous acronym was retained. World War II caused suffering and misery to millions of children; working with other agencies of the United Nations, UNICEF brought material assistance to millions of nursing mothers, adolescents, and needy children all over the world. More recently, it has shifted its emphasis toward programs of long-range benefit to children of developing nations. UNICEF places special emphasis on administering mass health campaigns against epidemics that attack children, on caring for young refugees, and on overcoming illiteracy among the young. It has trained a large number of paramedical and auxiliary staff personnel in many countries of the Third World. UNICEF depends on contributions from governments, individuals, and organizations and on a charitable sale of holiday greeting cards. Its grants-in-aid are usually matched by two or three times as much in local funds. *See also* WORLD CHILDREN'S SUMMIT.

Significance   The United Nations Children's Fund has been an integral part of the mission of the United Nations in all parts of the world, regardless of political and ideological conflicts. By its careful planning and nonpartisan administration, UNICEF vindicated the operational role of international organizations in social and human development. The solid achievements of UNICEF have won the highest universal acclaim—in 1965 it was awarded the Nobel Peace Prize. UNICEF fostered the 1990 World Summit for Children held at the U.N. headquarters, which brought 71 heads of state to New York just after the the start of the 45th General Assembly session. As a result of that summit, the priority for the safety of the lives of children and their healthy growth was upgraded. UNICEF is examining the impact of recent political and economic changes in Eastern Europe on the children of that region.

United Nations Commission on Human Rights   The body that considers questions concerning alleged violations of human rights and fundamental freedoms. The UN Commission on Human Rights has prepared recommendations and reports regarding an international bill of rights, international declarations on the conventions of civil rights, the status of women, freedom of information, and similar matters. The new human rights machinery includes the following: establishment of a variety of specialized theme mechanisms to take effective action wherever there are problems regarding critical human rights problems affecting individuals—such as disappearances, summary executions, torture, and religious intolerance; appointment of numerous special rapporteurs to examine conditions in individual countries (Afghanistan, Chile, El Salvador, Iran, and Romania being among the current subjects of investigation); establishment and expansion of the activities of new supervisory committees to monitor compliance with human rights treaties, several of which have new optional complaint mechanisms through which individuals can seek redress; substantial increase in the advisory program providing technical assistance in human rights; and development of a major initiative to expand UN public information on human rights in a new world campaign designed to advance awareness of rights and the UN machinery through which individuals can claim those rights. *See also* UNITED NATIONS COMMISSION ON THE STATUS OF WOMEN.

Significance   During the first 30 years, the United Nations' human rights program concentrated primarily on standard-setting; there were only a few modest attempts to develop procedures for enforcing human rights standards. Standard-setting work of the United Nations in the area of human rights goes on, reaching into new areas, such as the rights of indigenous peoples, migrant workers, human rights defenders, and others. Human rights advocates agree that the major challenge now is to strengthen the implementation of the standards developed so far. In addition to the Human Rights Commission, many principal UN programs have also dealt with specific human rights issues involving the violation of widely accepted norms for conduct. These organs have dealt with specific issues as violation of human rights in South Africa and Israeli-occupied Arab territories.

United Nations Commission on the Status of Women   Monitors, reviews, and appraises implementation of forward-looking strategies for advancement of women to the year 2000. The United Nations Commission on the Status of Women is currently examining in depth these priority themes selected in 1987 on equality, development, and peace: (a) equality in economic and social participation; (b) eradication of illiteracy, employment concerns, health and social services, population issues, and child care; (c) full participation of women in the development of their countries and in the creation of just social and political systems. The League of Nations concentrated on trying to eradicate traffic in women and children, established an advisory committee to study the problem, and encouraged cooperation in halting this traffic. Following the formation of the United Nations, the Economic and Social Council (ECOSOC) established the Commission on the Status of Women in 1946 as a subcommission of the Human Rights Commission. When this proved unsatisfactory to women, the subcommission was upgraded to the status of commission. In 1945 only 30 of the 51 original members of the United Nations allowed women to vote; today, only 8 countries of the 166 member states do not universally permit women to vote: Bahrain, Kuwait, Nigeria (in six states), Oman, Qatar, Saudi Arabia, the United Arab Emirates (UAE), and Yemen. *See also* UNITED NATIONS COMMISSION ON HUMAN RIGHTS.

Significance   The movement to recognize the equality of men and women has gained some momentum since the establishment of the United Nations Commission on the Status of Women. Yet one can legitimately ask whether the efforts of international organizations have had an impact on this movement. Women, in general, have gained a high degree of equality with men mostly in Western countries and in socialist nations, but not in the Third World. However, women from developing nations now have come into contact with those from the developed countries—not only through meetings at the United Nations but also under governmental programs and international seminars that address problems involving the status of women. Advisory services have also been made available to countries desiring to improve the lot of women citizens. As women in many countries have begun to assert their claims to equality, they have become an international interest group, constantly lobbying before international organizations. Under such pressure, the concerned international organizations have passed various conventions granting more rights to women.

United Nations Conference on International Organization (UNCIO)
A major international conference called in San Francisco in 1945 for the purpose of writing the Charter of the United Nations. The United Nations Conference (or San Francisco Conference) met from April 25 to June 26 in full session and in small committees and designed the 111-article Charter of the United Nations. The 50 participating countries, along with Poland (which did not attend the meeting because of a controversy over whether the London-based, Western-supported government or the Soviet-sponsored government should represent Poland), became the original members of the world body. The Soviet Union had succeeded in the Yalta agreement to have the conference admit the Byelorussian Soviet Socialist Republic and the Ukrainian Soviet Socialist Republic in addition to the Soviet Union as UN members; in this way the Soviet Union obtained three voting members in the United Nations General Assembly instead of one as with other members. The San Francisco Conference was attended by 282 delegates representing the 50 participating nations. More than 1,500 specialists and staff members advised these delegates. The charter came into being on October 24, when the five permanent members of the Security Council (China, France, the United Kingdom, the Soviet Union, and the United States) and a majority of the other signatories filed their instruments of ratification. *See also* DUMBARTON OAKS CONFERENCE; YALTA CONFERENCE.

Significance   The United Nations Conference on International Organization shaped the resultant body under the obvious influence of American planning and leadership. The unequal weight in the scales derived not only from American military and economic power but also from the worldwide prestige of President Franklin Roosevelt, who died shortly before the San Francisco Conference. He had done so much to inspire enthusiasm for the United Nations among U.S. senators and congressmen that there was a momentary fear that his death might weaken its impetus. But President Harry Truman's support for the new organization was undiminished. While on the surface the big powers presented a more-or-less solid front, Soviet intransigence and suspicion did not contribute to political harmony. However, the framers of the charter were resolved to disassociate the

United Nations from its predecessor—the League of Nations—and from any postwar peace treaty, such as that of Versailles after World War I, that might hamper the development of the new world forum. The charter was written two months before the dawning of the nuclear age with the dropping of the first atomic bomb on Hiroshima. If it had been written after that momentous event, it is possible that even more emphasis would have been placed in the charter on such subjects as peacekeeping and disarmament. Yet, 46 years later, the nations selected by the San Francisco Conference to exercise the veto power as permanent members of the Security Council remain the five great powers definitely known to possess arsenals of nuclear weapons (in addition to India, which possesses some nuclear weapons). This demonstrates some foresight on the part of the writers of the charter.

United Nations Conference on the Human Environment (UNCHE) A world conference to protect the human race from the threat of pollution and other environmental hazards. The United Nations Conference on the Human Environment, which met in Stockholm in 1972, approved a plan for international action to protect man's habitat on earth. It also called for the creation of a new agency within the United Nations Environment Program, a secretariat to staff the agency, a special voluntary fund for technical assistance projects, an intergovernmental council to supervise the new agency, and a new body in the UN Secretariat to coordinate the work of the existing UN agencies that were already working on various aspects of the environmental problem. Other recommendations of the conference envisaged the following: a 58-member Governing Council for Environmental Programs; an Environment Fund, to which governments would contribute voluntarily; and an Environment Coordination Board, to be established under the auspices of the Administrative Committee on Coordination. Representatives of 110 countries attended the UNCHE, also known as the Stockholm Conference. As a result of this conference, the General Assembly in 1972 established the United Nations Environment Program (UNEP). *See also* UNITED NATIONS ENVIRONMENT PROGRAM (UNEP).

Significance   The declaration of the United Nations Conference on the Human Environment is very general and, of course, is nonbinding on the member states. This does not, however, diminish the importance of the declaration. Its function is inspirational and educational, and its stature in this respect is enhanced by the fact that it was adopted unanimously. It is recognized that most effective measures for preventing deterioration of the human environment depend primarily upon national regulations and enforcement. It is unlikely that sovereign nations will subject themselves to supranational authority in ecological matters. Nevertheless, the problem of global ecocatastrophes from many existing sources present to humankind one more opportunity for cooperative action for the benefit of the human race. An encouraging development since the conclusion of the UNCHE is the emergence of a common pattern to hold intergovernmental conferences on environmental matters, with formal and informal participation. In terms of catalyzing environmental action and creating a worldwide awareness of the danger of environmental degradation, the UNCHE has succeeded greatly.

United Nations Conference on Trade and Development (UNCTAD)
A permanent organ of the UN General Assembly established to develop world trade policies. The United Nations Conference on Trade and Development aims to formulate a coordinated set of principles and policies, to be adopted by all member countries, designed to accelerate progress toward self-sustaining growth of the economy in each developing nation. Established in 1964, it attempts to promote international trade with a view to accelerating economic development, providing lower tariff rates for exports to poorer countries, and promoting multilateral trade agreements. UNCTAD reports to the General Assembly annually through the Economic and Social Council (ECOSOC). The conference has 166 members and normally meets every four years; its Trade and Development Board, which is the permanent organ of UNCTAD, meets in a regular session each year. The board has six main committees, open to all members—Commodities, Manufactures, Financing Related to Trade, Shipping, Transfer of Technology, and Economic Cooperation Among Developing Countries—as well as the Special Committee on Trade Preferences. *See also* GENERAL AGREEMENT ON TARIFFS AND TRADE (GATT); NEW INTERNATIONAL ECONOMIC ORDER (NIEO).

Significance   The United Nations Conference on Trade and Development has made continuing efforts toward the realization of the goals of the United Nations Development Decades and the Charter of Economic Rights and Duties of States. It was created when the developing nations became displeased with the existing international trading system and perceived the General Agreement on Tariffs and

Trade as being directed toward the rich nations. The developed nations that resisted UNCTAD's creation as an overlap of GATT's role were consistently outmaneuvered by the numerically greater group of Third World nations. However, after 26 years of its existence, UNCTAD reports note that the growth in gross domestic product (GDP) in most of Africa and Asia remains lower than the population growth, while in Latin America the rate of growth in GDP per capita declined in 1987, 1988, and 1989.

United Nations Day   The commemoration of the anniversary of the founding of the United Nations on October 24, 1945, when the necessary number of ratification documents were received and the United Nations was officially and legally "created." UN Day has been celebrated since 1948, following the drafting by the Big Five powers (China, France, the United Kingdom, the United States, and the Soviet Union) and a majority of states-signatories. On October 31, 1947, the General Assembly decided that October 24 should thenceforth be officially called "United Nations Day." The charter spells out the purpose and principles of the organization, along with the institutional arrangements and procedures to be employed in achieving them. The primary purpose of the United Nations is to maintain peace, advance socioeconomic cooperation, and promote respect for human rights. The United Nations is based on the sovereign equality of all its member countries, which undertake to (1) fulfill in good faith their charter obligations and (2) settle their international disputes by peaceful means and without endangering peace and security. Member nations celebrate UN Day with special programs, and national leaders urge organizations such as national UN associations to commemorate it with emphasis on peace and human welfare. *See also* CHARTER OF THE UNITED NATIONS.

Significance   More than four decades have passed since the first UN Day was celebrated to remind the world that the charter has a difficult mandate entrusted to it. After the suffering and devastation caused by World War II, the most difficult task was to rebuild a world in which peoples live and develop in peace. Thus it was, and still is, necessary for people to reaffirm a faith in a peaceful future, to cut through the atmosphere of distrust and hostility, and to learn to coexist despite differences among nations. The United Nations is still in its infancy, but immense progress has already been achieved. The United Nations has kept many crises from turning into conflicts. It has silenced the guns in many disputes that were brought before it. The United Nations has provided a channel of communication and a forum for East and West and North and South during the worst periods of the cold war and hostility among nations. It has awakened the conscience of humanity and helped more than 100 nations to achieve independence. It is therefore fitting that the leaders of the world, and all people of goodwill, join their hearts on UN Day to remeber the great step taken in 1945 when the world organization was born.

United Nations Development Program (UNDP)   The world's largest organization in the field of multilateral technical assistance. The Development Program is intended to help the poorer countries of the world increase their wealth and to provide them with adequate care for their people through programs of education, housing, employment, and health care. Part of the UN Secretariat, the UNDP is the central coordinating organization of the United Nations for development activities. It has its headquarters in New York and local field offices in over 115 countries. The establishment of the program dates back to 1965, when the General Assembly merged two UN bodies—the Expanded Program of Technical Assistance, set up in 1949, and the Special Fund, which had been set up in 1958 to provide preinvestment assistance. The amalgamation of the two in the UNDP gave some assurance that both programs would operate under a single operating framework. The UNDP is financed by voluntary contributions from governments. It has undertaken over 5,000 projects in 170 countries and dependent territories. *See also* INTERNA-TIONAL BANK FOR RECONSTRUCTION AND DEVELOPMENT (IBRD); INTERNATIONAL DEVELOPMENT ASSOCIATION (IDA); INTERNATIONAL MONETARY FUND (IMF).

Significance   The United Nations Development Program is a coordinating mechanism for the various UN organs and affiliates engaged in strengthening skills and human resources needed by the Third World. It seeks to develop in those countries a reliable inventory of natural and economic resources, a skilled work force, and an effective management apparatus. UNDP projects cover virtually the entire economic and social spectrum of nations and peoples. The process of programming in the UNDP invokes a meeting of minds among donors and recipients, technical experts, and generalists. Although project approval may be an international decision, getting projects into operation and ensuring their maximum effectiveness have been difficult. The controversial climate of national and international politics, inadequate financial support, overlapping administrations, longstanding traditions and taboos, all create resistance to modernization in many developing nations.

United Nations Disarmament Commission (UNDC)   An arena of the United Nations to promote consideration of arms control and disarmament. The United Nations Disarmament Commission is convened in full session on rare occasions; it has been called into plenary session on two occasions—in 1960 and 1965. It was founded in 1952 from the merging of two previous commissions on atomic energy and conventional armaments. The UNDC includes all members of the United Nations, and it has been meeting at UN headquarters in New York, usually in May and June of each year. The commission operates under its own rules and procedures and reports to the UN General Assembly. The UNDC accomplished little until 1954, when a five-nation subcommittee (the United States, the Soviet Union, Canada, the United Kingdom, and France) was formed. From 1965 to 1978 the commission remained dormant but was revived following the most recent United Nations Special Session on Disarmament in 1979. *See also* ARMS CONTROL AND DISARMAMENT.

Significance   The United Nations Disarmament Commission is a deliberative, rather than negotiating, body and was formed to give Third World nations an opportunity to put themselves on record regarding arms control and disarmament issues. It functions primarily as a forum for world public opinion, in order to influence the policies of the six known nuclear powers: China, France, India, the United Kingdom, the Soviet Union, and the United States. The UNDC has been controlled by Third World countries, which have focused most of their attention on comprehensive disarmament strategies and programs. Critics can point to many shortcomings of the UNDC, but it has accomplished much that remains unpublicized. Like the United Nations itself, the UNDC is a meeting place where the ideas and concerns of the entire political world can be expressed and considered.

United Nations Economic and Social Council (ECOSOC)   One of the six principal organs of the United Nations, responsible for serving as a central forum for the discussion of economic and social issues of a global or interdisciplinary nature as well as the formulation of policy recommendations. The UN Economic and Social Council carries on worldwide functions aimed at improving the welfare of the peoples of the world. Other main intentions and powers of ECOSOC are: (1) to initiate or undertake studies and reports, including recommendations, on international economic, social, cultural, educational, health, and related matters; (2) to promote respect for, and observance of, human rights and fundamental freedoms for all; (3) to call international conferences and prepare draft conventions for submission to the UN General Assembly on matters falling within its competence; (4) to negotiate agreements with the specialized agencies defining their relationship with the United Nations; (5) to coordinate the activities of the specialized agencies by means of consultations with and recommendations to them, and by means of recommendations to the General Assembly and the Members of the United Nations; (6) to perform services, approved by the General Assembly, for Members of the United Nations and, upon request, for the specialized agencies; and (7) to consult with nongovernmental organizations concerned with mutual concerns. *See also* UNITED NATIONS (UN); UNITED NATIONS: COMMITTEES.

Significance   The Economic and Social Council was established by the UN Charter as the principal organ to coordinate the economic and social work of the United Nations and the specialized agencies— known as the "United Nations family of organizations." Although accorded the status of principal organ, the ECOSOC functions under the authority of the General Assembly. In many respects its activities resemble those of other main committees of the General Assembly, even though ECOSOC is a large body and has 54 members. As an umbrella organization ECOSOC loosely oversees the activities of the UN specialized agencies and funds such as the United Nations Development Program (UNDP), United Nations Children's Fund (UNICEF), and the United Nations High Commission for Refugees (UNHCR). While ECOSOC has succeeded in developing these areas, "the failure of so many of ECOSOC's debates to materialize into effective action programs has produced a mounting frustration among the developing nations, aggravated by present rivalries and deep-rooted antagonisms of the past."[43]

United Nations Educational, Scientific and Cultural Organization (UNESCO)   A specialized agency of the United Nations that promotes collaboration among nations through education, science, culture, and communication in order to further a respect for justice, for the rule of law, and for fundamental freedoms. To realize these aims, the United Nations Educational, Scientific and Cultural Organization encourages the expansion of educational opportunities so as to enable the people of each country to participate more effectively in their own development; helps in establishing the scientific and technological foundations through which each country can make better use of its resources; and emphasizes the importance of preservation of national cultural values and heritage so that the maximum advantage can be derived from modernization without a loss of cultural identity and diversity. It develops communication channels for a free flow and a wider and better-balanced dissemination of information and promotes the social sciences as instruments for the realization of human rights, justice, and peace. Formed in 1946, UNESCO now has 156 members. See also SPECIALIZED AGENCIES OF THE UNITED NATIONS.

Significance   The United Nations Educational, Scientific and Cultural Organization was created on the premise that ignorance of each other's ways and lives causes suspicion and mistrust among peoples, often leading to war. According to the philosophy underlying UNESCO's activities, to prevent wars there must be a wide diffusion of cultural understanding and an emphasis on the necessity for the education of all humanity in the search for justice, liberty, and peace. In the natural sciences, UNESCO's programs include man and the biosphere; in the social sciences, it has produced studies on such subjects as tension leading to war, racism, the socioeconomic factors of development, and the relationship between man and his environment; and in communications, UNESCO surveys needs and assists developing countries through its International Program for the Development of Communication. The United States withdrew from UNESCO in 1984 after complaining that the organization limits press freedom and shows bias against Israel. The United Kingdom also withdrew from it on similar grounds. Despite promises of program reforms by UNESCO, the United States and the United Kingdom refuse to rejoin it—a decision sharply attacked by a growing number of U.S. congress members and other political leaders who advocate American and British reentry.

United Nations Environment Program (UNEP)   A program that provides machinery for international cooperation in matters relating to the human environment and promotes joint efforts toward preventing pollution of air and water and toward making wider and more careful uses of natural resources. The United Nations Environment Program assists governments and other bodies to promote a better human environment through development and management of human settlements and improved technology. As a result of the United Nations Conference on the Human Environment, or Stockholm Conference, held in 1972, which alerted nations to the emerging environmental crisis and challenged them to do something about it, the UN General Assembly established the United Nations Environment Program immediately. The aims of the organization, which is based in Nairobi, Kenya, are to facilitate international cooperation in the environmental field and to further international knowledge in this area, to keep the global environment under review, and to bring emerging environmental problems of international magnitude to the attention of governments. The basic policy guidelines concerning the development and coordination of environmental activities within the UN system are adopted by the Governing Council, composed of representatives from 58 countries.

Significance   The United Nations Environment Program has contributed substantially toward focusing world concern on growing dangers to the environment. The reason a program for environmental protection was founded stems from the lack of concern on the part of the globe's inhabitants for degradation of natural resources and existing environments. When many negative environmental incidents occur, sometimes liability and responsibility become displaced. It would be premature to expect a substantial across-the-board reduction in the volume of pollutants entering the environment. Yet, the events that rivet the world's attention generally are man-made disasters; often these have dreadful environmental consequences. As Eastern Europe opens up to outside scrutiny, the extent of environmental devastation from unconstrained industrial development becomes increasingly obvious.

United Nations Fund for Drug Abuse Control (UNFDAC)   A trust fund that acts as an international funding agency, planner, coordinator, and evaluator of projects to control drug abuse. The United Nations Fund for Drug Abuse Control supports activities in education and information; treatment and rehabilitation; crop replacement/agricultural development; research; and drug-law enforcement. The projects are executed by the government concerned, other UN agencies, other international organizations, and nongovernmental organizations. The UNFDAC was established in 1971 by the UN secretary-general to assist countries in complying with their obligations under international drug control treaties. It assists them by designing and implementing programs to combat production, trafficking, and use of illicit drugs. Headquartered in Vienna, Austria, the UNFDAC has been joined by 90 countries. Projects supported by the agency are concentrated in the Third World countries faced with illicit cultivation, trafficking, or abuse of narcotic drugs. The fund is financed entirely by voluntary contributions. The International Narcotics Control Board, which began operating in 1968, is responsible for the continuous evolution of strategy for governmental implementation of drug control treaties. *See also* INTERNATIONAL NARCOTICS CONTROL BOARD (INCB).

Significance   The control of drugs has been of global concern ever since the first international conference on the subject was held in Shanghai, China, in 1909. The international control system has been built up step-by-step, beginning in 1920 under the auspices of the League of Nations, and since 1946 by the United Nations. A series of treaties adopted under the auspices of the United Nations require that governments exercise control over the production and distribution of narcotic drugs and psychotropic substances. These treaties are a watershed in advancing international cooperation among law enforcement officials and legal and judicial officers aimed at curbing drug trafficking. Based on the premise that both the demand and the supply of drugs have to be addressed if the problem is to be mitigated, the UNFDAC in 1989 alone invested a budget of $62.5 million in 152 projects in 49 countries: 33 percent for reducing demand, 33 percent for reducing supply, 25 percent for controlling the distribution of narcotics and psychotropic drugs produced for medical and scientific purposes, and 9 percent for other expenses. The agency continues its leadership role in administering the fund, which remains the key multilateral tool in the global struggle against drug problems.

United Nations Fund for Population Activities (UNFPA)   A subsidiary organ by which the UN General Assembly provides additional resources to the UN system for technical cooperation activities in the population field. The Fund for Population Activities promotes understanding of population factors, assists governments in developing population goals and programs, and provides financial assistance to implement them. The United Nations has been concerned with population problems since 1946, when the Population Commission of the Economic and Social Council (ECOSOC) was established with a view to improving demographic statistics. Global population, at 5.3 billion in 1990, will grow by 90 million to 100 million people per year. By the year 2000 the world will have added a billion people—the equivalent of another China. The largest increases will be in the poorest countries, which by definition are the least capable of meeting the immediate needs of their citizens. Virtually all of the population growth—94 percent—is taking place in the Third World countries of Africa, Asia, and Latin America. According to a UN prediction, world population is predicted to exceed 10 billion soon after the dawn of the twenty-first century.

Significance   The United Nations Fund for Population Activities plays a positive role by strengthening voluntarism in the population program. It has supported modern contraceptive production to improve the typically low quality of contraceptives manufactured in the Third World. One of the major issues confronting the United Nations in its efforts to control population is that of abortion. The fund has made considerable progress toward focusing international attention on the different aspects of population control and encouraging efforts to that effect. It has financed projects in more than 125 countries and territories. The population problem continues to take the form of a race between the threat of disastrous population pressures on scarce resources and the rate at which food production can be expanded.

United Nations General Assembly   One of the six principal organs of the United Nations, in which all members are represented. The General Assembly is the plenary organ of the United Nations; each member has one vote but is entitled to five representatives. Decisions on substantive questions are passed by a majority or by a two-thirds vote if "important questions" are involved. New member states are admitted by the General Assembly on the recommendation of the Security Council; currently, the United Nations has 160 members. Under the UN Charter, the functions and powers of the General Assembly include the following: to consider and make recommendations on the principles of cooperation in the maintenance of international peace and security; to discuss any question relating to international peace and—except where a situation is currently being discussed by the Security Council—to make final recommendations; to discuss and (with the same exception) make recommendations on any question within the scope of the charter; to initiate studies and make recommendations to promote international law and the realization of human rights; to make recommendations for the peaceful settlement of any threatening situation; to receive and consider reports from other UN bodies; to consider and approve the UN budget; and to elect members of the various organizational arms of the United Nations. *See also* LEAGUE OF NATIONS ASSEMBLY.

Significance   The UN General Assembly is a deliberative body that acts through its recommendation and cannot make decisions that are binding upon its membership. Although the General Assembly has no palpable authority to enforce its decisions, it makes its viewpoints known to the world in one of the following ways: by declaration, resolution, or convention (treaty). The General Assembly is the central focus of the manifold activities of the United Nations. It has settled many disputes, helped to restore peace in many parts of the world, adopted the Uniting for Peace Resolution, helped promote economic growth, developed norms of international conduct, and worked to protect human rights. The influx of new members from Asia and Africa into the organization has contributed to the expanding role of the General Assembly. As the new nations demand equality, and the organization becomes more amenable to this concern, the concept of one nation–one vote becomes more meaningful on the General Assembly floor.

United Nations High Commission for Refugees (UNHCR)   An agency that promotes solutions to international refugee problems. The United Nations Commission for Refugees seeks guarantees that refugees will not be sent back to a country where their lives or liberty would be threatened. The Office of the High Commission for Refugees was established by the UN General Assembly to replace the International Refugee Organization. Originally set up for a three-year period, the UNHCR has had its mandate renewed for five-year periods since 1954. Based in Geneva, the agency has over 70 field officers with responsibility for providing assistance to more than 12 million refugees. It has a regular staff of 1,100, of whom more than 700 are in the field. The program is carried out under the directives of the General Assembly and the Economic and Social Council (ECOSOC). Part of the administrative costs of the UNHCR are covered by the regular UN budget; its programs are financed through voluntary contributions. *See also* UNITED NATIONS: REFUGEE PROGRAMS.

Significance   The United Nations High Commission for Refugees frequently plays the role of a catalyst, coordinator, and initiator in programs supported largely by individual governments. But it continually faces ambivalent world attitudes toward refugees. In the face of these uncertain responses, the United Nations has developed several strategies. Recognizing that many refugees seek entry to countries already impoverished and unable to provide sufficiently for their own population, the General Assembly passed a resolution in 1989 stressing the need to link aid to refugees to general development strategies. It is also working to develop an early-warning system, designed to predict when a large group of people may migrate into a country; thereby the UNHCR may be better prepared to handle such migrations. The efforts of the UNHCR have met with a high degree of success. It has, in the view of those who have studied the situation, been particularly successful in making the best use of funds available to it for refugee work. As a humanitarian organ of the United Nations, the UNHCR has been notably involved in worldwide social service programs. Quite appropriately, the UNHCR was twice awarded the Nobel Peace Prize, in 1954 and 1981.

United Nations Industrial Development Organization (UNIDO) The newest of the 16 specialized agencies of the United Nations, UNIDO was created to promote and accelerate the industrialization of the developing countries, with particular emphasis on the manufacturing sector. The United Nations Industrial Development Organization began as an organ of the General Assembly in 1966 as an action-oriented body, replacing the Center for Industrial Development, which had been operating within the UN Secretariat since 1961. UNIDO's conversion to the status of a specialized agency, proposed by the Second General Conference of UNIDO (Lima, Peru, 1975), was made effective in 1979. Based in Vienna, Austria, UNIDO promotes industrial development through operational activities involving direct assistance at the field level and supports activities in the form of studies, seminars, expert-group meetings, and training programs. The principal organs of UNIDO are the General Conference, which determines the guiding principles, approves the budget, and adopts conventions and agreements; the 53-member Industrial Development Board, which reviews conference-approved programs; and the 27-member Program and Budget Committee. The General Conference, composed of one representative from each country, normally meets once every two years to formulate overall policies. *See also* UNITED NATIONS CONFERENCE ON TRADE AND DEVELOPMENT (UNCTAD); UNITED NATIONS: TECHNICAL COOPERATION FOR DEVELOPMENT.

Significance   The United Nations Industrial Development Organization is the UN system's central coordination body for industrial development. Its main activity is to apply continual pressure on the industrial states to provide greater help to Third World countries in their modernization efforts. Activities cover macroeconomic and microeconomic aspects of industrial development. At the macroeconomic level, questions are considered concerning the formulation of industrial development policies, application of modern methods of production, and programming and planning. At the microeconomic level, assistance is provided with regard to problems of technical and economic feasibility, external management, and marketing. UNIDO also evaluates industrialization strategies, policies, and trends at the country, regional, global, and sectoral levels; and through its system of communications, it develops approaches to solving problems of international industrialization. Special advisers are stationed in developing countries to coordinate all technical assistance dealing with industrialization.

United Nations Institute for Training and Research (UNITAR)
An agency of the United Nations established by the General Assembly to train individuals for work in economic and social development, particularly for technical assistance programs. The United Nations Institute for Training and Research devotes particular attention to the needs of developing countries and provides training in international cooperation, international law and international negotiation, and multilateral diplomacy for delegates to the United Nations. Established in 1963 as an autonomous body within the UN system, the institute carries out training and research programs, with increasing emphasis being placed on further studies. The training program is also intended for members of permanent missions to the United Nations and other diplomats, staff members of the specialized agencies, and national officials of developing countries. With headquarters in New York, training programs are conducted at the U.N. headquarters (New York), in Geneva, and in the field. The institute works under the overall policy direction of a board of trustees and is headed by an executive director. The board consists of up to 30 members who are appointed by the UN secretary-general for a three-year term. *See also* UNITED NATIONS DEVELOPMENT PROGRAM (UNDP); UNITED NATIONS INDUSTRIAL DEVELOPMENT ORGANIZATION (UNIDO).

Significance   The United Nations Institute for Training and Research has trained thousands of diplomats and staff members of many permanent missions to the United Nations and delegates to the UN General Assembly. Its training programs deal with subjects of practical value to members of permanent missions and other trainees. They include orientation courses on the United Nations; courses on international economics; and workshops on the drafting and negotiation of international legal instruments, on dispute settlements, and on UN documentation. One of its programs involves special training for young people from the Third World in preparation for careers as foreign service officers or UN Secretariat officials. UNITAR researchers ways to improve the quality of training and promotes technical cooperation among developing nations in the field of training. Current research priorities include research on the United Nations itself and on issues of concern to it, includeing a major program on "the United Nations by theYear 2000."

United Nations International Court of Justice (ICJ)   The principal judicial organ of the United Nations. The International Court of Justice is the successor to the Permanent Court of International Justice of the League of Nations. Established in 1945, the ICJ (or the World Court, as it is commonly called) has jurisdiction over all cases referred to it by parties to the Statute of the Court and all matters especially provided for in the Charter of the United Nations or those treaties and conventions in force. Other states can refer cases to it under conditions laid down by the United Nations, which may itself lay a legal matter before the court. The ICJ consists of 15 judges, called "members" of the court. Elected by the United Nations General Assembly and the Security Council, each votes independently for a nine-year term, with the possibility of reelection. They are elected as individuals, regardless of their nationality, but no two can be nationals of the same state. The ICJ has its seat at The Hague in the Netherlands, but it also sits elsewhere. Normally, decisions are made by the full court, with a quorum of nine being sufficient to conduct business. The ICJ has no procedures for enforcement of its decisions. *See also* INTERNATIONAL COMMISSION OF JURISTS; PERMANENT COURT OF ARBITRATION.

Significance   The International Court of Justice represents the highest court of decision in securing the rule of law in the world community, but its decisions have no binding force. The concept of sovereignty remains a potent barrier to adjudication by the court. In theory its authority extends to all international legal disputes, but in reality the ICJ is limited by the reluctance of independent nations to submit to its jurisdiction. These nationalistic attitudes toward international adjudication are also prompted by concern that the ICJ itself is politicized and that its judgments are influenced by the national interests of the judges. For example, when the ICJ ordered the release of U.S. diplomats held hostage in Iran, as well as payment of reparations, Iran contested the jurisdiction of the court and ignored its ruling. In another case, *Nicaragua v. USA*, the United States refused to accept the jurisdiction of the ICJ and its decisions. In addition to its jurisdictional role, the court has authority to hand down advisory opinions. Only governments can bring cases before the court; international organizations cannot file cases, but they can seek advisory opinions on legal matters that arise within the scope of their activities.

United Nations Relief and Works Agency for Palestine Refugees in the Near East (UNRWA)   A United Nations organization established to care for Palestinian refugees. The United Nations Relief and

Works Agency for Palestine Refugees in the Near East was set up in 1949 to help the refugees who left their homes and livelihood as a result of the Arab-Israeli conflict in Palestine in 1948, pending the settlement of the dispute. The 1948 Arab-Palestinian-Israeli war created nearly three-quarters of a million refugees out of the 1.3 million Arabs who lived in Palestine. Today, the agency extends a wide range of welfare services to over 2.1 million designated refugees in the Middle East. It provides education for 350,000 Palestinian students in Jordan, Lebanon, Syria, and the Israeli-occupied territories of the West Bank and the Gaza Strip. Under the professional guidance of the World Health Organization (WHO), the UNRWA provides medical services to over 1.7 million eligible refugees. It also supplies shelter materials, emergency medical supplies, and food relief for more than 108,000 Palestinians considered to be special hardship cases. Since the Israeli invasion of Lebanon in 1982, the UNRWA has mounted a series of emergency operations to assist refugees (and sometimes nonrefugees) who have suffered death, injury, destruction of their homes, or dislocation. The agency's operations for 1989 were budgeted at $227.4 million; the largest contribution came from the United States ($61.3 million). *See also* UNITED NATIONS HIGH COMMISSION FOR REFUGEES (UNHCR); UNITED NATIONS: REFUGEE PROGRAMS.

Significance   The United Nations Relief and Works Agency for Refugees in the Near East has failed to resolve the Palestinian refugee problem by resettlement, repatriation, or other methods of assimilation, largely because the refugees earnestly desire to return to their home, now under Israeli control. Few members of the United Nations perceived in 1949 that the Palestine refugee problem would endure over 42 years—since the creation of Israel in 1949—with still no end in sight. In addition to acknowledging their love for their homeland and their consequent nostalgia, the UNRWA's humanitarian effort came to underline the Palestinian claim to land that is now a part of Israel. Anarchy and violence in Lebanon have imperiled both UNRWA clients and personnel, making the agency's work extremely difficult and dangerous. The Palestinian *intifada* (uprising) in the Israeli-occupied territories and measures taken to quell it have also hampered UNRWA programs and created the need for new efforts, especially in medical, food, and other relief services. Unless there is a solution to the Israeli-Palestinian dispute, the UNRWA's responsibility to help the Palestinians cannot be easily terminated, even though it suffers from the fact, because many nations are weary of making voluntary contributions year after year.

United Nations Secretariat   One of the principal organs of the United Nations, and the office of the secretary-general. The UN Secretariat consists of officials and other civil servants who perform administrative, budgetary, secretarial, linguistic, staff, and housekeeping functions for the other principal programs of the United Nations. More than 25,000 persons, from over 150 countries, work at the U.N. headquarters in New York and in other UN offices around the world. These international civil servants are expected to perform their duties in a professional and objective manner. Under Article 100 of the UN Charter, each member state undertakes to respect the exclusively international character of the responsibilities of the secretary-general and the staff and not seek to influence them in the discharge of their duties. To achieve high levels of competence and a fair geographical balance, the secretariat recruits staff members from all over the world. *See also* UNITED NATIONS SECRETARY-GENERAL.

Significance   The Secretariat of the United Nations has always found it difficult to implement the recruitment policy that its staff be truly international and independent. Many members of the secretariat are either on loan from member states or are former national civil servants, and in a national civil service it is taken for granted that its members promote the national interest. It would be incongruous to expect a staff associate to give up his private opinion or national predisposition, but he is asked to subordinate those to the interests of the United Nations. The function of the secretariat is as varied as the list of problems dealt with by the United Nations. It includes informal and formal mediation to resolve international disputes and the administration of peacekeeping operations. The secretariat staff is also engaged in conducting surveys of world economic and social trends and problems, studies of specific situations in human rights, and a multitude of other issues of concern to the people of the world.

United Nations Secretary-General   The chief administrative officer of the United Nations, who heads the secretariat. The secretary-general is chosen by the General Assembly upon the recommendation of the Security Council. Under Article 99 of the UN Charter, he is empowered to introduce situations relating to peace and security before the Security Council. The secretary-general also sits in on meetings of the General Assembly and Security Council to give advice when asked. Some of his responsibilities are the preparation of an agenda for major organs, compiling a budget and expending fund, initiating new plans and programs, and supervising day-to-day operations of the secretariat. At the first session of the United Nations in

1946, the General Assembly chose Trygve Lie of Norway as secretary-general for a term of five years. Since then, Dag Hammarskjöld of Sweden, U Thant of Burma, and Kurt Waldheim of Austria have served as secretary-general. Javier Pérez de Cuéllar of Peru is now serving his second five-year term as secretary-general; his term was due to expire in December, 1991. *See also* LEAGUE OF NATIONS SECRETARY-GENERAL.

Significance   The secretary-general of the United Nations influences the functioning of the organization to a degree that is not clearly indicated in its charter. This influence derives from his directorship of a secretariat staffed with international civil servants and experts who take an oath of loyalty to the United Nations and are not permitted to receive instructions from member nations. Therefore, the secretary-general is presiding over a strongly supranational bureaucracy. Lie, the first secretary-general, conforming to this concept, followed a pragmatic approach. Hammarskjöld, the second secretary-general, expressed firm views about the way the organization should operate and his personal role within it. U Thant and Waldheim—the third and fourth secretaries-general respectively—conceived of their office as primarily concerned with administrative duties. Pérez de Cuéllar follows his own personal instinct to play an active and public role.

United Nations Security Council   One of the six principal organs of the United Nations, primarily responsible for maintaining international peace and world security. The Security Council is composed of five permanent members—China, France, the Soviet Union, the United Kingdom, and the United States—and ten nonpermanent members, with five elected each year by the General Assembly for two-year terms and not eligible for immediate reelection. The number of nonpermanent members was increased from six to ten by an amendment to the charter that became effective in 1965. According to an agreement or general understanding concerning the nonpermanent seats, Asia and Africa have five, Eastern Europe one, Latin America two, and Western Europe two. Any nation that is not a member of the Security Council may be invited to participate in the council deliberation if it is party to a dispute under consideration. A member directly involved in a dispute must abstain from voting when questions concerning peaceful settlement procedures or terms are brought to vote. Voting decisions in the Security Council are made by a vote of any nine members of the council on procedural matters; but on substantive questions, the nine or more votes cannot adopt the measure if one of the permanent members casts a negative vote, i.e., a veto. *See also* LEAGUE OF NATIONS COUNCIL.

Significance   While other organs of the United Nations may make recommendations to member states, the Security Council alone is invested with the authority to make decisions that all members are obliged to carry out. The Security Council acts upon the principle that the Big Five—the permanent members—are primarily responsible for peace and security, but allows their functions to be shared with the nonpermanent members of the council. Because it is primarily an organ of emergency, the council (as is required by Article 28) is so organized as to ensure an ongoing operation. The assumption underlying the Security Council's voting system is that the great powers will develop unanimity on issues being considered, but that each of the permanent members possesses a veto; therefore, no great power can use the organization against another great power's interests. There have been times when the Security Council has dealt with disputes successfully and thus helped to stop armed conflicts in many parts of the world, but when great power interests among its members have collided, the council has been paralyzed. Since 1950 and the adoption of the Uniting for Peace Resolution, the General Assembly has been empowered to take jurisdiction over a security issue if a veto is used to block action in the Security Council. In 1990, for the first time, the Security Council voted unanimously to levy economic sanctions on an aggressor—Iraq. This action has led supporters of the United Nations' peacekeeping system to develop new hope that the organization will be able to continue to function in a way that the founding fathers of the United Nations had planned.

United Nations Trusteeship Council   A principal organ of the United Nations assigned the task of supervising the administration of trust territories placed under a trusteeship system. The Trusteeship Council oversees the operation of the system in accordance with the principles of the United Nations Charter; it was designed to provide international supervision for 11 non-self-governing territories formerly colonies of Germany, Turkey, and Italy, to be administered by 7 UN member states. By 1990, 10 of the 11 trust territories had been granted independence or were united with a neighboring country on the basis of a United Nations-supervised plebiscite. The Trusteeship Council acts under the authority of the UN General Assembly or, in the case of a "strategic area," under the authority of the Security Council. As the number of administering countries has decreased, so too has the size of the Trusteeship Council, now consisting only of the five permanent members of the Security Council (China, France, the United Kingdom, the Soviet Union, and the United States), which serve as the administering states. Article 85 of the charter states: "The functions of the United Nations with regard to trusteeship agreements for all areas not designated as strategic, including the approval of the terms of the trusteeship agreements and of their alteration or amendment, shall be exercised by the General Assembly." Voting in the Trusteeship Council is by simple majority; each member has one vote. *See also* MANDATES SYSTEM OF THE LEAGUE OF NATIONS.

Significance   Trusteeship is a method of governing territories that have been taken from a defeated enemy state but are not considered ready for immediate independence. The trusteeship system was established in 1946 by the United Nations to replace the former League of Nations mandates system. The aims of the trusteeship system have been fulfilled to the extent that only one of the original 11 territories remains in the system—the Trust Territory of the Pacific Islands (Micronesia), a *strategic* territory administered by the United States under an agreement by the Security Council in 1947. It has been the only trust territory to which the Security Council veto has applied, this because of its strategic nature involving military bases and nuclear testing, and because the United States liberated these islands from Japanese rule during World War II at heavy cost in casualties. However, the Trusteeship Council has been able to fulfill the major goals of the system in promoting the advancement and ultimate independence of the trust territories. The Trusteeship Council is the only principal organ of the United Nations whose success has eliminated the need for it. Perhaps it can be converted into an environmental council.

United Nations University (UNU)   A Japanese-based autonomous academic institution with a worldwide network of associated institutions, research units, individual scholars, and fellows. Like a traditional university, the United Nations University is concerned with the creation and transfer of knowledge and the critique of that knowledge. Established in 1973 with the issuance of its charter by the General Assembly, UNU began operations in 1975. The university's program, composed of three divisions—development studies, regional and global studies, and the global learning division—has initiated research into the roots of peace and violence, poverty, more integrated theories of development, and the dynamics of rapid social change. UNU's priority areas of concern under its Second Medium-Term Perspective for 1990–1995 are (a) universal values and global responsibilities, (b) new directions in the world economy, (c) sustaining global life-support systems, (d) advances in science and technology, and (e) population dynamics and human welfare. It has activities in 60 countries and aims to strengthen research and training capabilities in Third World countries. *See also* UNITED NATIONS EDUCATIONAL, SCIENTIFIC AND CULTURAL ORGANIZATION (UNESCO).

Significance   The United Nations University, with autonomy in the UN system, is an international community of scholars brought together in a global network. As an academic arm of the United Nations, UNU has become a geographically dispersed network of international centers for research and training. It has no students of its own, no faculty, and no campus, but it provides fellowships for postgraduate training in the university's network. The fellows are selected from among scholars and policymakers in institutions, governments, the private sector, and voluntary organizations. UNU does not receive any subvention from the United Nations' regular budget; its basic income is derived from an endowment fund toward which member states of the United Nations make voluntary contributions.

Uniting for Peace Resolution   An assumption of responsibility by the UN General Assembly for peace and security problems. Under the Uniting for Peace Resolution, adopted by the General Assembly in 1950, the assembly may take action if the Security Council, because of a lack of unanimity of its permanent members, fails to act against an aggressor. During the Korean War (1950–1953) the United States, the United Kingdom, and France led the drive, in the face of Security Council impotence, to have the General Assembly recommend collective security measures in Korea. Other provisions of the resolution called for summoning the General Assembly into "emergency session" within twenty-four hours in a peace and security crisis and establishing a Peace Observation Commission and a Collective Measures Committee to aid the assembly in such situations. The resolution was adopted over the objection of the Soviet Union and other communist states; they maintained that the UN Charter, according to Article 11, prohibited any organ other than the Security Council from calling for collective security action. It was pointed out that the Security Council alone was named in Chapter VII to determine the occasions and the measures of UN enforcement action. This assembly backup role was used in several cases, including the Suez crisis in 1956, when Britain, France, and Israel attacked Egypt. The General Assembly acted in that crisis under the procedures set forth in the Uniting for Peace Resolution by setting up the UN Emergency Force. *See also* CHARTER OF THE UNITED NATIONS; UNITED NATIONS GENERAL ASSEMBLY; UNITED NATIONS SECURITY COUNCIL.

Significance   The main defect of the Uniting for Peace Resolution lies in the fact that the recommendations of the General Assembly are not legally binding upon members of the United Nations. Politically the resolution was a lever to be used by the Western nations to contain communist expansion in Korea. The Soviet Union strenuously denied the legality of the Uniting for Peace Resolution. Even the International Court of Justice (ICJ) described it as based upon a "courageous" interpretation of the charter. The supporters of the resolution maintain that in fact it does little more than spell out a role for the General Assembly that, if not obviously implicit within the terms of the charter, is at least not excluded. The General Assembly's competence is further justified by referencing Article 10's broad proviso, which authorizes it to discuss and make recommendations directly to members of the United Nations, as well as to the Security Council, concerning "any" matters—including collective security measures. In the early days of the United Nations, the Soviet Union was criticized as being obstructionist for suggesting that peace resolutions were devised by the Western nations in order to bypass the Security Council.

Universal Declaration of Human Rights   A proclamation by the UN General Assembly intended to establish a "common standard of achievement for all peoples and all nations" in the observance of civil, political, economic, social, and cultural rights. Prepared by the Commission on Human Rights and the Economic and Social Council (ECOSOC), the Universal Declaration of Human Rights was approved by the General Assembly on December 10, 1948, by a vote of 48 to 0, with 8 abstentions (6 East European members, Saudi Arabia, and South Africa). Articles 1 and 2 of the declaration state that "all human beings are born free and equal in dignity and rights"; Articles 3 to 21 set forth the civil and political rights to which all human beings are entitled; Articles 22 to 27 set forth the economic, social, and cultural rights; and Articles 28 to 30 recognize that everyone is entitled to a social and international order in which these rights and freedoms are fully realized. See also UNITED NATIONS: HUMAN RIGHTS.

Significance   One of the first major achievements of the United Nations was adoption of the Universal Declaration of Human Rights. The UN declaration is not a legally binding agreement, but rather was designed to serve as a model for more specific future codification efforts. So in 1954 the General Assembly began work on two draft covenants—one containing civil and political, the other economic, social, and cultural rights—to implement the concepts contained in the Universal Declaration of Human Rights. At first glance, it may seem that the protection of human rights is strictly a domestic issue. Whether this is true or not, violations of human rights within a country become an international problem when they trigger an influx of refugees seeking asylum in foreign countries. The UN General Assembly each year adopts a number of resolutions dealing with some aspect of human rights, broadly defined. Many deal with political, economic, and social conditions in general terms, but some are addressed to particular violations of those rights. Some critics charge that the Universal Declaration was incomplete because it failed to mention sexual rights, such as the right of freedom of choice regarding abortion and the right of homosexuals to enjoy their life-styles without recrimination.

Universal Postal Union (UPU)   A specialized agency of the United Nations established to secure the organization and improvement of the postal services and to promote the development of technical assistance and international collaboration. The Universal Postal Union's basic activity is to make provisions for the various international postal services carried out by member postal administrations. It was established in 1874 by the Berne Treaty, which was approved by 22 nations at Berne, Switzerland, and came into force in 1875. The UPU became a specialized agency of the United Nations under the terms of an agreement that became effective in 1948. The principal organs of the UPU are the Universal Postal Congress, the Executive Council, the Consultative Council for Postal Studies, and the International Bureau. The work of the UPU involves assisting national postal administrations to speed up mail deliveries, especially in rural areas; enlarging the number of post offices; expanding the use of airmail for international parcel services and to maximize air conveyance in all categories; extending financial services, such as money orders and savings banks, where they do not already exist; and improving staff management. There are 169 UPU member countries. *See also* INTERNATIONAL TELECOMMUNICATION UNION (ITU).

Significance   The Universal Postal Union has made it possible to send mail from one state through several others to yet another by simply using stamps from the sender's country. Before this system, a letter with a foreign destination required special handling and the payment of postage to each country through which it passed. This illustrates the need for such international technical cooperation. Thus, among the specialized agencies the UPU has, in effect, made decisions binding on national governments, for no country has been willing to incur the consequence of exclusion from the union for failure to carry out the prescribed regulations, however much it might dislike them. Postal services are considered essential, and quite naturally the UPU, like the International Telecommunication Union, has a comprehensive membership that includes essentially all countries of the world, regardless of ideology or political systems. The UPU's success has encouraged the creation of additional functional (technical) international organizations.

V

Veto A mechanism to block the passage of a resolution at the UN Security Council. A veto, in effect, is a negative vote cast by any permanent member of the Security Council (China, France, the United Kingdom, the Soviet Union, and the United States). Most international organizations operate under the principle of unanimity, which gives each permanent member the authority to veto decisions. *Veto* does not appear in the UN Charter, yet it has come into frequent usage because of the voting procedures involved in making two types of decisions in the Security Council. Article 27 of the charter states that each member of the council has one vote. Decisions on procedural matters are made by an affirmative vote of any 9 of the council's 15 members. But decisions on substantive questions are made by an affirmative vote of 9 members, "including the concurring votes of the permanent members." This sentence has been interpreted to mean that an abstention from voting by a permanent member does not constitute a veto. Thus any of the Big Five can unilaterally defeat any Security Council proposal by voting "no," except for one relating to procedures; however, the charter requires that the party to a dispute, whether a permanent or elective member, must abstain from voting when the council considers pacific settlement procedures. *See also* CHARTER OF THE UNITED NATIONS; UNITING FOR PEACE RESOLUTION.

Significance The so-called veto power accorded to the five great powers by the framers of the UN Charter was regarded by them as central to the world organization's important role. Thus, in an action undertaken under Chapter VII of the charter, dealing with a threat to international peace and security or aggression, if the great powers were divided on the issue, without a veto the organization could be used by one group to undertake collective action against another group. This would not be collective security; it would be a major war. The evolution of the veto in the Security Council constitutes an important

246

step in the charter's progress toward multinationalization of the special role of big powers in international organizations, going beyond the limited attribution of unequal weight to the major powers accorded in the Covenant of the League of Nations. The use of the veto power has declined in recent years as the permanent members of the Security Council have recognized that failure to sanction a measure in the council merely transfers the issue to the General Assembly under the Uniting for Peace Resolution. Its decline is further evidenced in the recent Persian Gulf crisis over Iraq's annexation of Kuwait—the Security Council passed a dozen resolutions without any veto by the great powers.

Vietnam War   A civil war between North and South Vietnam, which escalated to involve interested foreign powers—France, the United States, and the United Kingdom in support of the South, and China and the Soviet Union for the North. The Vietnam War had its origin in French Indochina, which the Japanese occupied during World War II. With Japan's defeat in the war, a radical group under the leadership of Ho Chi Minh proclaimed Vietnam's independence in 1945. The French returned soon, initiating a war that lasted until its defeat in 1954. This resulted in the division of Vietnam into northern and southern political entities. Ho Chi Minh pressed for Vietnam's reunification. The United States, which began its involvement with a 35-member U.S. military assistance advisory group in 1950, undertook air strikes against North Vietnam in 1964 and inserted U.S. combat troops into the conflict a year later. By 1969, U.S. forces in Vietnam totaled over half a million men. Finally, in 1973 President Richard Nixon ordered the withdrawal of U.S. troops. In 1975 the North Vietnamese began an offensive in South Vietnam that led to the collapse of the regime in the South and reunification of Vietnam in 1976. *See also* AFGHAN CIVIL WAR.

Significance   Even today Americans often react to the word "Vietnam" with mixed feelings of failure and frustration. For 25 years, the United States attempted to create a viable noncommunist state in the Southeast Asian nation. But this effort achieved less than the desired results, ending ignominiously with the collapse of the South Vietnamese state. More than a million Vietnamese—both Southerners and Northerners—were killed, along with almost 58,000 Americans. The war in Vietnam cost the United States nearly $150 billion. Both sectors of Vietnam were devastated, and the Americans suffered their gravest defeat in history. Military and political leaders held that the war was essential to block communist expansion in Southeast

Asia, and that if it was not blocked, a "domino effect" would result in which country after country would fall to communism in the future. Later events refuted this theory. The lessons of Vietnam proved the inefficiency of trying to fight a massive land war in Asia and demonstrated that it is impossible to successfully wage a war when the will to resist on the part of the people being defended is not forthcoming. The Vietnam War also demonstrated that a determined combatant, imbued with revolutionary fervor and strongly supported by its friends, eventually prevails.

W

War   Armed hostility between two or more nations. A state of war exists in the legal sense when official declaration is made by one or more disputants. Social scientists do not agree on any single cause of war. However, a review of the literature on the origins of war by Couloumbis and Wolfe reveals at least seven conditions that have precipitated armed hostilities: human aggression, elite and popular fatalism regarding war, small-group conspiracy, economic imperialism, nationalist expansionism and irrendentism, systemic inadequacy, and the general cycles of history.[45] The level of modern warfare may vary, from the use of conventional land, sea, air, and marine forces, to a total confrontation utilizing nuclear, chemical, bacteriological, and radiological weapons of mass destruction. The greatest wars of our time were the two world wars, 1914–1918 and 1939–1945. During World War II the use of weapons of mass destruction forced the Japanese to surrender to the United States, thus ending the prolonged hostility. *See also* WORLD WAR I; WORLD WAR II.

Significance   A war can be fought for many objectives, with all means available for marshaling national powers. Prior to the evolution of the Covenant of the League of Nations (1919), war was a legitimate instrument to which sovereign states were entitled to resort in pursuit of national interests. The covenant did not prohibit war altogether, but the Charter of the United Nations (1945) formulated international law prohibiting not only resort to warfare but also the threat or use of force inconsistent with the purpose of the United Nations. The United Nations was established to maintain world peace through (1) peaceful settlement of disputes, (2) collective security action, and (3) building a world order through disarmament and economic, social, and humanitarian programs. Although a world war has been avoided since the creation of the United Nations, many local and regional wars have occurred in various parts of the globe.

War Crimes   Violations of the laws and rules of war. War crimes are violations of the laws of war by persons from vanquished states, as specified in Article 6 of the Charter of the International Military Tribunal of 1945 and reaffirmed by the International Law Commission and the UN General Assembly in the Principle of International Law, recognized in the charter and judgment of the Nuremberg Tribunal (1950). War crimes include, but are not limited to, "murder, ill-treatment or deportation to slave labor or for any other purpose of civilian population of or in occupied territory; murder or ill-treatment of prisoners of war or persons on the seas; killing of hostages; plunder of public or private property; wanton destruction of cities, towns, or villages, or devastation not justified by military necessity." Among other violations qualifying as war crimes are the abuse of a flag of truce or of the Red Cross or similar emblems; wearing civilian clothes or enemy uniform while in combat, poisoning streams or wells; the killing of any enemy who laid down arms; assassination; violation of surrender terms; breach of parole; and wanton destruction of enemy prize. *See also* WAR.

Significance   The legal nature of war crimes has undergone a revolutionary change since World War II. After that war 22 major German war criminals were tried at Nuremberg by the International Military Tribunal, representing France, the United Kingdom, the United States, and the Soviet Union. Charged with crimes against peace, war crimes, and crimes against humanity, 12 defendants were sentenced to death, others received jail sentences, and 3 were acquitted. Under the Charter of the International Military Tribunal for the Far East, major Japanese war criminals were tried in Tokyo on similar charges by judges representing the 11 countries at war with Japan. In 1945 an American military commission in Manila charged Japanese General Yamashita with failure to exert proper control over his forces and falling short of the standards of common responsibility established by the laws of war. The commission rendered a guilty verdict and imposed a death sentence. One of the legal arguments advanced against war crimes trials was that they were *ex post facto* — punishing acts that had not been criminal when committed.

Warsaw Treaty Organization (WTO)   A regional military alliance established to ensure joint defense of Eastern Europe. The Warsaw Treaty Organization, signed in 1955, is a military-political structure to counter the North Atlantic Treaty Organization (NATO). The treaty originally had eight signatories: Albania, Bulgaria, Czechoslovakia, the German Democratic Republic (GDR), Hungary, Poland, Romania, and the Soviet Union. (Albania withdrew in 1968, and East Germany's withdrawal was automatic following the reunification of Germany in 1990.) Headquartered in Moscow, the WTO averred that if one member was attacked, the others would take whatever steps were required, including military force. Major decisions were made by the Political Consultative Committee, which met sporadically. The Joint Secretariat resolved policy matters. The key organ was the Joint Armed Forces Command, responsible to the Soviet General Staff and headed by a Soviet marshal. The Soviets had also concluded bilateral status-of-force agreements with Poland, Hungary, and Czechoslovakia that provided for the stationing of Soviet troops in those countries. *See also* NORTH ATLANTIC TREATY ORGANIZATION (NATO); WESTERN EUROPEAN UNION (WEU).

Significance   The Warsaw Treaty Organization, also known as the Warsaw Pact because the agreement was signed in Warsaw, formalized a de facto Soviet hegemony over Eastern Europe. Although the pact might be considered the Eastern European counterpart of NATO, its conclusion was not an immediate riposte to the formulation of NATO in 1949, but rather a response to the rearmament and incorporation of West Germany into the Western system of collective security—that is, into the Western European Union (WEU) and NATO. The recent development of polycentrism in Eastern Europe and the dissatisfaction of WTO member nations with Soviet domination of the alliance corroded its unity. The annual strategic survey of the prestigious British International Institute for Strategic Studies, released on May 24, 1990, expressed doubt whether the crumbling Warsaw Pact "could act as a single organization in warlike circumstances." The East-West Conventional Arms Reduction Agreement of November 19, 1990, concluded in Paris, further eliminated the need for the WTO, and finally the alliance was abolished in 1991.

Washington Naval Treaty (1922)   An agreement by the leading sea powers to limit the size and construction of their capital vessels. The Washington Naval Treaty was a post–World War I effort to limit arms outside the League of Nations framework. In 1921 the Washington Conference, convened by the United States and attended by the United Kingdom, France, Italy, and Japan, set the pace for arms limitation negotiation. A treaty was signed in 1922 that limited capital ships to 35,000 tons for 16-inch guns, and aircraft carriers to 27,000 tons. Construction of vessels in these classes was terminated for ten years, and the United States, Britain, and Japan agreed to scrap a number of older ships. The treaty did not cover submarines, cruisers, and destroyers. Efforts at the Washington Naval Conference of 1921–1922 failed to reach agreement to limit other naval craft. *See also* ARMS CONTROL AND DISARMAMENT.

Significance   The Washington Naval Treaty served as the basis of a ten-year naval "holiday" during which the British Empire, the United States, Japan, France, and Italy limited the expansion of their navies. It was a rare agreement by big powers to an arms control measure as early as 1922. As the producer of a fully-foolproof system of arms control, the Washington Naval Conference was but a qualified success. It brought about not as much effective disarmament as it did stabilization. The mutual decision to scrap planned or incompleted units meant a halt to further capital ships competition. The treaty did not provide for inspection and enforcement, and it was scrapped by the 1930s with the resurgence of German military power. The United Nations has continued the League of Nations' tradition by sponsoring persistent efforts to achieve general disarmament agreements.

West African Economic Community (CEAO)   A regional organization established to promote trade and economic cooperation in western Africa. The West African Economic Community's objectives are to be attained through an economic and customs union for a harmonious and balanced growth in the economies of the member nations. Membership includes the former French colonies of Mali, Mauritania, Niger, Senegal, Burkina Faso, and Cote d'Ivoire. The treaty creating the CEAO was concluded in 1973 by the representatives of the member countries and went into effect in 1974. It replaced the Customs Union of West African States. The institutional structure of the community is based on three main organs: the Conference of Heads of States; the Council of Ministers; and the General Secretariat. A growing role is played by two financial institutions within the community—the Development Fund and the Solidarity and Intervention Fund. The first one aims to provide compensation for certain types of trade losses and financing for economic development projects. The Solidarity and Intervention Fund is responsible for granting loans and subsidies and extending guarantees for feasibility studies and specific projects. *See also* ECONOMIC COMMUNITY OF WEST AFRICAN STATES (ECOWAS).

Significance   The West African Economic Community is a loose form of association as a first step toward eventual integrated economic planning and development. It closely follows the philosophy of the Economic Commission for Africa (ECA), which places special emphasis on a subregional approach to industrialization and on the solution of transport problems. The problem of regional economic cooperation in West Africa is complicated by the existence of French-speaking and English-speaking countries side-by-side, differences in political and administrative experiences, and the presence of two monetary systems (franc and pound sterling). Further, development of the community's activities are often inhibited by factors originating from economic disparities among member nations. However, substantial steps have been taken to increase the volume of intracommunity imports and exports through the abolition of internal taxes on nonmanufactured goods and traditional handicrafts. Several joint projects are under way, such as the creation of a solar energy research institute and a commercial fisheries organization.

Western European Union (WEU)   A defense grouping of the central European core members of the North Atlantic Treaty Organization (NATO). The Western European Union was established in 1955 when West German rearmament was believed to be crucial to the defense of Western Europe. It includes France as a full member and excludes the United States. The current membership includes Belgium, France, Germany, Italy, Luxembourg, the Netherlands, the United Kingdom, Spain, and Portugal. Politically, it acts as a forum for consultation on European foreign policy and subjects of current interest. In military terms, it concentrates on problems of security: defense questions, arms control, disarmament, and developments in East-West relations. The structure of the WEU includes (1) the Council of Foreign Ministers, which may be called into session by any member to consult on threats to the security of Western Europe; (2) an assembly that meets in Strasbourg and consists of delegates of WEU nations to the Council of Europe's Consultative Assembly; and (3) a secretariat. *See also* NORTH ATLANTIC TREATY ORGANIZATION (NATO); WARSAW TREATY ORGANIZATION (WTO).

Significance   The Western European Union functions within the larger NATO framework, serving as an agency to develop common policies. Within this general framework three bilateral defense relationships are crucial. The first is the Anglo-French axis, unique as a partnership of nuclear states. Since 1986 there has been intensified discussion on nuclear collaboration, which may eventually extend to joint procurement of new air-launched cruise missiles already replaced under the 1987 Intermediate-range Nuclear Forces (INF) Treaty between the United States and the Soviet Union. The second is the Franco-German axis. Here the defense relationship, existing within the system of regular summits, led in 1986 to the Treaty on Defense Cooperation. Under the framework of the treaty there have been changes in French nuclear strategy designed to bring territorial Germany under the protection of the French nuclear forces.

World Children's Summit   A meeting of the world's heads of states and governments at the UN headquarters in New York in 1990 to discuss the state of the children. The World Children's Summit was held on September 29–30, 1990, attended by 71 kings, presidents, and prime ministers who designed an action plan for the benefit of the children of the world. The plan identifies specific goals for the nurture and development of children in the next decade: between 1990 and the year 2000, reduction in the mortality rate of children under five years old by one-third or 70 per 1,000 live births, whichever is less; reduction of maternal mortality by half; reduction of severe and moderate malnutrition by half among children under 5 years old; universal access to safe drinking water and to sanitary means of excreta disposal; universal access to basic education and completion of primary education by at least 80 percent of primary school children by the year 2000; reduction of the adult literacy rate to at least half of its 1990 level, with special emphasis on female literacy; and improved protection of children in especially difficult circumstances. Sponsored by the United Nations Children's Fund (UNICEF), the summit's ad hoc planning committee was composed of representatives of the World Health Organization (WHO), the United Nations Educational, Scientific and Cultural Organization (UNESCO), the United Nations Population Fund, the International Bank for Reconstruction and Development (IBRD), the International Labor Organization (ILO), and the United Nations Development Program (UNDP), as well as 25 UN member states. *See also* UNITED NATIONS CHILDREN'S FUND (UNICEF).

Significance   The first World Summit for Children—the largest gathering ever of world leaders—provided a historic forum dedicated to the task of establishing the priorities that the world must now give to the care of its children. This extraordinary meeting is proof of the emergent ethos of a new United Nations—one that is focusing on the qualitative aspects of human development rather than the quantitative indices. These world leaders established the principle of "first call" for children—a commitment to ensure that the essential needs of children be given high priority in the allocation of resources. The cost of implementing the declaration has been estimated at $20 billion a year for the current decade. Despite an apparent multilateral consensus on the need to address the problems of the world's children, some critics caution against inflated expectations. Others maintain that despite the cost, the future of our planet and its children depends on the successful implementation of the dreams and the decisions that were enunciated at this great summit meeting.

World Federation of Trade Unions (WFTU)　An international organization to consolidate and unite trade unions of the world. The World Federation of Trade Unions strengthens the solidarity of the international trade union movement by encouraging systematic exchange of information and experiences in trade union work. It was born at a congress of world labor that convened in Paris in 1945. Representatives at that meeting were spokespersons for almost every labor movement of the world. The only ones absent were the new labor organizations of World War II, those from defeated Germany and Japan, and the American Federation of Labor (AFL), whose leaders had turned down numerous requests to take their place with the other trade union movements. Some of the major goals of the WFTU are (1) to organize and unite the trade unions of the world within its ranks irrespective of nationality, religion, or political opinions; (2) to assist, wherever necessary, workers in countries socially or industrially less developed in setting up their trade unions; and (3) to carry on the struggle for extermination of all fascist forms of government. Headquartered in Paris, the WFTU has members in 76 countries and territories. *See also* WORLD PEACE COUNCIL (WPC).

Significance　The World Federation of Trade Unions is one of the world's great labor movements and thus has a moral responsibility to assist workers everywhere in their efforts to achieve democracy, peace, and security. However, by maintaining close contact with the World Peace Council—a communist-sponsored international organization—the WFTU has created a climate of misunderstanding with some "capitalist" labor unions, such as the American Federation of Labor. At the same time, by playing the communist-capitalist equation, the WFTU has developed a consultative status with the UN Economic and Social Council (ECOSOC), the Food and Agriculture Organization (FAO), the United Nations Educational, Scientific and Cultural Organization (UNESCO), and many other international bodies. With the collapse of communism it is likely that all labor unions, including the WFTU, will move philosophically from the political left to the political right and become more capitalistic. Thus healthy relationships between the WFTU and the AFL, or other labor organizations in the capitalist world, are likely to emerge in the 1990s.

World Federation of United Nations Associations (WFUNA)   An international organization to provide a bridge between the people of the world, their governments, and the United Nations. The World Federation of United Nations Associations acts as a peoples' movement for the United Nations, coordinates and furthers the activities of its members, and promotes the establishment of new UN associations. Founded in 1946 in Luxembourg, the WFUNA's spirit is found in the opening words of the Preamble to the UN Charter: "We the peoples of the United Nations." The WFUNA has its headquarters in Geneva, an office at U.N. headquarters in New York, regional offices in Africa and Asia, and sends representatives to the United Nations Educational, Scientific and Cultural Organization (UNESCO) in Paris. It conducts educational programs, including education for international understanding; the new world information and communication order; the future role of the United Nations; peace; development of human rights; and molding of public opinion. It also identifies ways of making the United Nations and related international organizations work better so that they can fulfill their potential. *See also* UNITED NATIONS.

Significance   Backed by a strong worldwide citizen constituency, the World Federation of United Nations Associations can propose UN reforms, encourage governments to take a more active role, and provide policymakers with the research and public opinion information they need to make wise decisions for the good of all humankind. There are over 70 national WFUNA affiliates in countries of differing ideologies and political and economic systems. It provides links between the East and the West, between the developed and the developing countries. By promoting tolerance, understanding, solidarity, and cooperation among men, women, and children throughout the world without distinction as to race, sex, language, or religion, the federation is doing more to make the United Nations stronger than any of the other international nongovernmental organizations (INGOs). The WFUNA is the only international institution of its kind that promotes the idea that the United Nations is the framework keeping the world's pieces together—a unifying force that encourages international cooperation and dialogue.

World Food Council (WFC)   An organ of the United Nations committed to coping with food crises throughout the world. The World Food Council was established in 1974 by the General Assembly to deal with global food problems. Among major policy initiatives promoted by the council are steps to raise the political priority of food and hunger issues and coordinate assistance. In November 1974, the

World Food Conference was convened in Rome by the General Assembly to address the food crisis. The conference focused attention on the scale and complexity of world food problems and called on the United Nations to establish a World Food Council at the ministerial or plenipotentiary level to function as an organ of the United Nations. The idea of assembling government representatives for political discussions on the issues of world food production, world food security, and international agricultural trade was initially encouraged by the United States—as the largest producer and exporter of food grains—and also by Algeria, speaking for the nonaligned countries. *See also* FOOD AND AGRICULTURE ORGANIZATION (FAO); WORLD FOOD PROGRAM (WFP).

Significance Among policy initiatives promoted by the World Food Council has been an advocacy of measures to improve national and global policies directed at eliminating hunger and malnutrition. The council recognizes that past trends in food production and productivity in the majority of these developing countries has been unsatisfactory, primarily because of inadequate social and economic structures, wrong price policies, insufficient investment funds, paucity of trained labor, and unfavorable trade relations. The WFC undertook a comprehensive review of the world food and hunger situation in 1989. It concluded that, although the world now feeds one billion more people than in 1974 when the council was formed, the number of hungry and malnourished people has continued to rise—to an estimated 550 million—and nutritional diseases continue to cause widespread suffering and death in the world.

World Food Program (WFP) An organization that seeks to provide emergency relief and to stimulate socioeconomic development through aid in the form of food. The World Food Program is jointly sponsored by the United Nations and the Food and Agricultural Organization (FAO); it was established by the General Assembly in 1961 to dispense emergency food assistance. Member countries of the United Nations and the FAO make voluntary contributions of commodities, cash, and services (particularly shipping) to the program. The regular resources available to the World Food Program since its inception stand at a total of $8.3 billion. In addition to the regular resource pledges, used primarily to fund development projects, the program receives resources from the international Emergency Food Reserve exceeding 500,000 tons annually. The Committee on Food Aid Policies and Programs is composed of 30 members, half of whom are elected by the UN Economic and Social Council

(ECOSOC) and the others by the FAO Council. This committee is responsible for the overall policy direction of the program. A joint UN-FAO administrative unit carries out regular activities under an executive director. *See also* FOOD AND AGRICULTURAL ORGANIZATION (FAO); WORLD FOOD COUNCIL (WFC).

Significance   The World Food Program enjoys a wide base of support, and substantial amounts of food are being supplied by the world's large-scale exporters. Although the most frequently donated commodities are grains, the program also handles substantial quantities of other products, such as milk powder, high-protein food blends, cooking oil, and sugar. Food crises and economic crises in the developing nations are linked, and both are associated with underlying and fundamental crises in agriculture. That is why food aid is usually combined with some economic assistance to the recipient country. The program cooperates closely with many UN bodies, private agencies, and governments, together making bilateral contributions. In recent years more than half of the program's emergency assistance went to the drought-stricken Sahel countries of Africa, including Ethiopia, which was the worst-hit by food shortage and famine.

World Government   A vision of a global institution that would create a supreme authority to oversee certain affairs of the world community. The concept of world government envisages the establishment of a federation with a central authority vested with delegated powers. Various proposals to replace the present nation-state system arose out of the collapse of the League of Nations in 1939 and the advent of the atomic age in 1945. One such proposal contemplated a federal union of the American type as a precedent that should be emulated on the global level. Another proposal was to develop a detailed plan that would specify exactly those powers to be transferred to a federal world government. Collectively, the major "world government movements" have three distinctive features: (1) they received a degree of popular support and some consideration at the national level, (2) they were based upon the idea of a voluntary surrender or limitation of national sovereignty, and (3) they maintained that the social, economic, and technological interdependence of the contemporary world had made the nation-state system obsolete. *See also* WORLD ORDER.

Significance   The concept of world government boasts myriad defenders and detractors. Advocates of world government argue that an international organization like the United Nations at its current stage of development can assist in encouraging the idea of world government. Its theoreticians also argue that the integrative efforts of the United Nations can be strengthened by giving it (world government) tasks that (1) are conspicuously related to the United Nations, (2) have a good chance of success in a technical and administrative sense, (3) involve the talents of many influential people, and (4) bring tangible rewards to member states, including the possibility of preventing war. The practical problem is how to replace the present international system. Those who propose to establish a world government through functionalism—cooperation at the socioeconomic level—often underestimate the difficulty of integration at the organic, moral, and political level. They think of a world mutually dependent but often forget that the components of that world lack mutual respect. In our age, any attempt to create a world government by coercion is likely to trigger mutual annihilation. At the same time, we are living at the dawn of a new era of universal humanity. We need not merely a closer contact between nations, but a closer union, a meeting of minds and a union of hearts. Until then, interest in world government will wax and wane.

World Health Organization (WHO)   A specialized agency of the United Nations with primary responsibility for international health matters. The World Health Organization helps countries strengthen their health systems by increasing an awareness of health needs and services for the individual, family, and community and by creating and developing health institutions, referral systems, and technology. The constitution of WHO was adopted in 1946 at the International Health Conference, called by the UN Economic and Social Council (ECOSOC) in New York. The organization itself came into being in 1948 after 26 UN members had ratified its constitution. WHO currently has 162 members and is headquartered in Geneva. Membership is open to all independent states; territories (which are not responsible for the conduct of their international relations) may become associate members, and at present WHO has one associate member. The main organs of WHO are the World Health Assembly, the Executive Board, six regional organizations, and the secretariat. The World Health Assembly, the supreme governing body, meets each year and is composed of delegations from WHO's member states. The WHO carries out its work in various ways, including (1) sending teams of experts to appropriate areas to demonstrate techniques in disease control, (2) sending consultants to requesting countries to assist in the development of their academic and clinical resources, (3) enabling health workers to undertake study and research in countries more highly developed than their own, and (4) convening expert committees and seminars for the purpose of exchanging information and pooling knowledge on specific health issues. *See also* SPECIALIZED AGENCIES OF THE UNITED NATIONS.

Significance   The World Health Organization is one of the few international organizations with a universal membership and its record of service has been outstanding. The drives to eradicate such endemic and epidemic diseases as smallpox, cholera, malaria, and tuberculosis have met with success in most countries of the world. Efforts are continuing to eliminate these diseases from the face of the earth. WHO directs its efforts toward ensuring that all people may have equal access to health services enabling them to lead productive lives. It emphasizes the need for health improvement in developing countries. WHO establishes worldwide standards in all countries for food, environment, and pharmaceutical practices. It is now actively engaged in an international campaign to cope with AIDS (acquired immune deficiency syndrome) and cancer. Every year, April 7 is observed as World Health Day to develop and underline health consciousness among all peoples.

World Intellectual Property Organization (WIPO)   A specialized agency of the United Nations to maintain and increase respect for intellectual property throughout the world. The World Intellectual Property Organization favors industrial and cultural development by stimulating creative activity and facilitating the transfer of technology and the dissemination of literary and artistic works. Intellectual property includes industrial property (trademarks and patents) and copyrights in literary and artistic works. Headquartered in Geneva, WIPO was established by a convention signed in Stockholm in 1967 and entered into force in 1970; it became a specialized agency of the United Nations in 1974. The origins of WIPO date back to the 1883 Paris Convention for the Protection of Industrial Property and the 1886 Berne Convention for the Protection of Literary and Artistic Works. WIPO superseded the United International Bureau for the Protection of Intellectual Property. Some of WIPO's programs include assisting developing countries through the transfer of technology from highly industrialized countries and conducting technological assistance programs, including seminars, professional training, and drafting of model laws. Current membership of WIPO includes 123 states. *See also* SPECIALIZED AGENCIES OF THE UNITED NATIONS.

Significance   The central purpose of WIPO is to facilitate transnational utilization of intellectual achievements through harmonization of policies concerning proprietary rights. It has been actively involved in correcting some confusing situations in the relationship between research by scientists and patents by inventors. To assist in the protection of intellectual property, WIPO promotes the wider acceptance of existing treaties and their revision and, where necessary, encourages the conclusion of new legislation. Because its essential functions are of a regulatory nature, strains are often created and international disagreements on intellectual property rights arise at times.

World Meteorological Organization (WMO)   A specialized agency of the United Nations to facilitate worldwide cooperation in the establishment of networks of stations engaged in weather observation and reporting. The World Meteorological Organization promotes exchange of meteorological information and observations and the uniform publication of statistics. WMO had its origin in the International Meteorological Organization (IMO), set up in 1873. In 1939, IMO was succeeded by the Intergovernmental World Meteorological Organization. WMO's convention was drafted at a conference in Washington, D.C., in 1947 and came into force in 1950. The supreme body of WMO is the World Meteorological Congress, in which all matters are normally presented by the heads of the meteorological services of member national entities. It meets every four years to determine general policies for WMO. There are six regional meteorological associations—in Africa, Asia, South America, North and Central America, Europe and the southwestern Pacific. Headquartered in Geneva, WMO has 158 members states and territories that maintain their own meteorological services. *See also* SPECIALIZED AGENCIES OF THE UNITED NATIONS.

Significance   The World Meteorological Organization, as the world's authoritative voice on the atmospheric environment, coordinates and unifies international scientific and policy-making communities for effective, realistic, and equitable action on climate change and forecasting. Its role has grown in response to the expanding needs for reliable weather data to provide safety for the millions who travel by air and sea. WMO provides for surface and upper air observations from a worldwide network of stations, mobile and fixed ships, commercial aircraft, and meteorological satellites. Many scientists say that climate changes will have devastating effects on millions of people and the world environment, animals, and plants over the next century unless greenhouse effects are reduced. In the 1990s WMO faces the challenge of global warming and how to cope with it; it is giving high priority to space-based observation systems and the use of satellite communications to record and transmit meteorological information.

World Order   A concept that refers to the aggregation of norms, procedures, and institutions to give shape and structure to international society. Those who espouse this concept visualize it as a method for diagnosing present world problems, prescribing changes for the future, and inquiring into processes of transition—bearing in mind values of peace, economic well-being, social justice, and ecological balance. Failure to make this transition will, the world order theorists fear, result in the destruction of the planet itself—either through a nuclear holocaust or through environmental collapse followed by global famine and pestilence. There are three "schools of thought" for the achievement of world order: maximalist, minimalist, and reformist. The maximalists suggest a system of government in which the total sovereignty of the state is divided in such a way as to make the central government sovereign over some transactions, other smaller units sovereign over some other transactions, and the two cooperatively sovereign over still other matters. This system is designed to prevent full centralization and absolutism as is practiced in a federal form of government such as the United States'. The minimalists favor world order based on centralization of political power more in line with a unitary form of government as practiced in Britain. The reformists prefer to adopt existing national and international machinery in achieving "world order." *See also* SUPRANATIONAL ORGANIZATIONS; WORLD GOVERNMENT.

Significance   The establishment of a "world order" depends on the eventual development of a moderate international system, which will require an expansion and strengthening of international organizations. But it does not require the ultimate centralization of power that the minimalists have envisaged. It requires that international organizations, while continuing to flourish in the arena of world politics, be allowed to develop greater autonomy—not in the sense of ceasing to be expressions of the interests of particular states or other international actors but in the sense of also expressing what might be called systemic interests. Those long- and short-term interests of states that aim not at selfishly only maintaining the status quo, but at the maintenance of moderation, should also be active components of a world order. A moderate international system will have to be based upon two principles. One is the universalization of cocern; the other is the need for safety valves allowing change when the pressures for utilization of force build up. Whether such a system emerges hangs precariously on those measures that international organizations may initiate. These organizations will have many critical roles to play if the states are to cooperate in the eventual establishment of a "world order."

World Peace Council (WPC)   A leading communist international organization used to mobilize the people of the world for peace. The World Peace Council calls for bans on all weapons of mass destruction and the ending of the international arms race, abolition of military bases, and elimination of all forms of colonialism and racial discrimination. Founded in 1950 in Warsaw by the Second Peace Congress, in succession to the World Committee of the World Congress, the WPC exposes supposed warmongers and promotes peaceful settlement of international differences. It considers production of armaments in the West as a warmongering activity, while its members have regarded such production in the Soviet Union as necessary for arming "the defenders of the peace." The council is composed of individual "peace fighters," leaders of national peace committees, and representatives of 144 so-called front organizations. Individual membership in the WPC is being replaced with corporate membership composed of national and international movements and groups. The WPC in its 1990 session in Athens adopted a new charter designed to take greater account of political changes, human rights, and economic and social development in the Soviet Union and Eastern Europe. *See also* WORLD FEDERATION OF TRADE UNIONS (WFTU).

Significance   The World Peace Council serves as an adjunct (if sometimes disguised) arm of Soviet foreign policy. Debate within the WPC on its structure and objectives has been brought to a head in recent years by the events in Eastern Europe. Discussions reveal skepticism among the organization's officials as to whether it could reform itself sufficiently to adjust to the new situation. With communism crumbling in Eastern Europe and *perestroika* (reconstruction) clearly in mind, the WPC is reorienting its general and worldwide approach toward peace. The WPC has been seriously short of funds and its survival now depends on how independently it can run without its Soviet subsidy, which is under threat. Whether for political reasons or from financial prudence, the WPC was unable to agree to a common program of action when it met in Athens on February 11, 1990. In general, the atmosphere was strained, owing to the inability of the conservatives, composed mainly of delegates from the Third World, and the reformist group, dominated by Europeans and North Americans, to come to agreement.

World War I   A military confrontation from 1914 to 1918 between two coalitions—the Central Powers, led by Germany and Austria-Hungary (later joined by the Ottoman Empire and Bulgaria), and the

Allies, led by France and Great Britain. (The United States associated with the latter in 1917–1918). In World War I the Central Powers were pitted against the Allied and Associated Powers, an aggregation that included Russia and nearly all the other states of the world. The generally accepted explanation of World War I begins with the assassination of Archduke Franz Ferdinand, heir to the throne of the Austrian Empire, in Sarajevo on June 28, 1914. Austria-Hungary suspected that its small neighbor, Serbia, had approved the plot to kill Ferdinand and used this as the pretext for declaring war, which eventually destroyed the three great empires—the Austrian-Hungarian, the Ottoman, and the Russian. By the autumn of 1918 the weight of Allied manpower and materiel on several fronts forced Germany to sue for an armistice, which was signed on November 11. More than 5 million Allied servicemen and over 3.3 million servicemen of the Central Powers died from wounds, disease, or other causes (some estimates show the total casualty figure as 20 million). *See also* TREATY OF VERSAILLES; WORLD WAR II.

Significance   World War I was the first "total" war of modern times, in which civilian populations as well as military personnel played a vital part. Peace agreements after the war changed the map of Europe: new governments appeared in Austria, Czechoslovakia, Estonia, Finland, Germany, Hungary, Latvia, Lithuania, Poland, Russia, and Yugoslavia. The results of World War I were embodied in the Versailles peace treaty of 1919. Germany was not invited to participate in the Versailles conference but was instead handed the completed treaty and told to sign within seven days. Germany was ordered to disarm and pay for the war because of "war guilt." It is possible to construct an argument that the Treaty of Versailles was responsible for the rise of Adolf Hitler and hence for World War II. The defeat in World War I and the consequent collapse of its economy and the humiliating terms of the Versailles treaty obviously provided enough ammunition for Hitler to mobilize the Germans and prepare them for another and more devastating world war. On the positive side, the first global organization—the League of Nations—was established by the victors of World War I, with all states as members except for the United States, to look toward the preservation of peace and security and to promote international economic and social cooperation.

World War II   The military confrontation from 1939 to 1945 between the Axis Powers (Germany, Italy, Japan, and certain minor nations) and a coalition consisting of the United Kingdom, the United States, the Soviet Union, France, China, and many of the remaining states of the world. World War II was precipitated by three main causes: (1) the problems left unsolved by World War I, (2) the rise of dictatorships in Germany and Italy, and (3) the desire of Germany, Italy, and Japan for more territory. On September 1, 1939, Germany attacked Poland. After this successful test of lightning war methods, the German war machine crushed six countries—Denmark, Norway, Belgium, Luxembourg, the Netherlands, and France—in 1940. However, Germany failed to defeat Great Britain by bombing and naval blockades. In 1941, Adolf Hitler's armies conquered Yugoslavia and Greece—which Italy had attacked—and then marched into Russia. Japan's plan for expansion in the Far East led it to attack Pearl Harbor, Hawaii, on December 7, 1941, bringing the United States into the war. After a series of disasters, the Allies took offensives and halted Axis advances on all fronts. Italy surrendered on September 3, 1943, and Germany on May 7, 1945. Japan capitulated September 2, 1945, closely following the first use of atomic bombs, which were dropped by the United States on Hiroshima and Nagasaki. *See also* TREATY OF VERSAILLES; WORLD WAR I.

Significance   It was a convincing proof to much of the world that superior technology was the decisive factor in winning World War II. If a scientific breakthrough had given the Germans or the Japanese the first atomic weapon, the outcome of the war might have been different. World War II changed the structure of global politics. The United States emerged as a superpower, and slowly the Soviet Union followed suit. The Soviet Union's traditional enemies—Japan in Asia and Germany in Europe—had been eliminated by defeat in war. The total battle deaths and civilians killed during World War II were over 60 million, or 3 percent of the world population. World War II killed more people, cost more money ($150 billion), damaged more industry and property, affected more people all over the world, and caused more far-reaching changes than any other war in history. That is why the victors of World War II hastened to establish the United Nations: "to save succeeding generations from the scourge of war" by seeking to make it illegal.

Y

Yalta Conference A major summit meeting of the Big Three—President Franklin Roosevelt, Prime Minister Winston Churchill, and Premier Josef Stalin—during World War II. The conference was held at Yalta in the Russian Crimea in 1945 to develop a joint strategy in the final stages of the war against Germany and Japan and to resolve postwar issues. Though the Allies were in sight of victory, a number of military questions needed discussion. The Soviets, about to launch their final offensive against Germany, requested assurance of concerted Anglo-U.S. advances in Italy and on the western front, so that Germany could not transfer forces to the east. With regard to Asia, Stalin confirmed his promise to declare war on Japan after the defeat of Germany. Understandings were reached between the three leaders concerning the establishment of governments in liberated states, the delimitation of spheres of influence by the three powers, and the calling of a conference on world organization. The Soviet Union was assigned three seats in the soon-to-be-established UN General Assembly (one for the Soviet Union, one for Byelorussia, and one for the Ukraine), and a UN trusteeship system, it was agreed, would replace the mandates system of the League of Nations. The five permanent members of the Security Council (China, France, the Soviet Union, the United Kingdom, and the United States) were given veto power in the council. *See also* UNITED NATIONS CONFERENCE ON INTERNATIONAL ORGANIZATION (UNCIO).

Significance The Yalta Conference helped resolve many remaining issues among the Big Three, and these decisions greatly affected certain features of the postwar world. One of the major objectives of the Yalta Conference was to develop a world community of interests on which to build a stable peace. The leaders recognized that cooperation and compromise among the great powers was essential for achieving that objective. Because no general peace treaty was signed at the close of the war, decisions of the Yalta Conference served as a basic instrument to harmonize postwar policies by the victors of World War II. These included the establishment of the United Nations system with its special membership and veto provision. The Soviets wanted to maintain their hegemony in Eastern Europe; defensiveness, expansionism, and ideology all played a part in the urge to dominate. The establishment of communist states in Eastern Europe, the outbreak of the cold war, and the creation of military alliances in Europe are all indirect effects of the Yalta Conference.

NOTES

1. Robert E. Riggs and Jack C. Plano, *The United Nations: International Organizations and World Politics* (Pacific Grove, CA: Brooks/Cole, 1988), 1.

2. Ibid., 325.

3. Ibid.

4. Walter S. Jones, *The Logic of International Relations* (Glenview, IL: Scott, Foresman, 1988), 552.

5. Marvin S. Soroos, *Beyond Sovereignty: The Challenge of Global Policy* (Columbia: University of South Carolina Press, 1986), 237.

6. Ibid., 248.

7. *Arms Control and Disarmament Agreements: Texts and Histories of Negotiations* (Washington, D.C.: U.S. Arms Control and Disarmament Agency, 1982), 25.

8. Thomas Schelling and Morton Halperin, *Strategy and Arms Control* (New York: Twentieth Century Fund, 1961), 171–172.

9. Linus Pauling, ed., *World Encyclopedia of Peace,* Vol. 1 (Oxford, England: Pergamon Press, 1986), 61.

10. Walter Jones, op. cit., 176.

11. Thomas Hovet, *Bloc Politics in the United Nations* (Cambridge, Mass: Harvard University Press, 1960), 30–46.

12. Ibid., 112.

13. Walter Jones, op. cit., 508.

14. Riggs and Plano, op. cit., 24.

15. John G. Stoessinger, *The Might of Nations: World Politics in Our Time* (New York: McGraw-Hill, 1990), 78.

16. Stephen Goodspeed, *The Nature and Function of International Organization* (New York: Oxford University Press, 1967), 9.

17. Ibid., 26.

18. Henry A. Kissinger, "The Congress of Vienna," *World Politics,* January 1966, 264–265.

19. Marvin Soroos, op. cit., 185.

20. Daniel S. Papp, *Contemporary International Relations: Frameworks for Understanding* (New York: Macmillan, 1988), 453.

269

21. James Lee Ray, *Global Politics* (Boston: Houghton Mifflin, 1990), 418.

22. John Stoessinger, op. cit., 332.

23. David Mitrany, *A Working Peace System* (London: Royal Institute of International Affairs, 1946), 7.

24. Stephen Goodspeed, op. cit., 26.

25. John Stoessinger, op. cit., 116.

26. Norman A. Graham and Robert S. Jordan, eds., *The International Civil Service: Changing Role and Concepts* (New York: Pergamon Press, 1980).

27. Werner J. Feld and Robert S. Jordan, *International Organizations: A Comparative Approach* (New York: Praeger, 1980), 62.

28. Theodore A. Couloumbis and James H. Wolfe, *Introduction to International Relations: Power and Justice* (Englewood Cliffs, NJ: Prentice-Hall, 1990), 271.

29. Frederick S. Pearson and J. Martin Rochester, *International Relations: The Global Condition in the Late Twentieth Century* (New York: Random House, 1988), 13.

30. Walter Jones, op. cit., 231–234.

31. Charles R. Beitz, *Political Theory and International Relations* (Princeton, NJ: Princeton University Press, 1979), 71.

32. John G. Stoessinger, *Why Nations Go To War* (New York: St. Martin's Press, 1990), 198.

33. Georg Schwarzenberger, *A Manual of International Law* (London: Stevens, 1950), 134.

34. Frederick H. Hartman, *The Relations of Nations* (New York: Macmillan, 1983), 99.

35. Richard L. Jackson, *The Non-Aligned, the UN and the Superpowers* (New York: Praeger, 1983), 4.

36. *New York Times*, July 7, 1990.

37. Donald C. Blaisdell, *International Organization* (New York: Ronald, 1966), 234.

38. Clyde Eagleton, *International Government* (New York: Ronald, 1957), 488.

39. Hans J. Morgenthau, *Politics Among Nations: Struggle for Power* (New York: Knopf, 1973), 9.

40. Inis L. Claude, *Swords Into Plowshares* (New York: Random House, 1964), 61.

41. Riggs and Plano, op. cit., 54.

42. Inis Calude, op. cit., 64–65.

43. Riggs and Plano, op. cit., 41.

44. Couloumbis and Wolfe, op. cit., 300.

45. Ibid., 187.

INDEX